# More praise for **Sister & Brother**

"Original and an absolute must-read. It is a revelation to see how many gay men and women share complex and abiding relationships. What is perhaps most compelling in this anthology is the reminder that it isn't only enemies that homosexuals have in common."

—Genre

"*Sister and Brother* charts our gay family values—the dinners, the fights, the reunions, the changes, the births and deaths, the big and small events. The lineage is itchy, varied, dystopic, yet hopeful and human."

—Kate Clinton

"This book overwhelmingly celebrates the differences of the participants—differences, as one writer points out, that 'did not alienate us but enhanced us both.' Highly recommended for all gay and lesbian collections."

—*Library Journal*

"Nestle and Preston have brought together some of the best writers the gay community can boast, and have created a powerful reading experience—touching, amusing, enlightening—while helping to discredit the hurtful and largely false myth of mutual indifference between gay men and lesbians."

—Larry Duplechan, author of *Captain Swing*

"Good writing, at times funny and painful, and often quite moving. *Sister and Brother* is a very welcome new book."

—*Lambda Book Report*

"The essays in this book explore a kind of love that's hard to imagine between any other combination of genders or sexual orientations. It's uncomplicated by romance, but surprisingly sensual. It struggles with a nuanced analysis of sexual politics, but remains, on some deep level, simple. As the writers in *Sister and Brother* pursue their relationships with the opposite sex, they ultimately lay bare the nature of friendship itself."

—Alison Bechdel, cartoonist, *Dykes to Watch Out For*

"This unprecedented collection opens the doorway for frank discussions about the difficult and wonderful ways that lesbians and gay men remain loyal to each other even as lovers come and go."

—*New York Native*

"An excellent addition to gay and lesbian studies."

—Booklist

# Sister
# &
# Brother

LESBIANS &
GAY MEN
WRITE ABOUT
THEIR LIVES
TOGETHER

# Sister & Brother

EDITED WITH AN
INTRODUCTION BY

**Joan Nestle
&
John Preston**

HarperSanFrancisco
*An Imprint of HarperCollinsPublishers*

*To all the lesbians and gay men*
*who honored each other with their love*
Joan Nestle


*To Joan Pickard*
John Preston

Throughout the essays in this work, some proper names, place names, and identifying details have been changed to ensure the privacy of individuals.

Grateful acknowledgment is made for permission to quote from "No More Encomiums," "How Like a Man," and "Sexual Preference," from *Living as a Lesbian,* by Cheryl Clarke, Firebrand Books, Ithaca, New York. Copyright © 1986 by Cheryl Clarke.

FIRST HARPERCOLLINS PAPERBACK EDITION PUBLISHED IN 1995
*Book design by Ralph Fowler.   Set in Minion*

Library of Congress Cataloging-in-Publication Data

Sister and brother : lesbians and gay men write about their lives together / edited with an introduction by Joan Nestle and John Preston. — 1st ed.
    p.   cm.
  ISBN 0-06-251055-X. (cloth) — ISBN 0-06-251056-8 (pbk.)
   1. Lesbians—United States.  2. Gay men—United States.  3. Friendship—United States.
I. Nestle, Joan, 1940– .  II. Preston, John.
HQ75.6.U5S577  1994
305.9'0664—dc20                           94-9158
                                            CIP

95  96  97  98  99  ❖HAD  10  9  8  7  6  5  4  3  2  1

# Contents

# Acknowledgments

Michael Lowenthal was an enormous help at two crucial moments in the creation of this manuscript. We thank him for his professionalism and his generosity.

Polly Thistlewaite and Lee Hudson also provided us with invaluable help as we created this book.

JOAN

NESTLE

&

JOHN

PRESTON

# Introduction

*July 9, 1964*
*Aurora, Colorado*

*Dear Bob,*

*I shouldn't have to tell you that your letter made me cry. You are the only person I miss from Great Falls—I miss talking with you and being with you. It is much easier for me to say things by writing them, and there is something I have wanted to tell you for a long time. As a person, you are rare. I don't know if you realize it or not, but it is almost impossible for a girl to be a friend to a boy . . . .*

from a special collection of the Lesbian Herstory Archives

This excerpt is from a store of letters one gay man has been treasuring for close to thirty years. The letters reveal the close and complex relationships that exist between some lesbians and gay men. The writer goes on to discuss the gay books she was reading, her girlfriends, her support for Bob's sense of style, and her joy at his excitement in the face of his new life in California. She commiserates with him at their mutual oppression and the codes they were both forced to use to survive the homophobia around them.

In 1970, the young woman who wrote these letters lost her life suddenly in an automobile accident. She had entrusted her dreams of erotic adventure and literary success, her passionate vision of what life could be, to Robert, who was himself just venturing out into his own gay world.

When Robert, now a gay man in his fifties, heard of the anthology John Preston and I were working on, he offered the letters as a way to commemorate his enduring friendship. He also donated a battered photograph of his friend that he had carried in his wallet—one where she is dressed in peg-leg pants, a collared shirt, and boots, with her foot pointing forward. Once again private documents open up a new window on our lives.

My own relationships with gay men began in 1959 when I found myself on the campus of Queens College, part of the City University of New York. Here in this working-class Berkeley of the East, I met Carl, the son of a trade unionist who had been purged from the union he had helped to organize in the first wave of red bashing in the forties. Tall, broad, with a permanent cowlick over his forehead, Carl was part of a whole family of red diaper babies who still believed in the vision of the International. This group of committed activists gave my own class anger a historical setting; my first date with Carl was to see Lotte Lenya portray Jenny in Brecht and Weill's *Threepenny Opera*, in a small Village theater. Afterward we sat in a huge and sparsely populated automat where he explained Brecht's vision of the theater to me, the coffee cups piling up and the ashtray spilling over.

That night we attempted to make love as my mother slept in the next room. I was naked, and Carl was stroking me, when my mother sleepwalked into the room. Carl threw his body over mine, and I said in a stern voice, "Mother, go back to sleep." Obediently, she turned herself around and marched out the way she had come. "What will I tell her in the morning?" I wondered out loud to Carl. "Tell her," he said quietly, "we were trying to find each other." All night we talked, not about Brecht or Joseph McCarthy but about Carl's first sexual experience with another man the night before and my own sexual explorations with women. We talked until the Queens sky turned orange with the new day; I still wanted Carl to make love to me, but I already knew that my womanness was not a softness that he sought.

We kept our erotic searchings to ourselves while Carl and the others continued my cultural political education; songs and voices filled my heart—Martha Schlamme, her voice heavy with European history, singing "Peat Bog Soldiers"; Pete Seeger, his head held high, singing "The Banks Are Made of Marble"; Odetta, like a reincarnation of Paul Robeson, making us believe in an international community of peace. We organized, petitioned, rode buses to Washington, picketed the Queens Woolworth for its discriminatory racial policies, rode freedom buses to Baltimore and attempted to integrate restaurants and luncheonettes. We refused to take shelter and had our college IDs confiscated; we shut the school down to protest the Vietnam War.

I am still inspired and haunted by memories of that time; by the maliciousness of the McCarthy era; by the courage of the then young people like Paul Robeson Jr. and JoAnne Grant, who were called before the House Un-American Activities Committee because of their unauthorized traveling to China; by our insistence to support them, to be present in that hearing room that really was a courtroom, a conviction room. And while Carl and I did these actions together, while he taught me about the long tradition of radical protest in this country, we both went our separate ways in the night, to differently fleshed worlds.

In 1963, I left this country to travel in Europe with my woman lover. When I returned, things had changed. My friends interpreted my going as a betrayal of Carl; male homosexuality was easier for them to understand than my lesbianism. I became more and more involved in Greenwich Village bar life, while continuing my own involvement in the civil rights movement. Carl went away to graduate school; we wrote long letters giving each other courage to explore queerness. Carl was looking for a home with an older man; I wanted sex, street wanderings. I found the gay liberation movement. This past year once again I was in Washington, along with thousands of other gay and lesbian people, demonstrating for a more compassionate American society. As I marched in the Lesbian Herstory Archives contingent down a long wide avenue, Carl jumped out of the crowd and ran over to me. Still large, still in his suspenders and a white shirt, he hugged me and I thumped his chest. Through all the emotional commotion of our reunion, we never missed a step as a whole nation of gay and lesbian people walked into history.

*Joan Nestle*

I grew up in a small town in Massachusetts. The only lesbians I was aware of were two nurses who lived down the block and were friends with my grandmother. (They were actually two of the only three homosexuals I could identify in that village.) They were loud and raucous, and somehow I knew they were outlaws. But they had served in the same unit of the U.S. Army Nursing Corps with my grandmother during World War II. Whatever bonds they created while they lived through the Blitz in London were stronger than social disapproval.

The couple were in most ways a stereotype of lesbians at the time: they were large, wore pants (in the fifties!), talked with husky cigarette-smoke voices. They frightened me, but they were compelling as well. Somehow I knew I shared something with them.

Whatever link there was between us, I couldn't identify it for years, and even when I did I certainly never spoke to them about it. It was the fifties and sixties; very few people made the connections that seemed to linger just below consciousness.

As soon as I entered high school in 1959 I followed the lead of our minister and became active in the black civil-rights movement. I spent my summers and many weekends from then on and into college doing demographic surveys in Boston, tutoring students in the most deprived housing projects in Chicago, and finally becoming part of the freedom-rider movement in the South. To this day my father will tell you that my season in Alabama was the one time he was most proud of me, and the one time he was most scared by what I was doing.

I learned just how deep hatred is in the United States while I was doing that work. I was shot at, the tires of cars I drove were regularly slashed, I was constantly threatened by gangs of other white men, who saw my willingness to be close to black people as proof of my perversion. I *was* perverted, but not in the way they thought. The work for racial justice taught me about community organizing and the power that can come when people organize for a more equitable and just society.

Other things were changing: I was beginning to sense just what my connection with those two nurses down the street was made of. Activism had become a way of life for me. I could see the outlines of just how I could use my skills and experiences in a new and unexpected way.

In 1969, when the gay and lesbian movement was just being born, I moved to Minneapolis, then one of the hotbeds of the nascent cause. Activism in Minneapolis was especially and shockingly visible because the University of Minnesota had the first gay and lesbian student group in the nation. I found that my instinctive populist politics demanded that the activism be taken into the community and not be limited to the campus.

I founded the first gay and lesbian community center in the country—Gay House, Inc. The whole point of the enterprise was to create a place for gay men and lesbians to just be gay men and, separately, lesbians. It was meant to be a place where people could explore their new identities and their new politics. It was quickly apparent that it would not do to have a man as sole head of the center. Cindy Hansen joined me; we became the codirectors. That was fine, but I didn't expect what came of our partnership. I was doing all this to be with men, really, and was simply agreeing we'd share the huge building with lesbians.

Cindy and I worked together closely and got along famously. After we were finished with our tenure as codirectors, we decided to work together on other projects. We also agreed to share an apartment. Living with Cindy and her lover, Sharon, presented unexpected problems and pleasures. I had to go through the inevitable learning experiences of a man living with the new generation of liberated women—"When are you going to learn to put down the goddamn toilet seat?" (That was the least of it!)

There was also an air of sexuality in our apartment. At first I thought it simply the passion these two women openly expressed for one another. Then I realized the passion included me. Cindy and Sharon were both tall, athletic women. They would wander through our rooms nude after lovemaking or showering, and I, who had dreamed of creating an all-male gay world, found myself unexpectedly attracted to them and inquisitive about their bodies.

Sex finally came up in our conversation when Cindy and Sharon spoke of Sharon's desire to have a baby. Would I provide sperm? How did I ever get from being a gay male activist to sperm donor? The sperm would be given naturally—no turkey basters for these women—and I found myself liking the idea of having sex with one or both of these women. We became more physical, we touched more, talked even more openly about our bodies. The baby didn't happen, but the discussions about creating a child made our curiosity about our bodies all the more forceful.

We also quickly learned that such thoughts and activities were best kept to ourselves. The gay and lesbian community didn't want its leaders to be indulging in any exploration of heterosexuality. It was best to put our attractions and our occasional explorations into a new closet.

*John Preston*

I first met John Preston sometime in the early eighties when we were on a panel of pornographers as part of a conference of gay and lesbian journalists; a group of writers who had been censored for their subject matter were meeting in one of the ground-floor rooms of the newly opened Lesbian and Gay Center of New York City. I was the last panel member to arrive, and I remember Pat Califia asking the whole panel to rise so I could wedge myself in behind the long table. John Preston was one of my colleagues that day. He sat straight and tall, unflinching in his gaze, as he chronicled his career in erotic writing. Intrigued by his honesty and dedication to his writing, I began to read his books and keep an eye out for his name as he toured the country.

Over the years, I would get warm, encouraging cards from John, words that I needed in the face of some of the more ugly responses to my erotic writing. We were comrades in our dedication to telling the tales of how touch and taste and yearning encouraged life. My other good gay friends—Jonathan Katz and his lover, David; Allen Bérubé; Bert Hansen; and Eric Garber—were all supportive of my history work, but it was John who read my books as portraits of sex.

*J. N.*

Joan and I have been on many panels together over the years. But she's wrong about this one being our first meeting. We originally met at a conference in the late seventies sponsored, I think, by the National Writers Union and its lesbian and gay caucus. I wasn't on the podium with her. I had attended that particular panel—it had been my highest priority for the trip—only to see her, listen to her, and meet her.

It was at the height of controversy about Joan's writing on themes that thought police had declared unacceptable for a lesbian. As a gay man who wrote much too much about sex, I had been fighting the same battles. Joan was sitting alone; she was the first presenter to arrive. The crowd was packing in, but there was no way to know, yet, if they were friendly or if this would be another public attack on Joan's honest writing.

I went up to her and introduced myself. "You are one of my heroes," I told her. She looked stunned—a little battle weary, I think—and said, "Thank you for telling me that. I'm so nervous!" We talked easily, but simply.

*J. P.*

In the mid-eighties, I grew aware of another dimension in John's work; he became one of the first creators of and spokespeople for a new eroticism: safe sex. He put his authoritative stance behind the possibility of hot, heavy gay male desire. Here we shared another parallel in our work. My erotic writings existed in a world where women lost their lives every day because of male violence. Every time I wrote of touch and entry, I had to weigh the consequences of my words; I had to ask myself whether I was serving life, the fuller life of women, by breaking erotic silences. Both John and I chose to keep alive the taste, the power, of homoerotic desire.

In 1991, John started writing me letters about his idea for a book, a book about gay men and lesbians. "Fondest of My Fantasies," he would greet me, "it is time for us to get to work on this project." His salutations became more and more baroque as our correspondence grew: Dearest Love Goddess, Dearest Erotic Icon of My Soul, and finally, Dear Divine Being of My Groin. How could a girl resist? The letters themselves, after their courtly flourishings, showed the hard work of a professional writer. We both had other editing, speaking, and touring commitments that kept pushing at the time we had put aside for this book, but finally in 1992, John demanded that we find the time for this project.

*J. N.*

The idea for *Sister & Brother* actually began with a 1991 conversation between my agent, Peter Ginsberg, and Susan Fox Rogers, who was then an editor for a large publishing house. They asked each other why the recent burst in lesbian and gay publishing didn't reflect the reality of their lives: that most gay men and lesbians had, in fact, warm and often powerful relationships with one another. Lesbian books, if they mentioned men at all, were most often furious with the other gender; gay male books mainly ignored lesbians and treated other women as stereotypes of the "fag hag."

Peter came to me and said I should do an anthology on the subject. I agreed, but it definitely needed a lesbian coeditor. Joan, of course, came to mind instantly. I would be able to work with my hero. And there would be the luscious benefit of hearing Joan's deep sensuous voice on the phone even more frequently.

J. P.

Sprawling on our couch, John's long legs extending far out into the living room, our dog at his feet. A sweltering summer day in New York, 1993. John's first meeting of Lee, my partner, who is a devoted fan of his *Flesh and the Word* series of gay erotic anthologies. From across the room, I notice how they resemble one another—both lean and gray, both marked by the slate blue of their eyes. John is tired and upset at the lack of interest in his proposed autobiography. He repeats the words of an influential editor he has just spoken to: "You know, Preston, the story of a middle-aged gay man who came out in the seventies and finds himself fighting AIDS in the nineties is not news anymore. It's been done."

His words bring back to me another conversation I had a few months earlier when I called a Jewish archives to see if they would be interested in receiving a copy of my neighbor's story of how he had survived the ghetto of Riga. I had worked with David, now a man in his seventies, as he translated his original Yiddish text into English. David would sit by my side as I sat at my computer and typed his journey of loss, of flight, of resistance, stopping only when his grief overcame his words. He had insisted that his story had to be remembered, beyond the confines of his immediate family, and so I made the call to a likely place. "Miss Nestle," the weary voice of the archivist informed me, "I know you find this story very impressive, very dramatic, very unique, but I am saddened to have to tell you that we already have thousands of such stories."

●━●━●

The next afternoon is the opening of the new Brooklyn home of the Lesbian Herstory Archives. Again the heat blared down, but I was so excited by the crowds of women, by the beauty of our new space, that I just plunged ahead. Through the streets of Park Slope we marched, our own small band drumming us along, over four hundred celebrants jamming into a building in Prospect Park to hear speeches, to eat, and, of course, to dance. I ran from table to table along with the other archives workers, making sure the chaos was pleasurable for our guests. Finally too tired, too hot to keep up the hectic scurrying, I stopped and just looked around at the moving, swirling mass of lesbians celebrating their own cultural institution. Then I saw John, his head towering above most of the crowd, standing with the sweat dripping down, his luggage pulling at his arms. I made my way toward him. "I just had to come," he said. "I knew how important this was to you. I can't stay, I have to make a plane home." He bent his head so I could kiss him good-bye and I felt his fever, like another sweltering August day, burning inside of him.

 *J. N.*

Joan and I have had a strange collaboration, one that worked for us but one that's unusual for editing partnerships. When we started, though I was certainly aware of my positive HIV status, I was physically well; Joan was in the throes of Chronic Fatigue Syndrome. She had a teaching job; I was living in Maine without any schedule that would impede my working on this book.

 I began the book. I was, I told Joan, the secretary for the venture. I sent out press releases, solicited the first set of essays, answered the correspondence. This book has taken two years to accomplish. As time went on, we began to shift responsibilities as Joan's schedule became more flexible and as I began to experience the first symptoms of AIDS. At the end, Joan took over the lead that I had once taken.

I had begun with an interest in making our collaboration a kind of model of a gay man and a lesbian working together. I wanted our partnership to be exemplary—and worried that critics would pounce on us if it weren't. Our individual health and our real-world schedules didn't allow for as much experimentation as I expected, but our partnership did end up being a study in equality and mutual respect.

We have both been constantly aware that this had to be a book that each of us could claim—that each of our voices and each of our priorities had to be part of the work. We have done, we believe, a very good job of accomplishing that. We had no disagreements over the inclusions in the book. It was important that for any given essay we were each allowed to say, "I need this essay for this to be *my* book as well as yours." That was our absolute, and we have both honored it. The rest was easy. I got to hear Joan's voice on the phone, and it was as voluptuous as my expectations of pleasure and love.

Some people are confused when I make remarks about Joan's sexiness, or bring up my history with Cindy and Sharon. Some have become angry, even defensive. I am a gay man, and I'm not supposed to respond to women this way. It actually makes me suspect in some eyes, because it means that I cross boundaries. One of the comforts of having a label for other people is that it creates clear limits; there are expectations on how a person will operate. The label of my being gay meant that people felt they knew how I would respond; any conversation about an erotic response—even when there was never any genital intent—by a gay man to a lesbian destroyed that illusion of containment. But I am totally a gay man, attracted to other men. One of the reasons Joan and I have been able to work so well together is that we are so clear that each of us is devoted to the work and love of our own gender. With that acknowledgment, there is then room for play, for gentle explorations. I would never seek out a sexual relationship with a woman, but I would also never understand how any man—any human—could not respond to Joan's voice, the sultriness of it, or the romance of dark eyes as they peer deeply into yours.

J. P.

One place John and I counted on seeing each other was at the annual OutWrite conference, a gay gathering of writers, editors, and readers. The conference of 1993 was our last chance to solicit manuscripts for this book, so we had several work-related meetings. One of these took place in the main lobby of the hotel in Boston, which opened its endless rooms to the almost two thousand participants who poured out over the hotel's corridors and coffee shops. A favorite gathering spot was a small bar and lounge on a raised platform in the bustling lobby. Here I joined John, who was seated in the center of a small couch; on either side of him were men—some young, some not, some California sun-tanned, some New York weary. I joined this circle and for a short time shared in what was John's world. The talk was about the previous evening's party for John's new *Flesh and the Word* book and the erotic adventures that flowed from it. The men teased each other, encouraged each other, and made promises to stay in touch. Even though the men were speaking to each other, they all sat half turned to John, who from time to time told them a story about a man he had made love to there ... here .... His voice hoarse and weary. He spoke again about the traveling salesman who had inaugurated him into the power and joy of sex many years ago, in the very hotel in which we were now sitting. In my younger years, I would have been uncomfortable in this setting, lost in my difference, but now in my mid-fifties, secure in that same differ-ence, I was content to listen to the stories, the erotic gossip that was laced with love. I soon understood that the men were paying their homage to John, that they were thanking him for years of writing and work about the gay male body and its travels.

    *J. N.*

To say that there are powerful relationships between lesbians and gay men isn't to deny that there are also political difficulties between the two groups. In 1993 I gave a speech on gay and lesbian history at Dart-mouth College, recounting the all too quickly forgotten history of how terribly hard it had been to begin to create our community. At the end of the lecture, a young man stood up and said that it had been helpful to him, because my words had let him see the ways in which his strug-gle was the same as women's.

I looked around at the women in the audience and realized they were not buying it, which didn't surprise me. I responded to the young man: "We gay men are aware of how much we've lost by coming out and how much we're hurt by society's prejudice. You have to realize, though, that lesbians look at us and see how much we still have—the power of being male in society, the privilege."

*J. P.*

Later that same day at OutWrite, a small group of us squeezed in a trip to the park that bordered the hotel so that a photographer could take publicity photos of John and me. Huddled against the November wind, John and I positioned ourselves on a bench, trying to find poses with which we both felt comfortable. Finally I gave up trying to find the pose that would not call up stereotypical male-female images and just let my body find its own position. I knew I wanted to hold John, for my own self, and so I raised myself up, and held his head against my breast. Immediately, I became aware of his fever, of the heat emanating from his body. Several months later when I saw the finished photos, I was struck by how our hands had found a way to hold on to each other's bodies.

Back in my hotel room that night, I wondered at how John Preston, New England gay man, and Joan Nestle, Bronx femme Jew, had ended up on that Boston bench together. Some answers to that question can be found in this book.

*Denver, Colorado*
*December 12, 1964*

*My darling, my darling Bob:*

*Your magnificent letter! I kissed it and tried to think how I could convey in words the love I feel for you. There is no way I can tell you how much I need you in my life—don't ever step out of it.*

# Gert

"Does it go too fast?" I asked her.

The three of us were sitting in a booth at "21," Gert and Roger and I, having supper after the theater. Robert Benchley's booth, as a matter of fact, a spitball's throw from the downstairs bar. Gert had such a vivid memory of its heyday that she could people the room with the regulars, Moss Hart to Cole Porter, transporting us back to a time of effortless glamour. No matter that Roger or even I didn't recognize half the names. I at least could keep up with her—*Wasn't he a set designer? Didn't she use to sing in musicals?*—enough to get her going and fill us in with stories fit for Damon Runyon. It astonished her how little the young remembered about the glory days of Broadway. How could it be—these giants who bestrode the glittering streets outside, the toasts of the town—how could they have vanished so?

At first she didn't appear to understand the question. "Does what go too fast?" She took a last delirious puff from an unfiltered Camel, oh how she could smoke, and I backed off a little, thinking perhaps the question had been too forward. "Oh, you mean *life*," she replied with a dawning smile, stubbing out the cigarette. "Not at all. It seems just as long as it ought to be. Well, the anniversaries maybe—they come round faster and faster every year. But don't worry, you're not going to feel you haven't had enough. Why are you thinking about *that?*"

Genuinely puzzled, a frown creasing the great wrinkled terrain of her face. A cross between Lillian Hellman and W. H. Auden, though more lovely than either of them, but the same fissured map that hid nothing of the cram of experience. Life drunk to the lees, plus five thousand cartons of Camels. She would have been seventy-five then, because there were forty years between us, and I retorted haltingly, "But I'm thirty-five already, and I've . . . I don't know, gotten such a late start." I meant in the theater, though the subtext was still all those wasted years in the closet.

Gert guffawed delightedly, sharing the laugh with, Roger. "But you're still a baby," she chided me, yet somehow without a shred of contempt. "You've got all the time in the world. I didn't even hit my stride till I was fifty-five."

I remember feeling very comforted by that—an antidote to the relentlessness of the California youth cult, the unwritten rule that put a writer out to pasture at forty, no longer hip. Or the equally sinister look that went right through you on Santa Monica Boulevard, the buffed pups of West Hollywood who never seemed to age at all. Their arms got bigger, their shoulders and chests bulging with good health, but never crossing the border into a full-grown man's experience. Staying youths as long as they could, no models for getting old anyway, not there among the clattering palms and the hydrocarbon smut of perfect weather. Old meant Palm Springs, tired old queens and their daiquiris, and the young avoided them assiduously, as if age itself were catching.

Thus did Gert become my role model for growing old alive. She was also my first lesbian, the first I really knew—though she kept to a rigorous code of silence when it came to the proclivities of the theater girls of her generation. I don't suppose she ever said the word directly, certainly not by way of self-identification, but that was all right with me. I wouldn't make her say it out loud, as long as she taught me the code. Besides, I was out enough for both of us. And of course I knew lesbians in Boston, writers and community activists, but these were still the years of separatist growing pains, a gulf of apprehension and mistrust between the men and women of the tribe. Still trapped by one another's stereotypes, and the past a matter of mostly shadows. Not enough sages and grandparents.

I met her in the most improbable place, at a Canton Academy graduation. This was the *girls'* school graduation, virginal to a fault, austere as a Shaker hymn. Afterward on the lawn the faculty mingled with the girls' families, picking at the lobster buns and petit fours that seemed to grow staler and more rancid by the year, an afternoon tea out of a cryogenics vault. And Gert—Miss Gertrude Macy—was the maiden great-aunt of one of my students, sitting knock-kneed on one of the grisly folding chairs that cluttered the lawn behind the library, still cobwebbed from storage. I was graciously introduced as the school poet. "I had no idea there were still poets around," remarked Miss Macy in her gravelly voice. "How encouraging."

It was only a moment before I was sitting cross-legged beside her chair, trying to hide from my dreary graduation duties in the shade of Miss Macy's presence. It turned out she had worked in the theater all her life, serving as stage manager and general factotum for Miss Katherine Cornell's company. Unarguably Cornell was the leading lady of American theater in the time between the wars. Gert started with her in 1928, through the yearly triumphs in New York—*Candida, The Barretts of Wimpole Street, Saint Joan, Romeo and Juliet, Antigone*—and then when the season was over, on the road with the touring company.

I was the perfect audience for the backstage version of all of this. I'd grown up bitten by the theater, done my share of teeth-jarring overacting while in college, and still went faithfully to the Boston tryouts of everything. I had even seen Miss Cornell onstage, her last tour, a two-character performance with Brian Aherne called *Dear Liar,* being the letters of Shaw and Mrs. Patrick Campbell. Not much of a play at all, really, with just the two of them standing at lecterns. And Gert would tell me later how grueling that tour had been, Cornell a ghost of the diva she once was. But at least I'd been in the presence, and so could imagine the Kit Cornell who swept through Gert's marvelous stories.

One year they were on their way to Seattle, the whole company on a train, *The Barretts* I think. It's difficult to imagine how profound the excitement was, when a star of Cornell's magnitude came to the provinces bag and baggage, a genuine New York production in tow. Alas, there was late spring snow in the mountains, and the train got mired. No way were they going to make Seattle for opening night, that very evening. Gert telegraphed ahead to cancel the first performance.

I think they pulled in to Seattle about ten hours late, exhausted and chilled. And the theater owner met them coming off the train, the sets and costumes being unloaded from boxcars. He announced to Gert that the audience was waiting at the theater in their seats. By now it was 10 or 11 P.M., and it would take hours to put up the set and light it. They clearly couldn't perform tonight. But the audience simply wouldn't leave, no matter how many announcements were made, or the offer of a special performance at the end of the run. They just sat there politely in their evening clothes. And because Kit and the others grew up in a time when the show just had to go on, the curtain went up a little before dawn, transporting them all back to Wimpole Street in the 1830s. A thrilling performance, according to Gert, though it could hardly have been a bust with such an amazing prelude. The burghers of Seattle clapped their gloves off.

Gert, of course, had known everyone, from Olivier to Brando, the latter playing Marchbanks to Kit's umpteenth revival of *Candida.* They didn't really know any *movie* stars to speak of, unless they had acted first on the stage. Hollywood was so far beneath the notice of Miss Cornell and her fellow stage immortals. All her life she turned down script after script, chance after chance to preserve herself on celluloid. But to her generation Hollywood was the opposite of "legitimate," not even close to what they in the theater called acting. Thus there is scarcely any record at all of the great lady's work, except for a moment's cameo in *Stage Door Canteen,* undertaken for patriotic reasons.

Gert wasn't so much of a snob herself, and admitted to an unapologetic fanship. Breathless the day Olivier brought his new wife, Vivien Leigh, backstage to meet Cornell. But the most overwhelming of all was the unannounced appearance of Garbo in the aisle seat in Row H, the seat beside her reserved for her fur coat. Remember, Gert reminded me, warming to her favorite anecdote, this was at a time when Garbo was mythic, thousands of women in New York affecting the slouch hat and the hooded look of the otherworldly star. Alerted to her presence, Gert and the rest of the company peeked through the crack in the curtains, gasping. Till Miss Cornell herself appeared and demanded to know what the ruckus was. She took a quick peek and declared the woman in Row H nothing but a wanna-be, or whatever they called them then. And besides, she declared imperiously, who *cared* about Garbo and all that nonsense. Places please, we have a show to put on.

As *The Barretts* reached its climax, Gert put in a fast call to L.A., to a publicist she knew who'd worked with Garbo. "Do you know where she is right this minute?"asked Gert when he took the call. As a matter of fact, he said, he had no idea at all, for Garbo had disappeared from a movie set about three days before, leaving the whole of the glitter kingdom in the lurch. Accustomed to such behavior by now, the studio bit its nails and waited.

When Kit came offstage at last, a dozen curtain calls and an armload of roses, Gert confronted her triumphantly: it *was* the real thing out there. Airily Kit dismissed the news and made for her dressing room. Gert fumed. Then five minutes later the Swedish diva herself appeared at the stage door, shy and practically muffled in her fox collar, pulled in like a turtle. "Miss Garbo to see Miss Cornell," mumbled that unmistakable voice to the guard. A stunned Gert stepped forward and led legend to meet legend. Kit wouldn't let Gert come in with Garbo. As Gert paced impatiently, about ten minutes later Kit stuck her head out of the dressing room, sweetly ordering her to take Guthrie over to "21" for supper. Guthrie McClintic, that was, Kit's husband and director for forty years—a gay man, as I later found out. Sent off like children, Gert and Guthrie ordered stiff martinis and caviar at the restaurant, defying Kit's rule that her guests could order anything on the menu *except* caviar, which even she in her extravagance thought too dearly priced.

When Gert and Guthrie came lurching home to Beekman Place, they found that Kit had brought Garbo to the house. The two actresses sat in the parlor before the fire, eating soup and a torn baguette. As Gert came in, Garbo was laughing (Garbo laughs!) and waving her bare feet in the air. "See how big they are!" she announced with glee. "Like a fishwife's!"

This was definitely a story of the Homeric Age, when stars were gods and goddesses. I didn't really think so much at the time about the gay subtext here. But for months afterward, whenever I told the story to friends old enough to know the cast of characters, they always interrupted me to say: "Oh yes, Miss Macy—she was Cornell's lover for years. And Guthrie had all the boys." Till it seemed like a secret that nobody kept. Except it somehow remained unspoken, protected by a wall of glamour that the press wouldn't have dreamed of trying to vault. It was, as I say, a certain understanding—a separate life conducted on the higher slopes of Olympus, underscored by a reflex of discretion. A bohemian aristocracy, if that's not too much of a contradiction in terms.

Gert and I parted fast friends, swearing we'd meet again before the summer waned, but who ever keeps such promises? As it happened, the '76 graduation was my last at Canton Academy. Biting the bullet, I'd decided I would never be the writer I wanted to be if I stayed in school. I would therefore take a year off and try to write a novel. I'd applied for a grant to see me through, but still hadn't heard about that. Roger said he'd support me, while I swore I'd wait tables if necessary.

I don't recall if Craig and I decided to go to the Vineyard before or after Gert's call. Craig was my closest pal in Boston—met the same night I met Roger two years before, and possessed by the glow of stars and all the attendant tinsel to a degree that made me look like an amateur. Of everyone I told, Craig was the one who ate up the story of Garbo in Row H like popcorn.

Anyway, Craig invited me down to Martha's Vineyard for an overnight, to stay with a friend of his youth from Williamstown. I knew Gert had a summer place at the Vineyard, but didn't have the number. Then, just days before we were ready to depart for the Woods Hole ferry to the island, Gert phoned out of the blue. She had a story to tell me, she said, about an extraordinary visitor she'd had at her house on the bluffs of the Hudson, which she'd been in the process of shutting up for the summer before making the trek north to the island. *Garbo*, I blurted in quick reply, and she laughed at my perspicacity. Delighted to hear I was coming over to the Vineyard, saying she'd save the details till then.

Thus Craig and I made our excited way to Gert's place on a drowsy morning in early July. It was hardly bigger than a fisherman's shack—a house for one, make no mistake—and perched on what amounted to a sandbar between the lambent surf of the bay and a reed-rimmed salt pond. So nicely isolated you could just see the roof peaks of Gert's near neighbors. Yet we had scarcely entered the little house—shipshape as a captain's quarters, an island all its own—still saying hello to Gert when the phone rang.

It was Nancy Hamilton, yet another of the charmed inner circle of Miss Cornell, like Gert an aging survivor of the golden years. Playwright and lyricist, famous wit, she had given the very best parties in the old days. Kit had left her The Barn on the Vineyard, her last home there, across the pond from Gert's. And now Nancy was calling to inquire suspiciously who were these two young men she'd seen driving up the ribbon of beach road to Gert's. She must've been spying with binoculars off the widow's walk to catch a glimpse of us. With a certain malicious glee Gert told Nancy she'd been expecting us, but not a word as to who we were.

We swam in the bay and lay in the sun, while Gert brought us out our first bullshot of the day (oh how she could put away vodka). Then, sitting grandly on her deck in her cobalt-blue-lensed sunglasses—a trademark of hers—in khaki shorts and an old army shirt, she regaled us with the tale of Garbo's visit. The legendary recluse had been longing to get out of Manhattan, where the weather that June had been unbearably sultry. A mutual friend suggested they spend an afternoon at Gert's place in Sneden's Landing, about forty minutes north of the George Washington Bridge. It took a week to coax her, but Garbo finally said yes, adding wearily, "Does she have to know who I am?"

*Now don't say anything about her career in pictures,* the friend warned Gert. Just a little lunch in the garden, and keep the conversation bland. Gert made sure her brood of dogs—a veritable pack of Shih Tzus and Pekingese, along with a dimwit Irish setter she'd adopted after a Sneden's neighbor died—stayed inside with the housekeeper. Garbo was offered a sunny spot, a shady spot, the view through the trees to the lordly river below. Nothing was quite right, because she'd left her sweater in the taxi on the way. She fretted about that sweater all afternoon.

I think she affected not to remember the evening she spent with Miss Cornell, showing off her big feet—it must have been thirty or forty years ago by then. The more Gert filled in the details, the more did Garbo seem to stiffen and grow aloof. "Not very bright, I'm afraid," Gert told us with keen disappointment. Garbo was wearing a blouse with a hundred buttons that went all the way up to her chin, and she kept patting at her neck to make sure it didn't show. "Miss Garbo," Gert asked her gently, "why don't you just unbutton your collar and feel the breeze?" After all, they were just three old ladies out here on the terrace, no paparazzi for miles around. But no, she stayed buttoned up.

The only other thing I remember from Gert's account of the day Garbo came to lunch happened over the stuffed avocados. Gert was chatting amiably with the mutual friend, Garbo staring moodily at the river below, when suddenly she announced apropos of nothing, "I hate it when somebody calls me Gigi." No one had done so. But Gert smiled gamely and observed, "Well, you don't have to worry about that, because everyone in the *world* calls you Garbo." And the look on the legend's face just then was a queer mix of offended dignity, as if someone had come too close, and a half-smile of satisfaction, basking in the world's notice.

That was all—no real bull's-eye anecdotes, no reverberating Garbo lines of the caliber of *I want to be alone* or the first words she ever spoke in pictures, asking for a whiskey in *Anna Christie.* But Craig and I pealed with laughter at every morsel, giddy as a pair of opera queens, and as if we were privy to the high jinks of a rare inner circle of our kind. For it didn't need stating aloud here, either, that the oh-so-subtle friction between Gert and Garbo was a confrontation of lesbians, a duel over the shadows of the past. And perhaps Craig and I were so gaga about the smallest details because these closeted stars were the only kind of role models we had from the past. The work to reclaim our history was only just beginning among the tribe's scholars and chroniclers. In our time we had to make do instead with high gossip, and Gert was there for the footnotes.

Craig was more brazen than I that day, oiled by bullshots and bluntly asking, "What was Tallulah like?" Or Julie Harris, whom Gert had produced in *I Am a Camera.* But the story that struck the deepest chord in me was the one about Marlene Dietrich. In '44 Kit and her troupe had volunteered to perform for the Allied boys, a six-month tour of *The Barretts* that took them through Italy and France, sometimes a bare few miles from the fighting. When they finally got to Paris they were wilted and beat, not having had a proper bath in weeks, let alone a hot one. Dietrich, who hadn't ever met Cornell, was being put up in the Imperial Suite at the Ritz, vacated in fact by U.S. Navy brass in deference to the supreme entertainer of the Allied forces. Dietrich put in a call to Kit's cold-water hotel and invited her up for a nice hot bath. Gert went along as an aide-de-camp—damned if she'd be shut out again the way she'd been with Garbo. Dietrich couldn't have been more gracious, leaving the other two women alone in a rose marble bath fitted out for a pasha. Kit and Gert luxuriated in the steam and cloudlike towels. After an hour they dressed and made ready to leave, not wishing to inconvenience the Kraut any further. But as they were saying goodbye, Dietrich cast a clucking look at the olive-drab uniforms sported by Kit and Gert. On a whim she flung open the imperial closet, revealing a whole Saville Row tailor's line of officers' uniforms, one for every branch of the Allied powers, and each one fitted to Dietrich's svelte figure. These were the clothes she wore to the front, a sort of reverse mufti, saving the beaded gowns and swansdown coat to perform in.

So for the next couple of hours the women played dress-up with the military gear—Gert a general, Kit an admiral, Dietrich a marine commandant, all of them merrily prancing and strutting. I can almost hear their laughter spilling out through the French doors to Place Vendôme, the bronze column in the center with Napoleon on top, commemorating a victory over Germans of another era. The Joint Chiefs in drag, as it were.

This was lesbian history of a very high order indeed. The image of the cross-dressed women wouldn't leave me, more erotic the more I thought of it. And three weeks later, when I started to work in earnest on my novel, the scene at the Ritz went into the story as part of the legend of my heroine—an aging chanteuse who was clearly based on Dietrich. Yet all my baroque imaginings were pretty weak tea compared with the reality—Dietrich the famous bisexual, notorious by then for the parade of lovers both men and women, the generals and the duchesses. More out than almost anyone in Hollywood, so confident was she of her vast unshakable womanhood. The opposite of Kit, with her backstage marriage to Guthrie and her offstage lesbian friends.

Indeed, I could hardly keep them all straight. Once I met an old actor who'd been in several Cornell productions, whose jowls quivered with passion as he waxed about Kit's genius. When the tone had finally lowered to dish, he talked of Gert and Kit as inseparable, then laughed about poor Guthrie, who was ever losing his heart to men who wouldn't love him back. Ambitious young actors and hustler types, who hung around for a while for the sake of the caviar, leaving Guthrie desolate in the end. Since he knew so much, I asked him offhandedly about this Nancy Hamilton woman, the one with the binoculars.

Ah, but Nancy Hamilton was the second great love of Kit's life— the one who came after Gert. Hearing it I felt a peculiar defensive pain on Gert's behalf, and couldn't figure out how Gert could stay so close after being supplanted. Her small pavilion among the trees at the edge of the bluff at Sneden's—another house pointedly built for one—was not far from the "big house" where Kit and Guthrie lived. On Martha's Vineyard Gert had bought the tiny fisherman's shack, after which Kit and Guthrie grandly acquired the whole nearby point. Perhaps they were all just very grown-up, willing to let their relationships elide and change, a loyal troupe no matter who was sleeping with whom. In any case Kit was the queen, the others her ladies-in-waiting. Or maybe *courtiers* is the better word.

I couldn't ever ask Gert to clarify; it would have been overstepping my bounds. She appeared to harbor not the slightest shred of regret or bitterness when it came to Kit's memory. She was keeper of the flame, after all, ever more so the more the world forgot. Didn't seem lonely in the least, any more than she ever seemed an old lady. The past had done the best it could with the compromises required to live in it, and there was no purpose in changing the rules now. Let the dead rest, for the theaters they had lit up with their names were all dark anyway, gone with the wind.

And yet, if the lavender truth of the past was off bounds, Gert was no less thrilled to see how the Stonewall generation had changed the rules forever. She adored hearing stories of my gay and lesbian friends, for whom being out of the closet was a necessary passage to living life for real.

Gert worried about the backlash, having an instinct for the savageries religion was capable of. Did I really think the Catholics and the Baptists were going to sit back and let our pride go unchallenged? Didn't matter, I said, because we would win. But she wasn't so sure, still uncomfortable when I spoke of Roger as my lover.

"Can't you just call him your 'friend'?" she wondered aloud on more than one occasion. "'Lover' sounds so . . . " She paused, at a rare loss for words. "Don't you think 'friend' is more intimate?" As a matter of fact I do, today anyway. But at the time I liked the shock value of "lover," my whole life having been recast since my long-belated exit from the closet. For a while there, shock was my favorite value. What we did agree about, Gert and I, was the thrill that came with a growing sense of community in the tribe. Indeed, our kind were everywhere now, and if Gert was more voyeur than participant in our newfound ubiquity, nevertheless she partook of the pride with a secret satisfaction.

After that midsummer visit with Craig I only saw her two or three times a year, especially after Roger and I moved to California. Because of her wizened countenance and her bad habits, I never knew if I'd see her again. There was always something poignant about that last wave farewell, as we left each other outside Sardi's and got into separate taxis. An inarticulate worry that maybe I hadn't said enough, hadn't probed deep enough. I don't think Gert shared my young man's anxiety of incompletion. She was very unsentimental about death, and fierce in her commitment to the right of self-deliverance. Meanwhile you did what you could with the present, just as you did with the past: no regrets. And the last thing anyone needed to stand on was ceremony.

Is that why I gave her so much leeway to counsel me? I remember I sent her my first book of poems, plus a sheaf of Xerox copies of my second, a group of dramatic monologues. When I came to see her at Sneden's she said she'd read them all straight through, and managed not to make it sound like going to the dentist. On the contrary she found them brilliant. Just one thing that troubled her: "Exactly who reads them?" I hastened to reassure her they were doing quite well among the little magazines, which suddenly sounded positively Lilliputian. And then of course there were my fellow poets, following one another's work—or was it just each other's career they followed, bristling at the fellowships and sinecures that should have gone to them?

"You should be writing for more than that," she observed. By which she meant not the small rewards, or even the chance of a wider audience, which she knew as well as anyone was mostly a matter of luck. Rather, she intuited a kind of constrictedness and self-absorption in the work, an overdetermined reach—strain, to put it bluntly—for the perfect image. All of which struck fertile ground, for I was beginning to question my own place in the ranks of the silver-tongued poets. The voice wasn't mine anymore.

"You should write a play," said Gert.

But I was writing a novel instead, which I assured her would have the same effect, unfettering my song. She gave me her most enthusiastic encouragement, all too aware that theater was an uphill climb, a world that had undergone sea changes since the halcyon days of Miss Cornell. I think she was also flattered to hear what an influence she'd had on the *femme d'un certain age* who stood at the center of my story. Gert was certainly first in line to read the galleys when the book reached print at last.

To celebrate, she had me to lunch at the Cosmopolitan Club, a ladies' club straight out of Ruth Draper. A palm-court dining room chockablock with women of a certain age, all of whom wore ice-cream-sundae hats as if in tribute to the queen mother. These were the self-same ladies, Gert confided drolly, who would fill up the matinee performances in the old days, so genteel. Turned out today in a vintage black suit of her own—"my funeral duds," she called them—Gert was distinguishable from the flock only by her blue glasses and bare head. Yet she clearly thought of herself as a kind of renegade among the ladies who lunched, with them but not of them. Just one of the curious paradoxes of the tightrope walk between Bohemia and a minimal gentility.

"And they'd all faint with shock if they read this book of yours," declared Gert. "I was a little shocked myself," she admitted with a deep-throated laugh. "So many sweating bodies!" I think she had rather relished the shock, unaccustomed as she was to sex that was rated X. And then she asked, but without any wish to moralize, more fascinated than disapproving: "Does it have to be quite so gay?"

Oh, indeed it did. The gayer the better. I launched into my half-baked credo, invoking the name of Forster, the writer to whom I was most in thrall, but the one who had somehow failed me the most as well. When Forster decided he dare not publish *Maurice,* for fear of the scandal and what his mother would think—when he locked that manuscript in a drawer for fifty years until he died—he silenced much more than himself. He put up a wall that prevented us, his gay and lesbian heirs, from having a place to begin. He had written an unheard-of thing: a queer love story that ended in love fulfilled. And so we would have to make do instead with the obsessive torments of *Giovanni's Room,* the broken flowers of Tennessee Williams. It wasn't just my book, but a whole new generation's worth—*Dancer from the Dance, Rubyfruit Jungle, Nocturnes for the King of Naples*—that would speak our passion without any compromise. No matter what our mothers thought.

Gert was unaccustomed to hearing me on a soapbox. She nodded gravely, ceding me the argument, then permitted herself a quick half smile: "Sometimes you remind me of Shaw, do you know that?" Shaw the haranguer, not Shaw the playwright. And I remember wondering even at the time, between the finger bowls and the pink parfaits, if I'd gone too far. Did she take it as veiled criticism of her own generation, with its locked drawers and its steamer trunks sealed? The truth about whom they really loved held hostage to their need to be discreet before all else? But if it struck her as any sort of accusation, she never let on. She always spurred me forward.

And in return, have I done the wrong thing here, spilling the secret that was second nature to them all, for the sake of a politics of openness of which they could scarcely conceive? I'm pretty sure Gert could've handled any revelation about herself, but she also would've drawn the line at Kit. After all, what do I have for proof but gossip, however high-toned? Hardly the stuff to withstand the scrutiny of history. Instinctively I feel that the veils shrouding our collective past should be rent, important that we claim as our own the Melvilles and Willa Cathers and Cary Grants. For God's sake, I managed to study Whitman for two years at Yale without it ever being pointed out that he was queer. *Whitman!* Begging the question of what a dunce I was for not figuring it out myself—but that, as they say, is another story.

During the next few years I was madly busy, churning out screenplays for Universal with one hand, up half the night writing fiction with the other. It's a wonder I didn't collapse, I was so driven. I certainly wasn't thinking much about what I was writing anymore. It didn't matter at Universal, where an army of underlings let not a comma go by without demanding a rewrite. And the novels, increasingly cerebral and unreal, seemed to have lost their compass too. I was far away from completing Forster's vision, love fulfilled and unafraid to shout its name. Gert never tried to steer me any differently. She didn't remotely understand how the movie business worked, beyond the adage that the writer was the lowest of the low in Hollywood. She gave me all the slack I needed, her fingers crossed that one of my antic scripts would get lucky and reach the screen. I was very full of myself in those years, fancying that I was developing quite a reputation as a wit, and that soon I would claim my place as a sort of latter-day Noël Coward, dry and effortless, skewering pretension.

It was somewhere in there that I visited Gert up at Sneden's, the trees on the river slope flaunting their gold in the sharp October light. We had birthdays just a week apart, and this was by way of a joint celebration, my thirty-three to her seventy-three. I think I was already starting to crack under the strain of my double career, a half dozen scripts under my belt that languished on various desks of people with less and less power—Hollywood's one-way ticket to Siberia. But I insisted to Gert I was still in the game, determined to battle the odds till I produced a script as sublimely funny and sophisticated as *Private Lives.*

"But that was a play," Gert retorted mildly. And then she gave me a very Gert look, wry and penetrating, the ash of her upheld cigarette precariously long. "You know, he stood right where you're standing once," she said, and it took me half a beat to realize she meant Coward. "And he said, 'I don't know that I ever really had love in my life. Not the way I wanted it.'" Gert had been stunned, partly because she knew the two men who'd been Coward's longtime lovers, one and then the other, and they certainly seemed to love *him.* Besides, Coward was the bard of romantic love: half the civilized world could whistle those songs of wistful longing for the perfect mate found in *If Love Were All.* Now it turned out that maybe even Noël Coward wasn't Noël Coward.

Within another year I'd hit the wall. I'd just finished writing a leaden script about vile people, called *The Hamptons*—suffice to say that it paid the bills and made me feel like slime on dirty water. That summer my union decided to go on strike against the producers, demanding a cut of the video market. The six-month strike managed to derail all careers as marginal as mine, the kind that were based on fast talk and no screen credits. At the same time my editor in New York up and quit the company that had published my last four books. For the next three years I would try to peddle first one story and then another, on the strength of a hundred pages and an outline, only to find myself summarily rejected. Not hot anymore. By the end of that downward spiral I had a raft of rejection slips, enough to decoupage the walls of my study and then some.

My lowest point was the fall of '81, compounded by the end of a ruinous affair—two months' obsession and general self-destruction on my side, an enervated dalliance on his. And when it was over I wouldn't let it go. It was as if my hands were frozen on the steering wheel, my foot slamming the gas pedal, reliving again the self-abuse of falling in love with straight boys. The endless crash-and-burn of my adolescent crushes, all the way up to my twenty-fifth year, coming round full circle and leaving me pining for a hustler. I'd thought my love for Roger would protect me from the heart's careening, but it didn't, not that year.

I withheld the truth from him instead, figuring the least I could do was keep the pain to myself. But didn't succeed at that either, only managing to blame my ashen countenance and sudden bursts of sobbing on the dead end of my work. I went back into therapy, three hours a week. I can't even stomach rereading my journal of those months of suicidal emptiness. There's nothing further to learn from it—except perhaps the tenacity of shame, still able to sting twelve years later. Roger and I came out the other side more or less intact, though the useless pain and grief took months and months to deaden.

It was in the middle of all of that I finally wrote a play. I don't even think I told Gert about it till after the first draft was done. In the beginning it had more to do with the mire I was in with Joel, the object of my fixation. He was writing a play himself, about Jews for Jesus, without the slightest anxiety about what he might face in trying to get it produced. I decided this was the proper attitude—that I'd spent too much time being channeled and second-guessed by producers and well-meaning editors, till my work felt like everyone's business but mine. I would just begin: Act I, Scene I.

A stubbornly old-fashioned play, as it turned out, a drawing-room comedy set twenty years in the past. Did anyone even *have* a drawing room anymore? It didn't deter me in the least, once I'd set my focus. I went back and forth to French's on Sunset, buying single copies of faded comedies from between the wars, plays that nobody bothered to revive, so stuck in the genteel past were they. They had butlers and cooks and intrusive in-laws, in and out through the French windows, all fifth business to the leading lady and leading man. And always a tart-tongued best friend for the lady, whiskey on her breath, as well as a smooth-talk troublemaker who snaked his way into Eden and turned the central marriage upside down.

By the time I finished the first scene I was hooked, taking pleasure in the act of writing for the first time in years. How was I to know it wasn't permitted anymore to write a play with eight characters, this being the age of downsizing? Bare stage, two or three actors—that's what producers were looking for now. I hadn't bothered to scope out the system at all: the nurturing of playwrights in the regional theaters, a close-knit troupe of itinerants where everyone knew everyone else. The one thing that hadn't changed since Gert's time was Hollywood as anathema, at best a necessary evil as long as you didn't make it a habit.

I finished the draft in about four months and began to work with a director friend who has since abandoned the boards to work in soaps, an easy half million a year and you get to live in New York. *He* was old enough to remember the fox-collar glamour of Kit Cornell and Ina Claire and the Lunts. He saw what I was trying to do with a long-abandoned form, saw it better perhaps than I, and didn't let me get away with a wasted line. I worked another four months on revisions, tightening up and trimming the excess foliage, jettisoning one character (but careful to save his best lines and sprinkle them around among the others).

At last I was ready to show it to Gert. I dispatched a copy to Sneden's Landing, waiting two weeks before I followed it up with a call. I needn't have worried: she loved it. So much so that she'd already called up two or three of her ancient producer friends to ask if they were in the market. A little while later she had to go into the hospital for minor surgery, and to have her regular confrontation with her doctors as to the volume of cigarettes and vodka she consumed. Her niece, Merloyd, told me that Gert's copy of *Just the Summers* was the prominent item on her bedside table, in case she could pitch it to some old friend with moneybags who came by to visit.

The old producers shook their heads. Marvelous play, they admitted, but far too many speaking parts and a world that was simply forgotten. Gert remained undiscouraged, no more willing to give it up now than she was the Camels and the Stoli. In the end I didn't need her connections, and managed to draw a coterie of enthusiasts on my own, which led to a group of staged readings, the closest I ever came to being produced. Fifty folding chairs in a loft, but if you squinted a bit you could almost believe you were in a theater, that the actors weren't reading from scripts but living every line.

It was years before it dawned on me that I'd written a play for an audience of one—and Miss Gertrude Macy was that one. Doubtless all of us writers are always out to please someone, Forster and his mother again. But Gert was something rarer than that. If I made it well enough to knock *her* socks off, then it would bear a seal of pedigree that went all the way back to the glittering streets of Broadway in its prime. Gert showed up at the loft on Ninth Avenue for the first reading, wearing her funeral duds, decades older than everyone else, and laughed her booming laugh at all the jokes she already knew. It was later that night that she took me and Roger to "21," when I asked if it went too fast.

By the following autumn the play had a producer and a director and an improbable semicommitment from Donald Sutherland to star. Thus we were suddenly locked into a Broadway production, raising our costs from the eighty thousand that would have sufficed for a ninety-nine seater to something over seven hundred thousand. It seemed an impossible gamble, but hard to resist. Our next reading was in a cavernous apartment in the Dakota, gargoyles peering in and a crowd of fat cats in the folding chairs, possible investors. "You can smell the money," murmured Gert as she leaned toward me.

I was out at Sneden's a couple of evenings later, still flush from the performance at the Dakota, how moving Sutherland had been as Julian, a man who'd chosen the closet in order to marry straight and rich. I remember Gert and I actually talked about individual theaters, which ones would work in the play's favor, and incidentally what great plays had trod the boards there previously. I was very high on the dream that night.

Around midnight we'd both stopped talking at last, a feat in itself, since the two of us could go on for hours. Gert was on to her nightcap as we sat before the fire, while I puffed on a roach—a tableau worthy of a post-mod *Candida*. And when she quietly asked about this "gay cancer" she'd been reading about, I realized it had been on her mind all evening. This must've been the winter of '83, before Cesar or anyone else I knew had fallen. So far it was all just shadowy rumors, an East Coast thing. I retorted with a careless laugh, assuring her it had nothing to do with Roger and me. The pinnacle of my earliest denial.

And I remember it didn't appease her, the worried crease only seeming to deepen in the firelight. But we let it go for the moment, for the sake of the circle of security we provided for one another. Only when I was leaving, as she dropped me off at the bridge to get a taxi, did she squeeze my hand and say, "Be careful."

There was one other time, a few months later. I was back and forth to New York quite a bit that year, having been hired to write a script about a model who becomes the billboard face of the moment. *15 Minutes*, it was called, and I cared about it a lot because it had an upfront gay character who was the girl's best friend and roommate, a mad queen. I barely had time to talk to Gert on the phone, but managed to hold an evening open before my return to L.A. There was snow on the ground at Sneden's, a late winter that stubbornly wouldn't yield to spring.

I can't say Gert was in somber spirits, or any less ebullient to have me for an evening to herself. Curious, but she never seemed to age during that decade I knew her—never aged *further,* I mean, than the beautiful wrinkled terrain of her face the day I met her. So I would've said that night that she was the same as ever, indomitable, but then I was the one who could still laugh off the darkness about to engulf us all.

"I have to go into the hospital again," she said with a certain breeziness. "They think there's a spot on my lung." She was puffing a cigarette even as she said it.

Then *I* was the one who got gloomy. Could it be cancer? Yes, of course. But they could treat it, right? They were catching it early, right? She shrugged, somehow not all that concerned. She'd always hoped to reach eighty, she said, but after that she knew it was a free-fall. And then she started to reminisce about the ones she'd lost to cancer, and here the passion surfaced. First her beloved younger sister, then Kit—both had died in the age of discretion, when genteel people thought it best not to tell the truth to the dying. "Oh, it was terrible. They got sicker and sicker, and we'd all put on our brave faces and tell them they were going to be *fine*." She fired that last word with fierce regret.

And what did she think death was, I asked her. Nothing, she replied, matter-of-factly. But what about the white light and the tunnel, I persisted. Lately there had been much to-do among those who studied near-death experiences, people who'd gone to the brink and back, the welcoming committee of loved ones beckoning them into the light. No, said Gert, she gave that no credence at all: "That's just the brain shutting down." There was something heroic about her lack of sentimentality, consistent with her belief that when it was time to go you made your own choice and pressed your own button. No extraordinary measures to keep the body pumping. I remember hoping I'd be that way myself when it got to be closer to my time—but that was forty years away, long enough to get used to death.

Merloyd writes to me that Gert's stoicism in the face of illness and death didn't mean she wasn't a believer in her own way:

> She would tell me in the last years of her life that at certain moments she would feel a kind of euphoria. She felt that perhaps it was what came to people who meditate. She somehow knew intuitively how to step outside of time. The very way she chose to live, facing the river, facing the sea, rescuing stray dogs and sticking by old friends and wayward family when anyone else's last shred of tolerance would have snapped, was a kind of celebration, even worship of life.

I didn't hear from Gert all that summer, assuming I would've heard if anything was wrong. Forgetting that proud instinct of hers, discretion at all costs and never a bother to anyone. When I thought of Gert I pictured her at the Vineyard, still clocking noon by mixing herself a bullshot. Indeed she was, says Merloyd, in a turban to mask the effects of the chemo, and stuffed avocados as usual on the deck. I don't even remember what my deadline was that summer, or whether Donald Sutherland had pulled out by then, or if the producer had already washed his hands of the whole thing.

In any case my poor play was moribund and orphaned, and I hated to think of telling Gert, who had been so much its champion. October came, and our birthdays. Because I couldn't rouse her on the phone, I sent flowers to Sneden's. The card read: "Happy 79 from Happy 38." Roger and I were busily getting ready for an autumn trip to Tuscany, so I didn't really think to follow up on the roses. But a couple of days later the florist called to say they couldn't deliver the order. Why not? "The lady's in the hospital, sir." Well then, I answered briskly, have them delivered there. A day later the stakes escalated. The florist again, apologizing profusely, but they couldn't deliver them to the hospital either. I knew and I didn't know. I placed a call to the hospital myself, and was told I should "talk to the family," the first I'd ever heard that particular sidestep. But then, the euphemisms of dying hadn't flooded my vocabulary yet.

I spoke with Merloyd, fumbling a condolence, hardly conscious yet of what I'd just lost. The family was planning a memorial lunch at Sneden's, but Roger and I had to decline because we'd be in Italy on that day. I lit a candle for Gert in Florence, in Brunelleschi's soaring graystone church of Santo Spirito, a believer in beauty if nothing else. Returning from that trip Roger and I were seized by the emergency of Cesar's diagnosis, and on and on till all of our friends were consumed one way or another, dying themselves or taking care of the stricken.

I hadn't much time for reflection once the plague had taken root. When I'd think of Gert it was always bittersweet—a word Coward practically invented—recalling a vanished world before the war. I understand now that it wasn't just a friend who'd been taken from me, but an elder and a mentor. Gert was my pioneer, a link to the dreams that made me different, the push I needed to go my own way. I don't think I ever thanked her in so many words, but following her lead, I refuse to regret that. No regrets. Of course, no one knows who the Barretts are anymore, or Kit or Coward or the Lunts. It won't be long, I suppose, before we come to a place where even Garbo and Dietrich will mostly draw a blank. All of them, I suppose, are just a sidelight anyway to the history of the gay and lesbian struggle. Glamorous though the closet was, the world Gert and her friends inhabited still had walls, such that they didn't even think to reach out to the pained anonymous legions of queers with nobody to look up to. Maybe history wasn't ready yet. In any case I can't bring myself to condemn them for their silence and their compromise. It needed a revolution to challenge us all, a moment after which there would be no going back: Stonewall.

I don't know if Gert reached out to me, or I to her. It was doubtless a mutual thing. In my play there's a character called Robin, a balmy old woman poet in a wheelchair who lived in Paris in the twenties and knew them all. She keeps calling the young man in the play Ernest, mistaking him for Hemingway. Robin isn't quite Gert, who never suffered a moment's lapse of clarity, but the same historical linkage was there. And at the end of the play, when the young man Tom has broken with Julian and is off on his own to Paris, he has one last question for his mentor. "Does it go too fast?" he asks. "You mean life?" retorts Julian. "Just the summers."

Gert proved wrong in the end. It has gone too fast, so swift and sudden I sometimes feel I've been left clutching the empty air as life rocketed by. Gert swore I wouldn't feel at the end I hadn't had enough, but then she couldn't know the seismic convulsion that AIDS would unleash. Frankly, I'm glad she didn't live to see the decimation of the arts, by plague and then by Philistines. Better for her to sit on the bluff of her memories, cheerfully giving it all away to me, though never stuck in the past herself. My friend from the far country of the eighth decade, first among sisters. Providing me my most intense experience of age, a cider taste of a world I would never reach myself except through her. All that and the Broadway years besides, *my* Broadway years. Caviar extra, but who can quibble with such a banquet? Or two on the aisle in Row H, as a thousand curtains rise.

# Old Squirrel Head, Mama, & Me

My mother, a widow living in the small Georgia town near Atlanta where I grew up, fell and broke her leg at eighty-six. That was in 1991. I am an only child, and most people would have called relatives, I suppose. I knew in my case that was a waste of time. Some of my relatives are the type who believe that someone has planted a transmitter in their head and tracked them with laser beams. Then, there were numerous cousins, who had not liked me for fifty years, and the feeling was mutual. I would not have asked them for the time of day.

So, from the sanctuary in Greenwich Village to which I had escaped long ago, I called Paul, my real family—a gay man who had been my friend for upwards of thirty years. After extensive wanderings, he had returned to live in our benighted hometown a few years back. I had talked to him at Christmas, so I knew he was OK. Not necessarily aging gracefully, but OK.

When he answered the phone this time, I just said, "Paul, I need help."

His reply was, "Is this the person I love best in the world?"

I said, "I guess so. It's me."

No excuses, no questions asked, Paul said that of course he would go over to the hospital and look in on Mama, who had not always been very nice to him. For years she had called Paul "old squirrel head," and had given me black looks when he came to call. Not because she thought Paul was gay—her mind instinctively avoided those meanderings—but because he was my friend. Mama did not like to share me with anyone, male or female.

But for my sake Paul went to the hospital to do battle with Mama's crazy sister, the one with the transmitter in her head; a raft of stolid cousins who felt very put upon to have been informed of their aunt's accident; plus a few doctors who wanted Mama shipped instantly to a nursing home, of which they were co-owners, where they could collect her Medicare for "rehabilitation."

By the time I flew in, Mama knew she had been rescued and had dropped all references to "old squirrel head." Instead, she was calling Paul her "precious friend," and they were doing everything but the bed-pan together.

A few days later, Paul and I ferried Mama home, where I had been engaged in a monumental scrub-down. Mama could not get about well enough herself to clean properly and had refused for a long time to hire anyone else to do it; stinginess and stubbornness were two more of her endearing traits.

Now, while my Bible Belt, homophobic mother slept peacefully in her own bed (thanks to the generous ministrations of "old squirrel head" and her daughter the dyke), Paul and I hung out in the kitchen. A coffee-klatsch of real, honest-to-God unnatural degenerates, as they would say in the local church, right there at Mama's kitchen table. This was, after all, Sam Nunn country, the native ground on which the story of my friendship with Paul had begun to unfold in the late 1950s.

"I don't have words to thank you," I told Paul.

"None necessary," he said.

I thought that there had never been any words for so much of what was between us. He had known me longer than any of my lovers, through years that spanned great changes in my life and transitions in our relationship. We had visited people and places together, studied the Italian Renaissance, planted gardens, and chopped down Christmas trees. Though he was only ten years older, he had showed me the world and how to make my way in it, better than most fathers, and was now behaving like the kindest of brothers.

Not that my youth was lacking in people wanting to point me in the right direction. Mama, of course, thought of herself as an infallible authority. But early on, it became obvious that we were not going in the same direction, simply because I started sleeping with women.

I had no name for that; I was just in love—from the age of fifteen with an older woman I had met and slept with in North Georgia at summer church camp. She was studying nursing in New Orleans. I wrote her steamy letters, received quite steamy ones in return, and saw her when she came back to Atlanta for vacations. It was great training for long-distance relationships.

At the outset, I did not suspect how that love would separate and distinguish me, but my intuition pegged it as verboten. I knew enough to keep quiet. First, the puritan code I had been raised by taught that anything that made you happy must be wrong. Then, Mama did not like to share, as I have indicated previously.

She came up with a definition for my great love from the dictionary—after she found some of the letters from the nurse. While Mama was pitching a hissy fit, I read and reread a sparse analysis of *homosexual* that said something about gorillas and chimpanzees. Daddy hovered sheepishly in the background, which was what he did best. I knew that I had to lie, so I used all my wiles to convince Mama that she was way off base. As a precaution, I started carrying all the letters with me everywhere I went.

Perhaps because of my great secret, my adolescence was something of an emotional blur, and only a very good cause could induce me to rake over that smoldering heap of coals.

That cause is our history, I suppose. Now that the general public and the media acknowledge the existence of the gay world, I believe that it is important for us not to get tarred by their brushes. Like America, we were here before they discovered us, right under their noses. If outsiders find the notion of lesbians as man haters provocative, that has nothing to do with my reality.

I am reminded of a talk show a few years ago where the hostess had two sets of lesbian guests: the man haters, or separatists; and women who had come out late after being married and raising children, and presumably did not hate men.

All I could say was that I did not fit either of these groups—the man haters or the women who had married men—and I had been around for a while. The emotional lives of most of the lesbians I had known had centered on women, as gay men's lives were centered on other men, and nobody had concerned themselves much about hating, or marrying, the opposite sex. You might want to banish to a faraway planet the lover who had betrayed you with another, but not the gay boy next door whose shoulder you had cried on. Straight men concerned me only as bosses, colleagues, or someone else to hide my identity from. Hating men, marrying or not marrying them, seemed to me problems for straight girls.

I do not know whether the story of my friendship with Paul will help to set the record straight, so to speak, or not. But I do believe that how we met and became friends and family says something about gay life as double life in an extremely repressive social order. A misstep could be costly, and survival back then in the fifties could depend at any time on loyalty and a mutual defense network that would cover your back, or come to your aid when you called.

Without women's organizations, men's organizations, task forces, or consciousness-raising groups, we had only each other. But perhaps in the end, when the politicking and the hoopla have subsided, that is all that any of us have. Like most young people, I suppose, I experienced a confusion, self-hatred, and anger that I would rather not remember. But being gay to boot made for a very murky wilderness where Paul became a beacon.

Flying blind most of the time in high school about where I fit in, I got lucky. I fell into Paul's American history class. The usual campus gossip circulated about him. Late twenties, unmarried, dark straight hair, and hazel eyes. All the girls—except me—speculated about Mr. MacPherson's love life. I was more interested in Paul's gifts as a historian, and his strength of character.

Paul was no nellie queen. He was perhaps the first intellectual I ever met; someone who read books and listened to opera and classical music. I was also impressed the day he threw some smart-aleck boy out of the classroom—I mean, literally threw him out, the kid still sitting in his desk and all. Paul had self-confidence and pizzazz, and earned respect fast.

If primitive lavender radar pointed me in Paul's direction, I was not the only one. A barrage of nice, white children—integration was not even a dot on the horizon—descended on his classroom after school. Each one of us was out of step in some way that must have homed in on Paul's flair for the bizarre. Since he had been around, he probably realized that we were all gay as geese.

Without realizing what we were about, we began gathering informally on the lawn for lunch, with Paul as our centerpiece, in warm weather—which was most of the time. You could always count on a certain group to show up because we felt safe and accepted, and laughed a lot. To me, Paul seemed a chink in a monolithic old-boy network, a male authority figure I could learn from.

I remember best the senior prom, when Paul was selected faculty adviser. As volunteers for the committee, my friends and I turned that dance party every way but loose. It was definitely the most artistic production ever in that tacky town. We painted flats and built arches for "My Blue Heaven," and strung streamers and spots around the ceiling, under the supervision of a sweet, gentle soul whose obsession was choreographing light and sound with fountains in his mother's garden. But a drag number to "I Burned Your Letters When You Told Me Good-Bye" was the hit of the evening.

We had a stellar cast, assembled by Paul. The headliner of that drag routine went on to become resident hairdresser to one of Atlanta's most notorious call girls, while moonlighting as director of music at a large metropolitan church. Another boy from the show met some trick years later who took him off to L.A., and then on to the New York cabaret circuit.

Tongues wagged at the prom, but what could they say? We looked almost like everybody else; we even had dates. I went with my friend Tommy, who also played the oboe and sax in the school band. Paul attended with Miss Madison, the physical-education teacher, who looked sort of like Mickey Mantle. But she was a woman.

As I look back, it occurs to me to ask why there was no woman to be my mentor. Why did the task fall to Paul, and the boys? I believe that a lot of women I could have revered in that time and place were too far back in the closet. An exceptional human being, Paul got the call instead. Years later, in New York, I found women who could take me the next steps on the way.

After the senior prom and graduation, it was definitely time to move on. My girlfriend in New Orleans was going to China, or somewhere, to be a missionary, and I was enrolled in the nice Baptist college that Mama had chosen for me. There, I would be safe from all the things that threatened the world's foundations in 1959: sex, alcohol, and fast cars, to quote Mama. When I said good-bye to Paul, he asked where I was going to be and expressed a concern for my future welfare.

I did not know what I was getting into, but as luck would have it, Macon, Georgia, where the college was located—a small city almost in the middle of the state—turned out not to be the haven Mama had promised. On the contrary, it was there that life began to reveal to me its true contours, and also the names for many things. In fact, I received the education of a lifetime in under a year, and gratefully escaped, largely because Paul was beside me.

In the first few weeks at the college, I had an affair with the junior girl who lived as a freshman counselor on our floor. She confessed to me a powerful lust for both men and women, though she played the piano every Sunday at the local church. I also met alcoholics studying to be ministers of the gospel, and thoroughly depraved youths from tiny towns bordering on large swamps in remote corners of the state.

This was more variety than I had expected, and somewhat confusing. Always looking for an identity, wanting to belong somewhere, I had gone out for sorority rush—which now seems truly like something out of *Believe It or Not.* Half in love with one of the sisters, by late fall I was shakily recovering from her sorority's rejection.

Had they rejected me because they had guessed that I was a "homosexual," I wondered. Like the chimps and the gorillas? More importantly, how had they figured it out, and would they tell?

Then, as that miserable semester slouched toward its end, Paul called me up out of the blue and told me he was in town.

"What are you doing here?" I asked.

He had forsaken teaching to try to make a little money in business, and the company was also located in Macon.

"How did you find me?"

"Does that matter?" he asked. Of course it did not, because Paul was back. We went out, surely my most interesting social engagement of the season, and how we laughed. What a relief! Adept as I was at concealing my feelings, I am sure I did not tell him how unhappy I was. Maybe he knew anyway. I think each of us was waiting to tell the other something important.

As things worked out, we would not have long to wait.

When we parted, Paul gave me two phone numbers—one at home and another at the house of friends.

"If you don't get me here, try this one," he said. He scrawled down a couple of names. "They're real nice people; I know you'd like them."

In that faraway time before answering machines, I missed Paul a few times but was too shy to try the other number. As a mild winter faded quickly into early spring, the forsythia was in bloom and it was time for a change. One fateful, sun-drenched afternoon, I fished the paper out of the drawer. Trumpets did not blare; sirens did not wail. But it was momentous, a real beginning.

I picked up the phone, and dialed.

It rang and rang, but I persisted. Finally, a great clatter erupted at the other end, followed by a voice that sounded like it was coming through a hollow log.

"Hullo," it drawled.

"Uh, I'm a friend of Paul's."

Silence.

"Is he there? I'm over at the college."

There was a brief pause, then a sort of giggle like the fluttering of hummingbird wings.

"Well, why don't you come on over? He'll be here in a while. We'll have a drink."

"You're Doug?" I asked. Two names—Doug and Sherry—adorned the paper.

"Yes, honey, Sherry's at work." He gave me the address, along with detailed instructions on how to get there.

Well-brought-up young ladies did not pay visits to strange men. But Doug's invitation dripped charm, and Paul was going to be there. I was not afraid of anything much anyway, except rejection by women. So, in about five minutes flat, I was out the door, striding along an avenue flanked by ancient shade trees and antebellum homes. It was as though I knew somehow that destiny was waiting for me, in that unlikely setting, arrayed in short shorts and a feather boa.

But I still had no words for any of that. Oh, they must be hippies, I thought when I saw the hallway of the apartment painted solid black and Dougie in his hostess outfit. He was tall and slim in denim cutoffs, in his early twenties, with straw-colored hair, bright blue eyes, and a face of angelic beauty. Shirtless and barefoot, the feather boa encircling his shoulders, he dangled a champagne glass from one hand.

Caravaggio should have had such a model.

Parenthetically, I am reminded again of straight people's need to be enlightened. Recently, a woman friend of mine was talking about some man she thought was a knockout, then turned to me with well-meaning apologies.

"Oh, but you wouldn't understand that," she said.

In defense of my discriminating lesbian eye, I reassured her that I did understand that there were attractive men out there. I had probably known many more than she had. Also, from long experience cruising with my buddies, I could tell a great deal about what they were looking for, and whether these men were worth the trouble.

Even then I knew, no doubt about it, that Doug, for example, was gorgeous. Plus he had a familiar devil-may-care air that I recognized would be the perfect antidote to those long faces, and all that hypocrisy and praying, at the college.

"Do you think it's too early for a drink?" he asked right off.

He could not depend on me to be disapproving.

We had several—Doug draped over a black butterfly chair near the window, and me watching him from the Danish modern couch. He did not ask me any difficult questions, and we found lots to talk about—the town, the college. After a while, he disappeared into the deeper recesses of the apartment.

I sat there woozy and content, wondering why I was having so much fun.

Then, Dougie was back, wearing a pair of sling-back pumps as an addition to his scanty costume. His eyes blazed brighter under pulsating lashes.

"Let's dance," he said and crossed the room to the stereo. A raucous rhythm-and-blues number echoed through the old house and out the open window laced with wisteria vines.

I noticed right away that Doug did not need a partner. He had begun to whirl nonchalantly, trailing the feather boa behind him. He dipped one shoulder toward the spinning floor and reversed directions with a burst of bell-like laughter. I applauded, and he was inspired. Sweat bathed his face as he swung the boa over his head and down about his smoothly gyrating hips. He was like a dazzling one-man chorus line, his long legs rising and falling. The music reached a crescendo, and as the last vibrant high note wailed, Doug took a deep bow.

Would straight girls—or boys—have found this display titillating? Disturbing? At my tender age, I saw Doug's performance as a great lesson in how to have a shameless ego, and kick over the traces. I am to this day grateful to him for it. I needed such lessons badly and in those days learned most of them from men, in or out of drag.

But Doug and I were no longer alone. A cry of distress sounded from the doorway.

"I told you not to wear my good shoes."

A plump, soft woman with a heart-shaped face charged Doug. She had short dark hair and wore a nurse's uniform. Right behind her, traipsing into the living room from the ebony hallway, was none other than Paul MacPherson.

"Hi," I said to Paul, as though our meeting at Doug's were the most natural thing in the world, planned well in advance.

"Hey, there," he replied, obviously very happy to see me there. "I wondered when I'd meet up with you again."

Of course, Paul had known all along that there was a place I belonged. But back then, the gay world was a well-kept secret. Without help, I could have spent a few more years wandering around, beating on the doors of closeted librarians and French professors, trying to make it with the sorority girls. But here was the gift up front. An underworld of my very own, where everybody knew the score and rolled with the punches. To meet Doug and Sherry was like a homecoming to a place I had never been.

I will never forget that it was Paul who gave me that phone number, and escorted me—without fanfare or trauma—through that door.

Sherry and Doug drifted into the bedroom for a major fight over her shoes, and certain drugs that were missing. Paul and I sat on the Danish modern couch and talked. He had picked Sherry up at the hospital. She and Doug were married, Paul explained, to divert suspicion, and that seemed to me a way of working things out. It never occurred to me to be shocked, or ask silly questions about Paul's sexuality, as we say now, or mine. I knew everything without asking, and divested myself of the last shreds of Mama's tidy world and its morality.

None of those rules applied here, and things that had been floating around in limbo suddenly fit into place. What startles me now, at this great remove, is how little it all startled me then. Having been an outsider for so long, I totally assimilated this rather tawdry scene with what now seems impressive rapidity.

For starters, Sherry made dinner, and wanted me to stay over when Doug and Paul went out. Paul told me he would drive me home, but I knew I would have more fun with Sherry. I was nothing if not compulsive, and figured they would never miss me at the dorm.

Sherry was lovely to me always, and did not seem to mind my sleeping around with all her friends. Except maybe Jackie, who was also a nurse and had meant a lot to Sherry, though that was over. Most of the local girls—like Mollie, Betty, and Harriet—worked in factories and drank a lot. Billy, who worked in a print shop, had been Jackie's first lover and had shot her in the leg when Jackie began to stray. It was a lively cast of characters. A woman who went by the name of Big 'Un played softball for some local team, and we often went to the games. Drunk as skunks. I drove, since I drank less than most of them because I had to go back to the dorm and study most weeknights.

There were parties, where Paul dressed up in Sherry's nurse outfit and pretended to be Florence Nightingale. Numerous servicemen from the nearby air force base came and went, and the occasional rough trade showed up, intent on robbing everybody and breaking up the party. We fought back, and one night Doug ended up in the hospital with a knife wound.

By that time, I had a name for almost everything: gay, straight, trick, trade, tearoom, queer, queer as pink lace, queen, dinge queen (the South was full of those), dyke, bull dyke (Macon was full of those), femme, butch. I was not clear on a few things, like *golden shower*, but I loved the fact that my underground fraternity had its own language. This was better than a sorority.

Then, after a couple of months of hedonistic debauchery, I woke up to some new vocabulary: purge, witch hunt, sodomite. Somewhere, it must have been determined that my baptism into the gay world would be fiery.

Paul, of course, called to give me the word.

"Don't go down to the bar for a while," he said.

Anne's Tick Tock Lounge was a ratty place anyway, but it was a hub of the town's social life.

"What happened?" I asked.

"See you later at Sherry's and Doug's," he said mysteriously.

That night I got the full story, from the three of them. It was not pretty. A local gay guy who had married a straight woman for big bucks was under investigation for her murder. He had the perfect alibi, because he was in the hospital with a hernia operation. The floor nurses on the night of the murder were none other than Sherry and Jackie. Suspicion had fallen first on the couple's Negro chauffeur, but the police had so broken him down that he had admitted to frequent sexual encounters with his boss man.

To make matters worse, the suspected murderer was an old flame of Doug's, and had invited Doug and Sherry to all his fancy society parties. The police confiscated a few guest lists, and bingo. What were those two—the floor nurse from the wrong side of the tracks and this unemployed hippie—doing at bashes with the elite?

The local police took the whole thing very seriously. They had already had Doug and Sherry downtown, for fingerprints and mug shots. A couple of anonymous phone callers in the middle of the night had whispered "Sodomite" and hung up.

The police had ordered Doug and Sherry not to leave town, and my friends were afraid the apartment was being watched. We agreed not to gather there for a while, to call only from pay phones, and to pass the word around to lie low.

I knew that Mama would not be pleased.

On the way back to the college, Paul cautioned me.

"Take it easy," he said. "The semester's almost over. Maybe you could spend a little more time studying."

"Oh, they're not gonna come around the college."

"Don't be so sure," he warned; he had seen purges in operation—in civilian and military life. "They're out for blood. They'll go after anybody and anything."

I had no illusions about how much cops hated queers, but I did not scare easy. Also, I did not want to give up the softball game with the girls, even if it was the night before finals. At least when they wanted to go to the bar, I remembered Paul's warning and said no. Back in the dorm, I sat up all night over my biology notes, and ended up getting a B.

When I staggered back sleepily after the exam, a message was waiting for me. "Call Paul," it said.

I did. The news was not good.

"Do you know Alice Holly?" he asked me. She was the only coed I knew at the college who was out-there gay. Unfortunately, she was not my type, though I had managed to sleep with her once or twice.

"The cops picked her up at the bar last night. They were checking IDs," he said. "They took her in, called the college, and they expelled her."

"She was graduating," I said lamely.

"They expelled her anyway," he replied grimly. "Mollie told Sherry."

"She was with Mollie?" I asked with a smirk, thinking that anyone who would go out with Mollie probably deserved to be arrested.

Paul brought me up short.

"They're making everybody they bring in now name names."

My name, I thought and froze.

"Are you through with your finals?" Paul asked.

"Last one was today."

"I'm gonna pick you up and drive you home for the weekend."

"You don't have to do that," I said shyly.

"I'd never forgive myself," he said. "Just get ready."

Paul could be very persuasive. As Doug used to say—"When Sister MacPherson says go, you go"—and it seemed I had learned more than enough for one semester.

I had to go back to the college only to get my clothes and check out. The purge picked up steam in the summer. People named more names, and gay people fled Macon pell-mell into the Georgia bush. As I found out later, Alice Holly had offered me up to the college authorities, who had chosen to ignore me because I was leaving anyway. I escaped by the skin of my teeth, and did not return to Macon for years.

Paul and I laughed about that spring. Alice Holly—the one who got kicked out of school—positively did not laugh, and I never heard anything about her again. I saw Sherry, who left Doug soon after, a few times, and a couple of the other girls. Since the drug culture of the sixties was right around the corner, I do not know if beautiful Dougie survived it all.

Paul and I shared many other moments, as I grew from daughter to sister in our makeshift family. We were in graduate school together, and I watched him expend incredible energies on callow youths I thought unworthy of his charms. But a couple of things I learned quick in the gay world: do not judge anybody, because who are you to say what makes them happy; and the only sin is to make people suffer. A far cry from my Baptist Sunday school upbringing. Because of Paul, I got to go many places that I would not have seen otherwise—from sleazy waterfront bars to Victorian mansions. We have discussed marriage, and tried sex together. But that is not the nature of our love.

Now Paul sometimes drives Mama to get her hair cut, and she calls him at least three times a week. I cannot stop her, and he says he does not mind. He came up to visit last summer, and has a new boyfriend, shockingly younger.

Mama seems to have forgotten the days when she called Paul "old squirrel head." She still carries on about sin and perdition from time to time, but it does not have the same ring of conviction. Abandoned by her crazy sister and the rest of that nasty tribe, she has, I think, almost learned to be accepting of and grateful for her daughter the dyke. Not to mention Paul, almost a surrogate son.

Mama is getting around to what I discovered a long time ago—that love equals tolerance and respect, and is the only family value that matters. If any comes your way, hang on tight!

# In Training

Nineteen forty-nine was my first summer in a Europe still filled with rubble from the war, where I discovered the delights of Italian men. In 1950 I returned once more before entering the Johns Hopkins University School of Medicine in Baltimore. I indulged myself as much as possible in what a denizen of that town, H. L. Mencken, archly called "Levantine deviltries." And now in the autumn of that year I found myself with a classmate returning from downtown Baltimore on a hot city bus, hanging on to the straps as we surged back and forth between stops, showers of sparks cascading from the electric lines as we clattered across tracks. My friend, Lindsay, who had gone to Princeton and was from a rich Washington family, hated sweating for anything, his monogrammed linen handkerchief becoming more stained and limp as he wiped his face. We had both joined the same club at Johns Hopkins and become friends, warily at first.

Bumping across a web of tracks at the bottom of Monument Street that threw us back and forth in a confined wave, we slid into another classmate, Mellanie Bantam, whom we'd met at a reception for students a couple of days before. Mellie was almost ten years older than the rest of us. Square, solid, she had a beautiful grin, dark hair, and Indian-dark eyes. Her thick molasses accent came with her from Red Hill, Arkansas. Just then the bus antenna slipped off the wires and we stopped dead in the suffocating heat. Someone groaned. A child on its mother's lap leaned over Lindsay's expensive tasseled loafers and puked a gush of chunky yellow vomit over his silk-stockinged feet, splashing on both of Mellanie's brown oxfords as well. The acrid smell of vomit filled the bus as Lindsay and I, eyes watering, retched loudly. Bucking the crowd like a squat surfer, Mellanie pushed us through the door to fresh air, Lindsay hopping on one foot as he shook meaty pieces out of his shoes.

"Ruined! My new shoes!" He made a face. "Yaaagh!" He flung the loafers into a garbage can. "Jesus! That brat!"

"Y'all were fixin' to make a mess yourselves," commented Mellie, wiping my face with a Kleenex as I gulped. She sat down on the curb, reaching up her skirt to pull off each cotton stocking, wadding them up as she thrust them into her shopping bag. Mellanie didn't shave her legs, and she wasn't going to start in medical school. She banged her shoes together, then dropped them in, too, as Lindsay moaned about his Italian tassels.

"These here ain't Eyetalian, but I sure cain't afford to chunk 'em in the trash," she commented. "Gimme those shoes. Somebody can use them." Mellie put them in her shopping bag and we set out, Lindsay barefooted, to walk up the Monument Street hill to Broadway, Mellanie singing, "Hey, good lookin', whaaaat you got cookin'. . . ," one of her favorite Hank Williams numbers. We made friends then, and medical school became a bit less scary. There were others in the same boat.

Mellie in 1941 had been a student at Brigham Young University— her presence there a legacy from Mormon missionary work in her part of Arkansas, where her biker state-cop brother became a Mormon bishop, although she never joined. BYU was a strange place for someone like Mellie, but it was an education. In that tight group she remained a "yaller dog" Democrat stoutly loyal to President Roosevelt, whom most Mormons regarded with suspicion. When Pearl Harbor was attacked, they called FDR a warmonger and hypocrite. Furious, Mellie left BYU and sent for her mother. They set out for California in winter over the Donner Pass, where their car broke down in a blizzard, with no help within a half day's drive. Mellie wrapped her mother in every piece of spare clothing they had between them, winding her stockings around her mother's hands while they waited in the deepening cold. A transcontinental rig finally appeared, and they were rescued.

When they returned home, Mellanie joined the Women's Army Corps. Amicably divorced, she left her young daughter with her mother and her ex-husband. Sent to England, Mellanie was assigned to the staff of the *Stars and Stripes* newspaper as a correspondent. Moving into Normandy with the invasion, she was swept across France and into Belgium. From there the Allied forces pushed into the Ardennes, where she earned a combat star for valor in the Battle of the Bulge.

After the surrender in Europe, Mellanie, interested in medicine after her experiences on the front line, returned to Red Hill, where she started work in a local medical clinic. There she met Marnie, a navy veteran and a registered nurse; they moved in together. Marnie helped her complete her university degree, after which Mellanie was accepted at the Johns Hopkins Medical School. A suitor who had been in love with Mellanie's mother when they were young and who later became an industrialist created a scholarship fund for her. Just before she entered medical school, her mother died of heart disease.

Mellanie entered with our class. She settled in at the Johns Hopkins Women's Medical Association, otherwise known as the Hen House—a pleasant row house down Broadway a bit from the medical school complex. I found a place in another row house where other students boarded opposite the old administration building. This building at Monument and Broadway, completed in 1893, is a colorful collection of patterned brick towers, cupolas, chimneys, and porte cocheres surrounded by an ornamental iron fence. It is flanked by the wards of the period, all of which fronts later additions extending a couple of blocks back. In one of the old buildings was the Brady Urological Institute, founded by Dr. Hugh Young with a gift from Diamond Jim Brady, a financial buccaneer of the Gilded Age whose plumbing was repaired by Dr. Young. Mr. Brady and his girlfriend, Lillian Russell, were delighted with the result; hence the gift. On every floor of the institute there is a portrait of Diamond Jim, his waistcoat buttons, cravat pin, and cuff links flashing gems as big as nickels.

In the white stone beaux arts library across the street hangs another portrait, a vast canvas by John Singer Sargent of the four founding fathers of the medical school, all swirling velvet and satin-banded robes. It is as much an advertisement of personality, power, and prestige as are the portraits of Diamond Jim, but this work has the Establishment imprimatur and is by the "right" artist. Mellie and I liked to compare the two. I think she liked Diamond Jim's frank flamboyance.

As our friendship grew, I'd go down the street to the Hen House to see Mellie—to study together or to hang out. Coming to Johns Hopkins, I inherited a set of expectations because two older brothers had also gone there. I resembled one of them closely, and his friends, now on staff and on the faculty, often called me by his name. I had met many of them on previous visits. My father, another physician and a pivot in my life, had died a few years before, and I missed him keenly. Mellie's mother, the center of her life, had died only the year before. In this we had a bond that we could talk about if we wanted to, relieved to grieve. I could tell Mellie some of my fears. One big one was that I had made the wrong choice by going to medical school and that I didn't have the guts to change it. I discovered that many of the other students, including Mellanie, felt like this at some point along their way.

More and more, Lindsay became one of the group. Fascinated, we listened to his accounts of his busy Washington social season, which he took very seriously, and to his accounts of the well-known figures in the musical and literary worlds he knew. *Life* magazine featured his art collection in an issue that year, and he took us to see it at his home. It included eight portraits of Lindsay himself in various media and poses. He was an opera freak, too, and was hilarious when he burlesqued singers and performances, besides being a consummate mimic of the faculty and staff. And Mellanie always felt easy enough, after a couple of hours of this, or when we had been out to dinner or a movie if we had time, to say, "Y'all go home now. I've got studying to do and so do y'all."

◖●◗

In the first year our first trial was human anatomy class. Early into the class Mellanie remarked that she noticed a certain jockeying for position going on, and this continued throughout the course. The atmosphere in anatomy class was oppressive. Dr. Allen Shefflin, our professor, taught by bullying and intimidation. He sat on his dais rapping out questions and orders, always ready to sneer and humiliate. Mellanie's accent and easy manner particularly annoyed him. His chief method was sarcasm; her answers were mild, but she held her ground.

Hopkins Medical School at that time did not issue report-card grades. One could get this information privately; usually we knew how we were doing. We also knew that if a letter from any of our course instructors appeared in our box, it meant academic trouble. Well into the course, Mellie found one when she picked up her mail. Facing possible disaster, she steeled herself for her appointment with Dr. Shefflin, only to find that he had called her in to reprimand her for minor damage to her microscope case, for which he fined her. She was disgusted by his pettiness. "He has a voice that could worm a dog," she said of their session.

Anatomy class consisted of lectures, then dissection and demonstration. Three students shared each cadaver, the cadavers becoming more and more ragged as dissection progressed. My group had a little old man whose time in the tank had obliterated any way of determining his race and (almost) his sex. He was as stiff, brown, and unhuman as a creosoted board. Most students had never seen a dead body before. Often the reaction is self-protective: feelings shut down in the face of such stark mortality. Sometimes this effect lasts an entire career.

Not so with Mellanie; war and her experiences in it, as well as her work in the rural clinic and her interest in human beings, had formed her long before this. Working with Lindsay and another woman classmate, Mellanie regarded her female cadaver tenderly. "I feel like I knew this pore soul," she said sometimes as they unwrapped the body for the session, ready for more whittling. She tried to imagine the trials and circumstances that had brought her subject to this place. As for the rest of us—the men—the stern lectures on respect for our subjects never stopped the japes when the instructors were out of the dissecting lab. By the end of the course our white lab coats had hems and cuffs of cadaver grease two inches wide. The effect on the other diners in the local greasy spoon where we sometimes ran out to lunch always made Mellie laugh. "Honey pot, that was a real hard case on the operatin' table this mornin'," she'd say, loud enough to be heard.

My first Christmas at Hopkins approached, with our holidays. I was ready to go home. Lindsay, in Washington, was already home. Mellanie would return to Red Hill and the faithful Marnie, who looked after things for her while she was gone. The Hen House always gave a traditional Christmas party for all students, staff, and faculty. There was always plenty to drink from the bar and at the big punch bowl in the basement. Starting in my freshman year, my handsome classmate Bob McGraw, after having several glasses of powerful punch, lifted me up by the heels and dunked me in the bowl head first. (He was big and I am small. Later this became a yearly practice.) When this was done, Mellie led a laughing, wet, bedraggled me to her room to towel me off, both of us a little drunk.

"Mellanie," I began, serious, slurring, holding the towel piled on my head. "I, uh, want to tell you something."

"Now what, honey pot? Is that likker still in yore ears?"

"No," I said, pushing the ends of the towel in my ear canals as much as I could. "I, uh, I, well . . . I like men."

"Sugar, so do I! They can be useful thangs sometimes. I have a daughter to prove it. And you're a man, and I *love* you." Mellanie's smile, always beautiful, comforted me.

"Oh Mellie! I mean . . . you know . . . "

"Aw, honey, I've known what you're gonna tell me since the day we met." She cupped my alcohol-stained cheek. "Martino, I've done my best to let you know I know, and it's all right. But you had to tell me yourself." She rubbed the towel vigorously over my hair. "And you know where I'm at, too." There was a comfortable silence.

"Is Lindsay? I mean . . . "

"Honey, anythang you want to know about Lindsay you ask him yourself. That ain't got nothin' to do with us talkin' here and now."

It was like coming up for air after trying to breathe underwater, and after that we never looked back. It was only much later when Lindsay and I came out to each other that I learned he had told Mellanie about himself at the same time I had—that first Christmas. Mellanie never gossiped about her friends to each other.

Mellanie listened patiently many times to the monotonous details of my unrequited crush. I'm certain she could see little in that person, but honoring the pain of each other's crushes is a kind gay and lesbian tradition. Once in a while Lindsay, whose topic was often directly or indirectly himself, gave us glimpses of his own world. Starting in his teens, and with his looks and elegant air, Lindsay had made many conquests, some of them famous people.

In the real world of student work on the surgical floors, I realized during one long duty evening that an attractive young African American orderly who jockeyed gurneys was interested, and interesting. At that time I shared an apartment over a corner drugstore with an upperclassman whose schedule brought him back only late at night. Soon Benjamin, the orderly, and I were spending evenings in bed behind a locked door; later, when we heard snoring, Benjamin would slip out. Late one night the telephone rang. I answered it no differently (I thought) than I had any hundred times before. It was Mellanie.

"Did you do those pages we were assigned yesterday?" she asked. We discussed what we were doing and had done, just as we had in all the other late calls about class. "Martino," she said out of the blue, "you've got somebody in bed, ain't you?" She sounded pleased. I was dumbfounded; I had been waiting to see how things went before mentioning Benjamin. I never discovered how she knew. She wouldn't tell me, but only smiled like the Cheshire cat.

Mellanie kept secrets and she attracted confessions, sometimes stormy ones. But she could almost always deal with them. Take Gaylord Gaines, for instance. Gaylord Gaines, a couple of classes behind us, was a Mississippi sissy from a powerful and rich family. We wondered how he got into Hopkins, for his partying took precedence over his studying. He worshiped Mellanie like a lost puppy. One night after leaving a local undercover gay bar with a trick, he fell into a trap. He and his pickup headed for the parking lot to make out in his Buick convertible. The trick's accomplice, claiming to be a security guard, shined his flashlight into the car, catching Gaylord and his pickup in the act. After a hullabaloo of curses and threats, a terrified Gaylord persuaded the accomplice, for a payoff, not to turn them in to the cops. Gaylord flew to Mellanie: my God, what to do? What would he tell his daddy?

Thinking the situation over, Mellanie called Mr. Gaines. After introducing herself, she went on: "Mr. Gaines, yore Gaylord here is jes' too much man. He's gone and got a young girl pregnant." She let Mr. Gaines digest this astounding news. "But . . . "—she hesitated—"he might not have to leave Hopkins and get *married* . . . " She stopped. Mr. Gaines was in her hands. The accent did it. "That is, if you make her a good offer." The blackmailer, she said, wanted thirty-five hundred 1952 dollars—not peanuts by a long shot. Mr. Gaines, having feared the worst with Gaylord's queeny ways, was pleased by both the problem and its solution. His son! At last he had something to brag about. He telegraphed the money within the hour. In 1952, going to the police was out of the question. Gaylord would have been hauled in on the quaint charge of having committed a "crime against nature."

(I remember, too, a straight best friend and classmate asking me with surprise, "Martino, did you know that *gay* means 'homosexual'?" We knew that, but the word *gay* didn't come out of the closet until nearly twenty years later.)

The teacher we admired most in our second year was Dr. Arnold Rice Rich, our erudite professor of pathology (and the father of Adrienne Rich, who was beginning her career as a poet). He wrote our textbook on tuberculosis, a disease with which he and many of his residents had been infected while performing autopsies. Dr. Rich held a question-and-answer session once a week during which he chose a student as a sounding board. His formal expositions were brilliant lessons in medical history as well as in pathology. In her turn, Mellanie knew her subject and did well. I felt lucky to have been called on only once.

In pathology we spent hours at autopsies in an amphitheater filled with the thick smell of fresh guts. It was in the autopsy room, not the anatomy dissection lab, that I came face-to-face with what was mortal in others and in myself: fresh mortality in the intestines we had to clean, in the dead hearts we had to handle and learn, in the livers mottled with cancer, the lungs black with smoke and lumpy with tumors, the stinking abscesses we met in these bodies dead that day. The red swirls of constantly flowing water rushing to who knows where silenced even the hardiest jokesters.

Mellanie claimed she was getting used to it. I never could. Pathology was a keenly interesting subject, though, and I could have chosen it as a specialty if only I had lacked a sense of smell. Lindsay, who had been a hospital corpsman in the navy and was consequently an expert in all things medical, insisted that carrying large gauze pads soaked with a diverting scent would solve the problem. From his mother's dressing table he confiscated a bottle of Chanel no. 5 for us to use. After trying this three or four times, Mellanie and I, and Lindsay as well, gagged as soon as he opened the square flask with its double *C*'s. To this day the mere sight of a bottle of that perfume tightens my throat with nausea. So it was back to the bodies and organs as is, with relief.

Such close attention to dead bodies made us pay closer attention in many anxious ways to our own live ones. It is during the pathology course that the suggestible students begin to develop everything from periarteritis nodosa to brain cancer and all stops in between. If this or that organ looks funny or doesn't feel right, up go the flags. Mellanie herself had breasts as large as small watermelons, and we saw what happened with tumors. Her feelings about her breasts conflicted. Pulling off her blouse one day when we were in her room, she showed me the bruised red grooves worn into her shoulders by her bra straps and told me that Dr. Egerton, chief of plastic surgery, whom she had consulted, had offered her breast-reduction surgery. It *did* reduce the chance of cancer, didn't it? "But mine are just like my mama's," she mused, "and I loved hers."

She told me then about the time an influenza epidemic hit her county, killing some and prostrating almost everyone. Among the sick was her mother, who at the time had a nursing baby, Mellanie's younger brother. Mellanie was eighteen months old and had been weaned long before. Her mother, too weak and ill to get out of bed to fix their food, pulled Mellanie into the bed and nursed her too so that she wouldn't go hungry.

Tampering with body parts this symbolic aroused strong emotions, but she had the surgery done. She awoke in the recovery room crying for her mother. Afterward she always felt a mixture of relief and regret with the result. She complained that her nipples had been planked back on wrong, pointing "straight up, like puppy noses. Honey pot," she concluded, "titties are a pain in the ass!"

As we began our third year, not unusual for that time and that setting was the attitude of our professor of gynecology, Dr. Andrew TerBosch. An aloof, fastidious man, he announced to the class soon after it began that "gonorrhea is the savior of the white race." By this he meant that its prevalence and complications in the African American population (a segment of which surrounded Hopkins) often resulted in sterility. At that time there were no African American medical students at Johns Hopkins, and the gynecology wards were segregated by race.

Race was never one of Mellanie's problems, although she was raised in surroundings where African Americans were routinely referred to as niggers. On the ward and off, people were simply individuals to Mellanie. She recalled an older woman student from Texas at the Hen House who told her, "I'm gonna run down every nigger I see in the street," because she thought the thief who stole her purse from her car was black. However, in Baltimore race has always been a factor.

Along with gynecology we had obstetrics. Mellanie appreciated Dr. Eastman, our professor (who also wrote our text), a kind, small man who stammered when he was excited; she thought his treatment of women in labor was more enlightened than most others. Having had a child herself, and having "caught" many babies when she worked in the rural clinic, Mellanie had firm ideas on the subject. Women in labor did best, she declared, when they walk about or "crawl all over," or stand or squat in a doorway to push. They should be able to eat or to have pop or tea or coffee if they want it. There were fewer complications as well as better cooperation this way.

This view didn't sit well at all with the busy OB residents, most of whom were male. Women in labor were in restraints and were monitored in one place, for convenience. Once in a while Mellanie could persuade a nurse to try it her way, but it had to be secret. We were fined if we were inattentive and the baby arrived in bed or slipped out, as small babies and "preemies" tend to do. Once Mellanie at delivery noted affably that preemies looked "just like skint squirrels before they go in the stew." The image has stayed with me. The attending resident was disgusted: Mellanie was older, she was female, and she had a southern accent—all stigmata of incompetence to him.

Men were not the only ones who were male chauvinists in medical school. One of our professors of psychiatry, Dr. Ellen Richman, played to the male gallery and had a reputation for sarcasm among the women students; she seemed to enjoy antagonizing them in our conferences. One particular day, Mellanie was to present Rose Anne, her patient from Appalachia, a woman clubbed mute by abuse, poverty, and desperation who had fallen into a depression postpartum. She had shoved her stillborn baby into the wood stove in her kitchen. Mellanie's own background wasn't too different, and she had worked hard with this patient. Before chemical treatment for depression, the chief therapy was electric shock, of which Rose Anne had had several courses, without improvement. So Mellanie had started what she called "talkin' and touchin'," finally coaxing a small response where all else had failed. When she entered the classroom, Rose Anne clinging to her hand, Dr. Richman's disapproval was obvious. Mellanie was not maintaining the clinical distance necessary for "objective assessment" in the case.

Then Richman struck. Was Rose Anne, ignorant as she was, even aware of what she was doing? Could anyone with *that* background be expected to improve at all?

I saw the struggle on Mellanie's face.

"Dr. Richman, have you ever been in the hollers?" There was outrage under her soft drawl.

She went on to evoke vividly a way of life familiar to her, if apparently brutish to an outsider. Her eloquence was the verbal equivalent of Walker Evans's poignant photographs of depression-era sharecroppers. Finishing, she put her arm around Rose Anne and led her from the room, slamming the door behind her. Dr. Richman moved quickly to the next case. Mellanie survived the course, but Rose Anne never improved again.

At the beginning of our third year Mellanie was elected president of the Johns Hopkins Women's Medical Association, a mark of the association's confidence in her ability and good sense. The Johns Hopkins University School of Medicine was a white male preserve, even though it had admitted women from its founding—a policy demanded by a group of women who had raised money to get the school started (Gertrude Stein was an early student, although she didn't complete the course). This caused tensions, which at that time were never dealt with openly. Our class had six women students out of seventy-five, about average for each year. The women came from a variety of backgrounds; some were foreigners. None were married.

Although Marnie, Mellanie's companion back in Arkansas, had never visited her, Mellanie spoke of her easily and had photographs of them together in her room; the connection was not hidden. Their backgrounds fit into each other's like nested Russian dolls. Most of the time Mellanie dealt skillfully with delicate situations arising at the Hen House, keeping the respect of those involved.

One determined and demanding woman, a classmate from New York City, developed a strong attachment to Mellanie, who handled the situation with kind attention but firm avoidance. Angry and vengeful, the frustrated and persistent classmate went to the woman faculty member who headed student services. This person was experienced, tactful, and fair, and was highly regarded by the students. The classmate complained that the Women's Medical Association was "a house full of lesbians," blaming her allegation, and the "atmosphere" at the Hen House, on Mellanie. These complaints could have produced an ugly rip in the tight stowage Hopkins maintained in matters of this sort, but the older physician prevented it. She listened calmly to the classmate, heeded her complaint, then guided her to a less heated view of the matter. Later she sent for Mellanie. When they conferred, she said simply, "Be discreet." In our fourth year Mellanie was reelected president of the association, an unusual honor.

But Mellanie did fall in love—with Louise, a young entering student, fresh and sensible, who boarded at the Hen House; her affection was returned. By then we were entering our last year, having worked our tails off to get there and with more work ahead. Even so, Mellanie and I had time now and then to explore Baltimore, which has some colorful neighborhoods, and the beautiful Maryland countryside. Mellanie's new friend and Lindsay often came along too. Lindsay sometimes took us into his various worlds, and was full of fun as a guide. We went to a local gay bar only twice that I remember, because it was risky.

As the term went on, Lindsay and I became aware that Mellanie's growing love for the young student was changing her. Mellanie wouldn't talk about it, but I reckoned that she was feeling guilty about Marnie and wasn't facing the problem directly, as she usually did with things. She became irritable and complaining: nothing was right; nothing suited her. She was becoming a different person. Lindsay and I tried different strategies, such as taking her to places she had enjoyed, or to happy hours, or to the races at Pimlico and Laurel. Nothing worked. To make matters worse, her student had to return home for Christmas while Mellanie at the time was too broke to buy a plane ticket to Arkansas. I was leaving, and Lindsay would be in Washington with his family. Mellanie faced the prospect of a bleak Hen House over the holidays.

The time for the annual Hen House Christmas party approached. Everyone bought silly toys to exchange, one of the party traditions; afterward the toys were sent to the pediatric wards. I got ready for Bob McGraw to dunk me one last time in the punch bowl. Once more Mellie toweled me off, this time in front of the fire in the parlor. All of us had been drinking, and Mellanie's guilt began to show. "Y'all," she began, "I know I've talked and acted real ugly lately, and I'm fixin' to make it up to you." She took Lindsay's hand. "I'm truly sorry. But I've had a lot on my mind lately, Lord knows." She sighed and looked at Louise. "I'm gonna miss y'all over Christmas."

The week before, Lindsay had gone to his mother and explained Mellanie's predicament. His mother, knowing how fond Lindsay was of Mellanie, generously wrote a check for two hundred dollars, providing Mellanie's round-trip plane fare. Lindsay and I then planned a surprise: we would give Mellie the check at the Christmas party. We got an empty box of Lydia Pinkham's Female Remedy, as familiar then as Wheaties, and stowed the check inside.

As we sat there after Mellanie dried me off, Lindsay, a great actor, started in. "You've been an *impossible* bitch lately." He screwed up his face at her. "Something's wrong with you." He pulled out the Lydia Pinkham's with a flourish. "This'll cure whatever ails you," he said menacingly, thrusting it in her hand. "Drink it! And shut up!"

Stung, Mellie was suddenly furious. "Goddamn you two! I ain't gonna do no such thang!" she exclaimed, flinging the box straight into the fire. Lindsay snatched it out just as it began to char, stamping on it until it broke open and Mellanie saw the check. We couldn't stop laughing. The bitching stopped, and Mellanie made it home—to Marnie.

●●●

That last year kept us busier than ever, especially preparing to present in grand rounds. Lists of the cases to be presented along with the students assigned were posted on the several floors where the specialties were: medicine, surgery, neurology, orthopedics, and so on. Making our way from floor to floor to see who and what was posted, we called these lists the Stations of the Cross, because presenting to the senior staff was often traumatic. But Mellanie loved grand rounds and the concentrated preparation they demanded. She compared them to being cast in a play: intimate and exciting. To her they were "a great learning process with superb teachers."

"Martino," she once told me, "it's a person's time to shine or to flop, but either way it's a *wonderful* experience." I see her now far down on the stage in Hurd Hall, presenting to Dr. Alfred Blalock, the professor of surgery, her soft drawl carrying in the rapt silence. Then Dr. Blalock's equal drawl rising to a small whine, as it did when he made a particular point. I remember her reflective mood after the final grand round.

"These have been four of the happiest, most interesting, most *strenuous* years of my life," she told me. "We've had the great teachers." I felt that she was referring not just to the medical school.

June 1954 finally came. After the graduation ceremony Lindsay gave a small champagne party for the four of us. Neither Mellie nor I had family at the ceremony, and Lindsay celebrated for us. Still having ambivalent feelings about a medical career, I felt particularly lonely; it was a comfort to be with the three closest to me. After this, Mellie, Lindsay, and I holed up at the Hen House every day for the next two weeks to study for our Maryland State Board medical exams, which we had to pass to get our licenses. I remember it as a summer of emerging cicadas whose deafening, constant rasp in the maple trees filled every cranny of our hearing. Every now and then we erupted in a frenzy of sheer craziness—food fights, ice fights, running outside screaming and laughing—to blow off our tensions.

We took our Boards and passed them; our separate internships were waiting. I was going to Tulane-Charity in New Orleans, Lindsay was headed for Baltimore City Hospital, and Mellanie was off to the University Hospital in Little Rock. It was an end and a beginning. The change would be complete.

That last weekend we exploded into freedom like warm Cokes at a summer picnic. Piling into Mellie's old Chevy (people often mistook the "AL" on its license plates for Alaska), Lindsay, Mellanie, Louise, and I headed out of muggy Baltimore west into the hills and hollers—Mellanie's country. By evening on that fragrant day we found a village where the lights and music of a gaudy little traveling carnival welcomed us. On the small ferris wheel each gondola bore the painted name of a town, all curlicues and flourishes, so we climbed into "Tallahassee," my hometown. The tinny crash of "Over the Waves" rose from the merry-go-round. Later each of us slammed down the maul to test our strength, with Mellie winning. We tossed baseballs at a clown, missing every time. The cotton candy was sweet.

Louise bravely held back her tears all evening. When we reached the lopsided photo booth, all of us somehow squeezed inside. "Come on, y'all, we're fixin' to get took for posterity. Look happy!" Mellie cupped a hand beneath her student's chin. "Everybody smile!"

And smile we did. I'm looking at our picture now—stained, wavy, and yellow around the edges. We look so young! And we were, those thirty-nine years ago. That night we stayed in the Van Gilder Hotel, "12 Rooms, 3 With Bath." Lindsay and I shared a room with gulping plumbing and we slept like babies. After a huge country breakfast, we took our time driving back to Baltimore. Our student couldn't stop weeping. The next weekend we went our different ways.

"Lord, sugar! Where the hell are you?" Mellanie's surprised voice crackled when she recognized me on the telephone. After consulting my Johns Hopkins Medical Directory for 1986, the latest available, I had called Mellanie's office listing. The number was out of service. Next I called the state medical society where her practice was last listed and asked for help. I was sure that she would be retired, off the list, unreachable. Perhaps dead. But they found her in the southern city where she has lived for years and practices still. She is in her seventies now. What is she doing?

"Honey pot, I was just gettin' ready to go over to the old folks' home." It was eight o'clock in the morning there. "Every weekend I go over there and dig out their fecal impactions. Nobody else'll do it for the pore souls. You don't know what it means to them." She laughed. "I know what it's like to be old."

We caught up a little, laughing and remembering in the tumble of almost forty years; together again. After training, Lindsay became a fine cardiologist. He married and had two children. Then, in his thirties, he died of leukemia, withdrawing from the world in those last months, not wanting us to see how cruelly the disease had changed his looks. Marnie died years ago in a fiery auto accident. She was buried with full military honors. Mellie's student had graduated and faded into family life.

"How did you find me?" she asked.

I told her, feeling as if, for once in these sad days, I had won the lottery against huge odds. "I think I'm the only person—for sure, the only doctor—in two hundred miles around here who voted for Bill Clinton." She paused, chuckling. "I ain't changed a bit!" There was silence. Then, "Martino, let's never lose each other again."

# Gay Girls
# & Gay Guys

## An Old Past, A New Future

Back in the fifties, when *dyke* and *fag* were still dirty words, gay girls and gay guys in South Florida had close relationships. Bonded by our common oppression in a society equally hostile to us both, constantly in danger of harsh penalties under laws designed to punish us for our "crimes against nature," we formed a tight group of deviate outcasts. Our gay society was rich in its culture and sense of community, diverse in population, and carefully stratified according to age and class. Still, we were all the same under the skin; we all could be, and many of us were, socially persecuted and criminally prosecuted if the members of the straight society knew whom we loved, knew what we did in bed.

Nevertheless, gay life in South Florida in the fifties was swinging and exciting, offering something for everyone and plenty for all. There were drag shows at the Onyx and Billie Lee's. There was dancing, drinking, and pool. We went to the Hi Room, the Nite Owl, Googie's, the Mug, and the Left Bank, where we would dance the madison in a long line out the front door, around the building, and in again through the back. We hung out at the Cas-Bar, where we painted our names inside our handprints on the "mad, mad wall." There were free brunches and dinner buffets, and always there were parties, parties, parties.

Although many of the bars were considered to be either "boys" or "girls" bars, there was a great deal of cross-visiting and mixing. Often, we partied together, danced together, drank together, and gave each other nurturance and emotional support. Gay girls and gay guys together, we camped and carried on, women imitating men's parodies of women's behavior.

On weekends we hung out at the Beach—the gay beach, located on the shore of the Atlantic Ocean between Twenty-first and Twenty-second Streets. There we congregated through all four seasons of the year, gay girls and gay guys together, young and old, in great numbers, in all our diversity, class boundaries giving way with the removal of our clothes. This block-long stretch of sand and sea was bounded on one side by a small hotel and secured at the other end by a long pavilion. Out into the Atlantic jutted the seawall, down the length of which we danced to music from the jukebox, gay girls and gay guys together; we danced, six plays for a quarter, to Della Reese, Frances Faye, Ray Charles, Dave Brubeck, Edith Piaf, Dinah Washington, Jackie Wilson, and of course, our all-time favorite, Johnny Mathis. We danced mambo, samba, pasa doble, and cha-cha. We did the fox-trot and Panama City bop, chicken, lindy, madison, and that famous outgrowth of the madison—the hully-gully. Whenever or whatever we danced, we paired ourselves off with partners of the opposite sex, gay girls with gay guys, to appear as nonqueer as possible to the eyes of the notorious and ever present but often unrecognizable plainclothes police who lurked the beach trying to catch queers who were guilty of being blatant, who were guilty of obvious perversity.

Sometimes, as we danced on the long pavilion in the heat of the sun, our glistening skin many shades of tan, our hair—which we combed stylishly immediately upon emerging from our swims—stiff with seawater, we would suddenly, unexpectedly, be approached by these officers of the law, grabbed, and pushed roughly toward the sidewalk. Sometimes, as we lay on our towels and blankets, sat on our chairs and chaises, floated on our rafts and inner tubes, we would suddenly be assaulted by an onslaught of uniformed and plainclothes agents, ordered to our feet, marched from the beach. Sometimes, as we ate our hot dogs and hamburgers, drank our beer and soda that we bought at the snack bar at the front of the pavilion, we would be pulled up by police and thrust toward the street, leaving our food behind. We all would be pushed, gay girls and gay guys together—the dancers, the swimmers, the diners, the sunbathers—into paddy wagons that lined the road, shoved into the backs of the vans, herds of half-naked bodies pressed together until the space was filled and the doors, with mesh-barred windows, were slammed and locked. Then off we would go to the local precinct station, there to be fingerprinted, booked, thrown into a cell, beaten, and sexually assaulted, with the promise of public humiliation yet to come. There at the jailhouse we were separated, gay girls from gay guys, to come together later, after we were released on bond, to comfort one another after our assaults and injuries.

How dare we filth have the nerve to swim, sun, eat, and be happy on a public beach?

*With what am I being charged, officer?*

*Vagrancy.*

*Vagrancy? But I have a job, a home, a family, a reputation. I have money and identification in my wallet. I was only sunbathing on a public beach on a Sunday. I am not a vagrant.*

*We have twenty-seven different counts of vagrancy we can charge you with. We can book you and put you in a jail cell and hold you for twenty-four hours on suspicion. We can do with you as we please. You filthy queer!*

Then, the following morning, the worst of all would happen— headlines in the local newspaper proclaiming the arrest and detention of the perverts, listing names, addresses, telephone numbers, places of employment. The building blocks of our lives tumbled down as our parents, our spouses, our employers read our names, read our shame. We were felons, the lowest of the low, guilty of "crimes against nature."

The bars were raided in a similar manner. Paddy wagons would pull up to the doors, and police would swarm onto the premises, alert to the deviant behavior or dress. They would carefully read the contents of our wallets, making lewd comments about our personal information. Anyone they wished to take in would be hustled off to the precinct house, physically inspected for three articles of sex-appropriate clothing as required by law, robbed, beaten, taunted, sexually assaulted.

In those days for many of us there was no social awareness of racism/sexism/homophobia. There was no gay pride/feminist movement/lesbian nation. This was before Stonewall/women's liberation/lesbian separatism. For gay girls and gay guys together, there were the constant threats of exposure, ruin, violence, extortion, prison, and confinement against one's will in mental institutions where we would be given electroshock therapy and heavy medication in attempts to cure us of our "inversion." Many lesbians and gay men came out of jails and mental hospitals broken, if they came out at all.

Sometimes the pressure and isolation got to be too much, and some gay girls and guys tried to escape into the safety of a phony straight life through marriage. This was often an unsuccessful, even devastating experience. Sometimes the only escape was suicide. And I never will forget the day that a young gay man jumped from a window in his extreme fear, and died in a hideous manner for being a queer. The story was in the local newspaper along with a photograph of the young man being carried to a waiting ambulance by several other men. The reason it took several men was that some of them were carrying him, and others were holding up the sawed-off section of heavy iron that was protruding from his chest and abdomen. The young man had been impaled on the decorative spears that topped the fence like spikes. This accident happened when he jumped from the second floor of the Miami police station, jumped in a panic, in a frantic attempt to escape, because he was a young Latino fairy without immigration papers who had been taken in a raid on a gay bar, arrested with scores of other lesbians and gay men. In his terror over what his future might bring when he was discovered, he brought his chance of any future at all to a stop by dying of his wounds.

Because our survival could be enhanced at times if we were able to pass as straight, gay girls and gay guys often helped one another to obtain a semblance of social appropriateness by cross-dating to appear "normal" through being seen in public with a person of the opposite sex. We would go together to employee functions and to family affairs. There, we'd put on great acts of being romantically and/or sexually involved, both to prove our "normalcy" and to discourage possible straight date seekers. Many gay girls and gay guys, especially those who had been disowned by their birth families, formed intentional families with each other. While there was a lot of real companionship, love, and support among us, there was little, if any, sexual interaction across gender lines. Whatever else we might become, we remained gay girls and gay guys.

At the beginning of the sixties, there was a rash of gay/lesbian marriages—for appearance, convenience, job and family security, citizenship. I married my good friend Jack to squelch the local rumors that we were queer. We remained in a platonic marriage for six years, attending family and job-related functions together, providing for each other the social safety of having a spouse, and playing the part of traditional married folks on the surface. Meanwhile, although we shared a living space, we had separate social lives, friends, and lovers.

After we parted ways, I married John, another gay man with whom I'd had a close friendship for many years, this time not for appearances but out of deep spiritual love and a shared commitment to the same goals and ideals in life. Although we each maintain separate personal and social lives, we have shared a home, lifestyle, and the parenting of five adopted children for the past twenty-five years.

Because when I was a young dyke I'd had so many close relationships with gay men, I was quite distressed to realize, as I grew up, that although there were individual gay men whom I deeply loved, I really didn't like being with them as a group very much anymore. They became lumped together in my experience with "men" in general, with "the patriarchy" in particular, and their collective behavior did nothing to change my mind.

In the seventies, I plunged into the swelling tide of the feminist movement, and my consciousness began to change. I became more and more aware of prejudice, oppression, and ways that social conditioning shapes our attitudes. I was slammed by the reality of sexism and oppression/exploitation of women, everywhere, in advertising and the media, in politics and administration, in all aspects of daily life, overwhelming me. As my awareness of sexism and, subsequently, other forms of oppression increased, my feelings toward my gay brothers began to change. By the eighties, I no longer found many of their campy behaviors cute, funny, or entertaining. I resented their caricaturing of women. I resented their flaunting of their privilege. I resented their hedonistic proclivities and lack of political awareness. I resented their lack of support for issues specific to lesbians. Most of all, I resented the fact that no matter how often and in how many different ways I called them on their misogynistic behaviors, tried to explain how they were hurting me, other lesbians, other women, and themselves, most of them just didn't "get it," and of the few who did, fewer still were willing to change their behavior.

◖◗◖◗◖◗

"You wouldn't dream of wearing blackface and a minstrel costume to a gathering." I am attempting to explain, through use of this analogy, why I am unhappy to Jerry, who is mincing around in a long gown, high heels, makeup, jewelry, and a beehive wig.

"It's only a costume," he replies. I remember the hippie costumes we wore in the sixties, with lots of glitter and glitz, flowing fabrics and paint and accoutrements that did *not* parody the patriarchal definition of what a woman "should" be like; and I wonder why these fellows choose *this* particular form of costuming. "Besides," Jerry adds, anticipating a possible rerun of my Tools of Our Oppression spiel, "drag queens get raped too."

◖◗◖◗◖◗

"I can't read this." I throw down the story I was looking at, a piece written by a gay man about other gay men. I am intensely offended by this piece. I wonder why, in referring to these men in what appears to be a humorous fashion, the author talks in terms of their tits and bras and cunts. They don't *have* tits and bras and cunts! Why is he making fun of women's body parts? I never hear gay men ridicule dicks and balls and buns! Why do they insist on using *cunt* as a derogation? Don't they realize they are demonstrating the same loathing toward women that straight men exhibit, the same loathing that straight people in general show toward queers?

◖◗◖◗◖◗

Mike is short-tempered, snappy. "What's the matter, baby," Bill asks him, "are you on the rag?" I am offended. I try to explain that this is not humorous to me, that I think Bill is being very inappropriate by ridiculing menstruation, which he has never experienced, and, specifically, the associated emotional changes, which can be a source of severe stress for many women and not a laughing matter at all. What I really want to say but don't is that I think they have no right to exert their grabby male privilege and use that idiom at all. Bill apologizes, but he doesn't really "get it."

During the March on Washington events, some well-known lesbian writers are reading at a benefit to raise money for breast-cancer research. Later, I ask a friend who had attended how many men were at the fund-raiser. "Are you kidding?" she laughs. "Since when do gay men support women's issues?"

Lesbians and gay men are working together on our local march and other events for the pride-that-dare-not-speak-its-name week. A group of gay men come up with the logo for this year—three male figures dancing in a circle. One of the lesbians who did not work on the logo protests after the fact, disturbed at being so erased. The men are angry at her protest. "What difference does it make?" they say in their egocentric ignorance. And my blood runs cold as I hear other lesbians, from their own position of invisibility, agree.

These are the nineties, not the fifties, but I wonder how far we actually have come. Sexism is on the rise again, and lesbians remain generally invisible except as objects of curiosity, contempt, or heterosexual titillation. The norm in our society still is that men are accustomed to receiving service from women, and gay men are raised to these roles in the same way as are their heterosexual brothers. This social conditioning is more subtle and pervasive than we might realize. Thorough and insidious, it enables us to behave in ways that are to our advantage without consideration of the fact that many events and circumstances in which we take pleasure may be hurtful or oppressive to others. Gay men share male privilege in our society, and most of them see no need to try to interfere with this pattern.

These are the nineties, not the fifties, but lesbians and gay men still face similar threats to our survival from members of the heterosexual masses. As we become more and more visible in public, as we demand to be treated equally as citizens of this nation, we become more accepted by some people, but we become still more loathed and feared by others. Violence toward lesbians and gay men has been increasing, and the right-wing Christian movement is gaining strength, purposefully threatening our civil liberties and our personal safety. Denying us our civil rights is the first step toward genocide.

In the face of this common enemy, we must join forces for our own protection, we must work together for our very lives. Even some lesbians who have long been separatists are now coming together in coalition with gay men to fight for our survival, our civil liberties, our human rights.

These *are* the nineties, and as we spiral toward the Age of Aquarius, I remain optimistic that we will find a newer, more healthy common ground, that we can develop a mutual respect for each other and learn to work together to make this world a better place for us all, lesbians and gay men together.

# The House
# O' Happy Queers
# at 281 State

It was close to one in the morning by the time I made it home. It had
been a torturous night at the Iron Horse—two sold-out shows of
Luther "Guitar Jr." Johnson spewing what the emcee called "raw-guts-
in-a-bucket, sawdust-on-the-floor Mississippi blues." I had washed
more empty nachos plates and beer glasses than I thought it was math-
ematically possible for the number of people in the crowd to have produced. About halfway through the second show I'd had this terrible
fantasy that the dirty dishes were alive and multiplying like rabbits, and
I was doomed to the dish room forever.

As I walked the mile back to our house, the January wind snapped
at my corroded dishpan hands like a nasty dog, biting off what felt like
quarter-sized chunks of flesh with every gust. My back was almost as
sore as my feet, or vice versa. I opened my eyes only every third or
fourth step, just enough to keep from stumbling into street signs.

The kitchen light was on, and I could see Beth through the window, cooking something on the stove. She was smiling and looked
happy as a Hallmark card through the frosted glass. I imagined she was
making up a big batch of popcorn, with plenty to share. I would walk
in, collapse on the couch, and watch a few minutes of The War on CNN
before going up to bed.

I pulled open the screen door and let my limp body fall forward,
ready to melt into the house. My shoulder smacked against cold, hard
wood.

"That fucker," I thought. "She locked the door again."

I slid to my knees, wrung out like a sponge. It was such a little
thing, I knew, but that doorknob not turning was the definitive proof

on this long, long night that the universe was stacked against me. Only this time, I knew the agent: it was Beth.

I leaned over to the kitchen window and rapped as hard as I could without breaking the glass. Beth whipped around with a white face, almost spilling whatever it was on the stove. Then she stared out the window for a long time, eyes as mean as a mule that's been kicked in the stomach. I doubt she could see out into the darkness, but I knew that she knew it was me.

Finally, she came over and let me in. "You are a fucking sexist asshole," she screamed.

I just walked past her. "Locked out of my own goddamned house," I grumbled on my way up the stairs.

I was too tired to argue, and I knew it wouldn't make a difference anyway. I could tell this was the big one. The grand finale. Our House O' Happy Queers was history.

With two months to go before our graduation from Dartmouth, Chris and I had had the Big Talk and decided to move somewhere together. We had been dating for a year, had done the monogamy-pact thing, and were ready to try life as full-time lovers. The only question was: where?

Our friends Beth and Jackie had graduated two years before us and moved to Northampton, Massachusetts, just a hundred miles south on the Connecticut River. Their reports convinced us that it was the perfect place to settle: a small, rural town, with mountains and farms within ten miles, but with a busy music and cultural scene and, most important, an active and visible queer community. The four of us—plus Spike the dyke dog—found a decent house with cheap rent to share, and in September we moved in to 281 State Street, calling it the Dartmouth House O' Happy Queers.

The house sat on the cusp of two neighborhoods. Walking out the front you entered a quiet, quaint residential area, with a park where junior high kids shot hoops every day after school. A hundred feet in the other direction and you were dodging delivery trucks at the loading dock of a Stop & Shop complex. It was the best of both worlds.

The house was barely big enough for the four of us. The downstairs had a kitchen, living room, bathroom, and study. Upstairs there was just enough room for the two bedrooms and what we dubbed the stoop-in closet. None of us had much furniture, so on our first day together we planned a commando raid on the shopping center's loading dock. We waited until midnight, when the stores had been closed for an hour. We crept over the backyard path and then, while Beth and I stood watch, Chris and Jackie made a break for it, carrying back almost a dozen milk crates of all colors and designs. The next day we built makeshift bookcases and a desk, using the crates and an old door with the hinges taken off.

A few days later, Chris and I gave in and finally bought our first "real" furniture—a crimson futon, which we placed proudly against the back wall of our room. We soon discovered that we were sleeping head-to-head with Beth and Jackie, just inches apart through thin drywall. It was soothing to wake up at one or two in the morning and hear the muffled moans and sighs of our friends loving each other in the next room. It was soothing and, after four years in a small, stifling college community, tremendously liberating: we were four young queers, inventing our adult lives together.

Northampton is something of a lesbian Mecca, to which all dykes must make at least one pilgrimage during their lives. (And many stay once they get there.) It's a town where lesbian softball teams outnumber the Little League, where tickets to a Kate Clinton show are coveted like free passes to heaven. As one of the few specifically lesbian "ghettos" in the country, Northampton has a distinctly separatist feeling. Lesbians and gay men interact closely in certain spheres, such as at the town's two mixed bars, in places of work, and to some extent in political organizations. But the public sense of community seems to stop at each group's front door. Lesbians generally live with lesbians, gay men with gay men, and there is not much social interaction.

In Northampton, political correctness is the law of the land. This is the town where a women's bookstore was reportedly firebombed by antipornography lesbian feminists because the store sold copies of *On*

*Our Backs.* When the title of the annual pride parade was changed to include *bisexual,* a contingent of "Lesbians for Lesbians" refused to participate and organized their own rally instead. The bulletin board in the downtown Laundromat is always crowded with advertisements like

> *Three lesbian feminists seeking fourth for substance-free, vegetarian, all-womyn apartment and Safe Space Available: No Meat, No Men. Pets Welcome.*

Clearly, 281 State Street was a different kind of beast. We were two men and two women (in the same house?!). We had a Weber grill that we planned to fire up for the occasional steak-and-beer barbecue. We had (promise not to tell) pornographic books and magazines.

Our mixed-gender household soon began to attract attention. "It's so cool you're living together," we often heard, and, "Wow, I really support that." Although we didn't hear much of it directly, we knew there was also a fair amount of "You couldn't *pay* me to share a house with two [lesbians/gay men]." Beth and Jackie, in particular, became the targets for some serious lesbian scorn.

Both sets of reactions to our household arose from a common assumption: that our living together in political, polarized Northampton was an intentional "statement." Friends and acquaintances viewed 281 State as a conscious experiment in gay male and lesbian cooperation, an emblem of a new wave of attempted unity. Our joint living arrangement was treated like a suspense novel or a soap opera, only with political implications. Everybody was dying to know: Could we get along? Were we on the same side of the struggle? What do *they* really do in bed?

I don't think any of us had moved into 281 State as a conscious political act. We were college friends, and living together seemed logical, convenient, and fun. But as long as others were automatically viewing our living arrangement this way, I welcomed the opportunity to play up our household unity as a political statement. I was well aware of the historical tensions between lesbians and gay men. I knew about countless coalitions in which the lesbians' concerns were always subsumed to those of gay men, who regardless of their sexual orientation had been socialized to be just as dominant and chauvinist as straight men.

I wanted to believe that this kind of behavior, and the antagonism it provoked, would disappear with a new generation of nonsexist, queer men. And I wanted desperately to prove—to the understandably dubious Northampton lesbian crowd, and perhaps even more to myself—that I was one of this "new breed" of men. I had based my political activism throughout college on this faith, but now was my chance to show that I could practice what I preached. Was I really as sensitive and nonsexist as I'd been saying?

Beth and Jackie, too, soon realized they had a stake in the success of our "experiment." After so many negative reactions from other lesbians in the area, they had to demonstrate that their decision to live with two gay men was politically progressive, not reactionary—that they were not traitors to the lesbian cause.

As we settled into life in Northampton, we worked hard on the story of our living together. We understood that the tensions between lesbians and gay men were essentially the same as those between all women and men, with one twist: because we as *gay* men share an experience of oppression, lesbians expect more from us than from straight men. Thus the stakes are that much higher; when gay men, as oppressed people, are themselves insensitive or oppressive, it is a double betrayal.

With this in mind, we concentrated on avoiding traditional gender and power roles, always trying to remain conscious of the ways we'd been socialized. Beth and Jackie were full-time graduate students and were usually gone all day. Chris and I had the opposite schedule, working nights at the Iron Horse, a restaurant–music club downtown. The four of us made a point of overlapping almost every evening for sit-down, "family" dinners. When we "boys" cooked, the "girls" did the dishes, and when they cooked, we cleaned. Beth and Jackie were usually in charge of barbecues; I did a fair amount of sweeping. We had house meetings to work out by consensus how we'd split the food and utility bills, and who would be responsible for different chores.

Through it all we had loads of fun together: racing carts down the aisles of the Stop & Shop, hiking to view the foliage in the nearby Holyoke Range, going to $1.50 movie specials at the Calvin Theater. We lived simply, hanging our wash on the line to dry, splurging with the occasional six-pack of Rolling Rock. There were small, stupid disagreements about things like paying for the cable TV hookup, but none of us thought much of these disputes.

Mostly, we just enjoyed the good company and took advantage of the opportunity to learn from one another. Chris and I leafed through their back issues of *Lesbian Connections* and asked questions about dyke politics, dyke sex, dyke everything. They read our *Men on Men* books and joked about which of us would look better in drag. We were like anthropologists on an extended field study, or like kids trading their prized baseball cards. We were acting our parts brilliantly: the new generation of postsexist, coalition-building queers.

In addition to operating our domestic household by our own standards of political correctness, we all wanted to be involved in larger causes. All four of us had been activists in college—where the number of "out" queers was so small that coalition politics was absolutely essential—and hoped to continue our commitment to gay *and* lesbian activism. Beth, who was writing a thesis on AIDS activist art, decided to organize a group of people concerned with HIV-disease issues.

In September a group of a dozen men and women gathered in our living room, and ACT UP Western Mass was born. We brainstormed about issues and actions we could take up: housing for PWAs, education and condom distribution at high schools, information campaigns on the public transit system. Realizing the potential of such a group, and the amount of work to be done locally, we advertised widely for the next meeting. Posters were plastered all over town, with our address and phone number listed as the place to contact. The response was immediate and overwhelming. Suddenly, 281 State became ACT UP Central.

The nature of the group that evolved was confirmation of the set of principles 281 State was coming to stand for. In contrast to ACT UP chapters in New York, San Francisco, and other cities where the group was male dominated to the point that many lesbians felt unwelcome, ACT UP Western Mass from the first meeting on had a majority of lesbian members. There was also a balance between college students and "townies," with no identifiable factions or infighting. Even the procedural logistics of the group reflected our political ideals: meetings operated entirely on consensus, with rotating male and female cofacilitators. We were one of the few coequally gay and lesbian organizations in Northampton.

To some degree, the birth of ACT UP in our house was a fluke of timing and logistics. With four of the original dozen members living there, and someone home to answer the phone days as well as evenings, it made good sense to base our activities at 281 State. But something more was also at work. From the start, people gravitated to the cooperative, mixed-gender atmosphere we had created. The magazines on the coffee table, the art on the walls, the books on the shelves were lesbian *and* gay, not one or the other. Those who came seemed comfortable in the house, able to put their differences behind them. The house was a shared space, neutral ground.

ACT UP Western Mass grew rapidly, and almost immediately outgrew our small living room. Meetings were moved to bigger homes, and eventually to a town community center. But 281 State remained a hub of activity, and the spirit of the house continued to set the tone for the group. We had fulfilled our friends' larger-than-life expectations for our living experiment. In quite concrete terms, 281 State seemed both an emblem of and a catalyst for a new wave of lesbian and gay male cooperation in town.

Unfortunately, just as our house was coming together publicly as a center for queer unity, inside we started falling apart. Conflicts erupted, were repressed, bubbled underneath the surface, and then exploded again. Most of the arguing was between Beth and me, much of it stemming from the difficulties of trying to live on so little money, but a good deal simply because we got on each other's nerves. We fought over absurd details: who had finally broken a long-suffering chair, cleaning hairs off bars of soap, why we should or shouldn't pay attention to the answering machine.

A classic guerrilla housemate war ensued. A typical morning: Wake up sweating and go downstairs to check the thermostat. *Seventy degrees! Hasn't she ever heard of sweaters? Turn it down all the way to fifty just to make the point.* Hunt around for breakfast. *All there is for cereal is Cap'n Crunch. She knows I hate this sugar crap! Hide the box behind a bag of rice and settle for instant oatmeal.* Wash the bowl. *She left her dishes in the sink again. Does it take that much just to rinse them off when she's done?* Turn on the tube to catch the morning news. *Oops. Since I didn't want the cable hookup in the first place, I'm not supposed to watch any TV.* Turn it off and get a book. *And on and on and on.*

Now rather than trying to overlap at home for sit-down dinners, I left for my night work shifts early, hoping to be gone before Beth and Jackie arrived. In the morning, I stayed in bed until I heard Beth's car pull out of the driveway. We went for days without speaking to each other.

Meanwhile, we were still the Happy House O' Queers to our friends in ACT UP. Somebody at a meeting would inevitably ask, "Everything still great at your place?"

How could we let them down? "Sure," I'd say. (*Don't make eye contact with Beth. Try not to show gritting teeth. Nod convincingly.*) "Everything's fine."

When the gay male a cappella singing group the Flirtations came to town to do a benefit for ACT UP, they came to our house for the postperformance bash. Beth and I were barely speaking to each other at this point, but we valiantly put on our happy faces and gave the group a tour, showing them our adjacent bedrooms. "Isn't that wonderful?" one of the singers said. "Dykes and fags living together like this. Things really are changing." At that moment, Beth and I both managed to have our mouths full of Doritos. "Mmmm," we agreed.

Clearly, we needed a way out. The thermostat, the answering machine, brands of cereal—these pet peeves weren't getting us anywhere. But then we found the Issue to End All Issues: locking the door.

In all my life I had never lived in a house where the door was locked: not growing up less than a mile outside of Washington, D.C., murder capital of America; not in my dorm rooms or off-campus houses in college. And that was very important to me. Keeping the door unlocked is a small way of practicing the values I preach: trust, openness, honesty. The realist in me knows the risks this entails, but the optimist in me wins out; in a world of fear and violence, where so much seems beyond our changing, an open door seems like one easily accomplished step toward making things the way they should be.

Beth, on the other hand, had never lived in a place that was left unlocked. She had grown up in Manhattan, where most people double-lock the door when they go down the hall to get the mail—and often with good reason. Locks, bolts, and bulging key rings were a part of life she had never questioned. So even though our residential, low-crime section of Northampton was no Manhattan, Beth locked 281 State like a zealot—when she went to the store for five minutes, when she walked the dog, sometimes even when she and others were inside watching TV at night, or doing the dishes.

Neither of us raised the issue at first. We just played a message game, on the same scale as the thermostat debate: I would get up first thing in the morning and unlock the door on my way to the shower. When Beth left for work in the morning she would relock the door behind her. When I went out, I left the door open. It was like an Abbott and Costello routine.

Then one day Beth confronted me, saying that I was threatening her safety as a woman by leaving the door unlocked. I was shocked. Shamed. Beth's words were like a punch to my jaw, jolting me from my egocentric, narrow gaze. What privileged presumption to think her reasons for locking the door were on the same level as mine! I could get used to carrying a key if I had to; how could Beth ever "get used" to being threatened or raped? As can happen only in moments of deep humiliation, I saw how blinding my own socialization could be. I felt like a skunk.

I started locking the door religiously, hoping to atone for my sins. I even locked the door when Beth was gone all day and would have no way of knowing if I had. But almost right away I couldn't help feeling that my best instincts had been played upon, that I'd been somehow double-crossed. Beth knew how hard I tried to be aware of and sensitive to women's concerns—doubly hard as a gay activist hoping to prove himself worthy of lesbians' trust. She knew I tried to be hyperconscious of my male socialization and to break free of its oppressive aspects. She knew that by accusing me of any kind of sexism or insensitivity she could stop me dead in my tracks. And she had.

My increasing suspicion of Beth's motives made me extremely uneasy; wasn't it sexist merely to question Beth, and thus her right to safety as *she* defined it? Was my sexism so overwhelming that I just couldn't see that I was wrong? But in my gut, I didn't trust her accusations.

Finally, I asked Beth if fear of being attacked was really the reason she locked the door so obsessively. If so, then why was it so vitally important to lock the doors when nobody was home? Why was it necessary to lock the doors when two or three people were in the living room at night, with the lights on, when not even the most deranged rapist would consider attacking?

Beth protested at first, but soon admitted that the only time she genuinely felt fearful was at night. The rest of the door locking was mere habit. I assured her I would be happy to lock the door during the night when everybody was asleep; she had a right to do anything she needed to feel safe. But I explained how alienating it was for me to come home exhausted after a night of dirty dishes, to see people relaxing inside the house, only to find the door locked. It made me feel like it wasn't my home. Beth agreed not to lock the door at night unless she went to bed before I made it home. It seemed like a workable compromise.

Then came the night of the Luther "Guitar Jr." Johnson show.

●—●—●

The next morning I woke up and, as usual, listened to see if Beth was still home. I could hear her in the kitchen, so I waited. And waited. And waited.

Finally, I had to pee so badly that I gave in and went downstairs. I walked to the bathroom with my eyes half-closed, pretending to be extra sleepy. Beth stopped me as soon as I came out.

"We need to talk," she said.

"I know," I answered, moving toward the stairs. "Can we pick a time later? Chris and I have plans to be somewhere soon."

"No." Beth was adamant. "Now."

The four of us sat down in the living room—Beth and Jackie on one side, Chris and I on the other. I felt like I had walked onto the set of

*Crossfire.* I was embarrassed for Chris and Jackie, who had done an admirable job all along of staying out of our fight. But Beth insisted on bringing them in. Then she began her tirade:

"What you did last night was completely unacceptable. I will not live with somebody who comes pounding on windows, storming into the house in the middle of the night. It just proves that you've never taken my concerns seriously. You've never respected me. You leave dirty dishes all around the house, just expecting me to pick it up. Well, I'm not your mother and I'm not going to pick it up anymore. When was the last time you cleaned the bathroom? I'm not a maid. I thought gay men might be different, but you're not, you're just a man. Same as any other. You're a typical male chauvinist pig."

And on and on. I didn't say anything the whole time; any defense of myself would just be more proof in the pudding: I'd be acting like a belligerent, aggressive, stubborn pig.

Chris and I moved out a few weeks later.

In the months that followed I tried to make sense of what had happened. I drafted countless letters to Beth, devised dozens of things I could have said to defend myself. At first I thought the best approach would be to respond to her point by point, answering each of her charges. I got bogged down in the nitpicking for weeks before I realized I might as well have been trying to climb out of quicksand.

When I finally gained some distance from the grimy details, I found, curiously, that I wasn't especially upset by Beth's accusations. Our original confrontation had devastated me and left me questioning my entire understanding of gender relations. I had been ashamed of myself, saddened to think that even as someone trying explicitly to live the new queer male paradigm, I had failed so miserably. But when Beth called me a sexist the second time, I didn't believe her.

Beth herself had provided the convincing evidence in the words she chose during our final blowup. Rather than discuss the specifics of the disagreements we were having as roommates, Beth lapsed into generic antimale rhetoric. Her use of stock phrases like "I'm not your mother" and her fabrication of "typical male chauvinist" infringements like not doing the dishes (which was patently absurd, given that I complained regularly about *her* not doing dishes) made it perfectly clear that Beth was not speaking to me as an individual about my particular behavior. Rather, she was speaking to a "Man" about typically male behavior that often leads to conflict with "Woman." She was dealing not with the specific differences we had as two people trying to share a house, but with generalized differences that cause tension between two vast groups of people.

This realization left me less troubled by my own behavior, but still groping for an understanding of why things had happened the way they did. Why did our personal incompatibility turn so suddenly into a question of Woman vs. Man, Dyke vs. Fag?

The answer came to me one night while I was watching *60 Minutes*. Mike Wallace was interviewing Paul Simon and asked for the singer's reaction to the fact that Joe DiMaggio's said he *hated* the verse about him in "Mrs. Robinson." Simon explained, "Well, his problem was that he hadn't started to think of himself as a metaphor yet."

What finally occurred to me as I listened to Simon's remark was that Beth—and probably all of us at 281 State Street—had had precisely the opposite affliction. Our friends had looked to our successful living arrangement as an emblem for something larger than itself, and in time we had come to believe this ourselves. We had become so wrapped up in the idea of our household as a *metaphor* for gay and lesbian cooperation that we sometimes forgot the *reality* that we were also just four individuals sharing the rent. So when things fell apart, we felt we had to justify our failure with reasons that were larger than life; it didn't fit the story to admit that we simply couldn't agree on what kind of breakfast cereal to buy.

Beth is the one who made the leap explicitly, but in our own thinking I'm sure we were all lured by the power of metaphor. It was just too tempting to view our breakup as one more chapter in the age-old story of lesbian and gay male relations: lesbians and gay men try to build cooperative efforts but the gay men soon disappoint the lesbians by showing their true colors—they're not gay men, they're gay *men*.

Telling the story this way was even easier given the door-locking episode. Whether it was sexism, lack of awareness, or simply differing personal preferences—and I remain confident it was the last—it is clear that I failed to make the extra effort, the substantive compromise, that is essential for successful coalitions. Unfortunately, in telling her version of our closing chapter, Beth read the metaphor in reverse; instead of using our specific example (281 State Street) to shed light on a general situation (relations between lesbians and gay men), she imposed the general situation on the meaning of our particular example.

Realizing the faultiness of Beth's logic doesn't make the implosion of 281 State Street any less painful a memory. It still hurts me that in Beth's eyes I will always provide more evidence for the idea that gay men and lesbians *can't* get along. It troubles me even more deeply that on some level Beth was justified. I had as much stake in the metaphor as she did, and yet I was far from the model I hoped to be.

Now, more than a year later, and one hundred miles north again on the Connecticut River, Chris and I are thinking about moving in with Susan, a lesbian friend of ours. She has told us she's trying to redefine the concept of *family*, and that our shared house could be a model to put her ideas into practice.

I love Susan dearly, and I think it would be wonderful to live with her. However, I've put two preconditions on the plan: first, she needs to read this essay so she is forewarned about what a stubborn, obsessive (and sexist?) person I can be; second, if we're going to live together there will be no more talk of the "new family." I refuse to live as a metaphor, and I don't think Susan should either. I bet we'll get along much better as real people.

**KATHERINE V.
FORREST**

# A Message
# for Steve

Maybe you can remember me. We met in one of Detroit's gay bars in May of the year the century turned sixty, a month after I turned twenty-one. I saw you perhaps half a dozen times during that late spring.

The particular night I met you I was with a group of friends at a small bar on Gratiot Avenue, a bar whose name I've forgotten, but maybe you'll remember. Later that year it ended its brief tenure as a haven for queers and became a "black and tan" bar—slang in that highly segregated city for a place that welcomed blacks. I remember the city in those days as being glamorously grungy and vital, but safe, not the violent, dangerous place it is today. But I also understand that I felt safe because I was young—and that some confidence of youth is taken away by the years. How I hope that yours remains undimmed.

The night I met you I was in the Gratiot Avenue bar with three other lesbians: Joan and Anne, with their short dark hair and men's pants and white shirts, visibly butch; and Carole, with her slumberous blue eyes and simply cut dark hair, a woman I knew from the company where I worked and whom I was nuts about (and would shortly lose to Joan—not that I exactly had her to lose). Carole was also butch but conventionally very pretty, as butch women often are, and she was playing femme for Joan—role switching that made better sense to me later on when I had more knowledge and some perspective on lesbian behavior.

We had come to the bar from a crowded coffee shop on Woodward Avenue where, over coffee, I had been immersed in the company of my lesbian companions, especially Carole. What had happened afterward still reverberated in me as I sat in the Gratiot Avenue bar, because I couldn't, wouldn't discuss my feelings with my companions. I didn't know what to say—and, for all I knew, I was the only one troubled by what had occurred.

We'd gotten up to leave the coffee shop and were single-filing our way through tables to the door when it began. My entire body seemed to burn in the rising cacophony of whistles, laughter, catcalls, taunts. While I had been obliviously drinking my coffee, everyone else in that place had identified us as lesbians—probably due to Anne's and Joan's butch drag—and they were now indulging in a litany of ridicule: "Come back, come back, we can save you," "It's your last chance, girls," called individual male voices accompanied by explosions of female giggles. "Don't go out that door"; "Turn back, it's not too late"; "You, the one on the end, there's still hope . . . " Carole was the one on the end. I can still see her sheepish expression as I turned back to look at her, her shoulders lifting and rounding as if warding off rain.

I had been singled out before, stared at during the one month in which I had become a regular in the bars. The bars were the only place I knew to be, and I was still acclimating myself, trying to figure out where and how I fit in, with very few signposts for deciphering such behavior as the cult of butch and femme. Likening this radical culture to heterosexuality was to compare palm trees to teaspoons. I seemed too tall and awkward in my skin to be femme, yet I could not envision myself adopting the clothing or the attitudes of a butch woman. So I was puzzling through the rules of the bar culture, its sexual signals and permissions.

I had been brought to these very bars one month earlier, on my birthday, by a heterosexual friend whose idea of formal introduction to adulthood was that I should look at the seamy side of life, that I should go look at queers. But what I had seen, with a lightning strike of unwilling recognition, was the truth about my life: that these were my people and this was where I belonged. I returned alone the following night, electrified with apprehension but pulled—as the tides are by the moon. So now I was one of the queers on exhibit, to be gaped at by slumming heterosexuals who came to sit in our dark, smoky bars and watch us slow-dance to wailing Connie Francis songs or twist to Chubby Checker.

But being stared at in a shadowy bar where I was an indigenous inhabitant was different from being singled out in the public world of heterosexuals. And so I sat in that bar on Gratiot Avenue with my insides thrumming with the aftershocks of that gauntlet I had walked through in the coffee shop—when you strolled up to our table.

I don't know where Joan knew you from, how the two of you fit into each other's lives, but you greeted each other with jocular familiarity. Those were the days before separatism and other hostilities, before the women's movement led us to a place in ourselves where we found such a depth of fury and rebellion that many of us lined up every male in the world in its focus. But back then wars and enemies were a far simpler matter, and so you sat down at that table with us, leaned back, crossed an ankle over a knee, and entered my life.

This isn't enough to have you even recognize yourself, much less remember me, so let me describe you.

You wore your straight blond hair in close-cut neatness except for a cowlick at the crown of your head that you couldn't tame no matter how much you patted or combed it. You had a fine broad forehead, wide-apart powder-blue eyes, pale blond eyebrows, a good nose, a wide mouth, and a quick smile. Your face was not bony, but there was boniness in the shape of it, that endearing element of rawness young men sometimes have. The sprinkling of acne scars across your cheeks only added to your attractiveness.

You weren't a student, but you dressed collegiate, in the fashion of those days: open-throated white shirts and what were called continental pants—a style using a two- or three-inch flap of fabric as self belting—pleasing on your trim body and long legs. In the chilly spring evenings, like that one, you added a crewneck sweater, usually navy blue, and I loved its rough wool and masculinity. Your pants were conservative dark colors, but once you wore baggy trousers in a snappy-looking houndstooth, and that night your pants were tweed, in a small checker pattern. You were never expensively dressed but always immaculately (but not meticulously) neat, and you smelled of a clean scent of after-shave lotion. You were always smart looking in the casual chic way that young people today would kill to achieve.

I immediately loved your looks and I still do, I still love it when any gay man (or better yet, a butch woman) dresses even somewhat the way you did. I envied your style, too. You exuded a charming combination of boyishness and maturity. You were a field of dreams . . . you still are.

I don't remember what any of us talked about in the bar that night, but it didn't matter. In that small, dark, intimate place your talk was light, free, confident; and your words were like music to me.

We went out into the brightly lit street. Your bearing and slenderness added to an impression of height, and most beautiful of all was the ease in the way you moved. You seemed to contain in your body the freedom of a dancer who dances for himself and then for others.

"I took this guy home last night," you said, talking to Joan. "He was a doll, a real doll . . . really sweet." But then, somehow your words—your welling laughter—became directed at me. "Let me tell you, I wasn't what he expected. We were in bed and I was making him very happy, and I just turned myself around and was he ever surprised at what he had in his mouth." And you flung your head back and laughed so joyously, and you strode so buoyantly at my side along the street, and your strides were so long and confident and cocky . . . "So he found out all about sixty-nine. He was such a doll . . . "

I laughed with you in my own sheer delight, not at the story you told to me in such intimate, audacious detail, but because I could take unalloyed pleasure in the company of a man without any fear of complications—for the first time.

Much more than that. Your joy in your life and your confidence in your sexuality were balm on those burns from the coffee shop.

The image of you striding along that Detroit street, your naturalness with the profound mysteries of sexuality, unfolds as easily and as vividly in my mind as if on film. At the time I didn't know anything else about why this image of you was so vital to me, why I clutched it so close inside myself, how much it meant to me.

Joan and Carole—and you—soon disappeared from my landscape, which is another story, and the following year I fled to California, carrying all the despair and confusion of my profound homophobia with me. A very long process followed, of struggle and anger and healing, of support from good people in aiding my growth and evolution, before I could find the ease within my own skin that you showed me on that Detroit street, before I could dance for myself and then dance for others.

You gave me the first of the building blocks on which I learned to shape my lesbian pride and self-esteem; you were part of the genesis from which the affirmative images of lesbian life and love came into being in all my books.

In the many years since that May night, friendship and camaraderie with gay men have taken their rich place in my life. Our two communities may have needed time apart in the seventies to explore our own identities and culture, but we belong together, and you were the first gay man to show me the promise of what we bring into each other's lives.

You were the first gay man I ever knew. I don't know your last name, I don't know what you did for a living, I don't know the name of the bar where we met, I don't know what happened to you.

I only know that on the lonely streets of that city all those years ago, you were light, you were hope, you were possibility.

Today all gay men are my brothers. But you, Steve, were my first.

CLIFFORD

CHASE

&

GABRIELLE

GLANCY

# Invisible Threads

I.

I have never written a portrait in memory of a relationship or in celebration of someone who was not dead or lost to me. The clarity of absence is not in operation here. Nor has my memory hardened into clear prisms like rock candy on a string. In this case, life has afforded me no such opportunities. Thank God. Cliff is alive as I write this, moving into the evening of a Sunday in New York City, as I sit here at my desk on a gray San Francisco afternoon. Even my grandmother, who died over four years ago, I can hardly walk all the way around. The journey is an expanding and contracting one, like Alice's chute down the tunnel, tangled with fine and intricate skeins of gossamer thread. With Cliff, the threads are living, resilient as corn silk, and still a little wet.

This, then, is the preface to a portrait of the best friend I ever had.

So I propose that I speak first and Cliff will respond in italics. Then Cliff will speak and I will respond in italics.

Okay?

*Okay.*

Cliff was a college friend, sort of. I met him in the Bach Society. Like me, he played flute. From the outset I was predisposed to like him because in high school I had been in love with a male flutist, Dan Kiely, who played with me in the band. So when I met Cliff, I transferred my feeling for Dan Kiely directly to him. Here was a male flute player with long hair, just like Dan's, though Cliff's hair was blond. I was attracted to him in a way, though he seemed, for lack of a better word, "closed." I would see him, I would like him, I would, for a moment, consider him sexually, and then I'd come up against a kind of wall. I had no idea he was gay. A few months earlier he had told me that he had been in love with my roommate—Linda Huffman—this beautiful weird girl who told me she couldn't stand living with me by smearing pumpkin innards on a note she posted on our door.

*I remember Linda Huffman . . .*

Cliff wore these loose khaki pants, neat, and a white shirt, also neat, and had a long blond ponytail that went down his back. I vividly remember his khakis and the color of his hair. He seemed to me, in some inexplicable way, mysteriously dull. He confessed to me later he thought I was dumb. In fact, I was just waking into my life as he was just waking into his. There was a time, perhaps four months, in which we lost touch. When I saw him again at the counter of Stevenson Coffee Shop, he had cut his hair and had a very trim, healthy reddish beard. He looked like a completely different person. Years later I would learn he had spent that summer in Berkeley, flirting with the idea of sleeping with his friend Wayne. As for me, by the time I saw him again, Linda Huffman had moved out of my dorm room and Lauren Stalman, who would turn out to be my first woman lover, had moved in.

Cliff was a Christian when I met him. I seem to remember him telling me he was in the fellowship at school. Once the Bach Society played at a Lutheran church on High Street, and I was conscious of his being more "involved" in the service than the other members of the group. He prayed and bowed and seemed generally pious, which caused me to respect him on one hand, and to dismiss him on the other. Religion seemed to me then like a fault in someone's character.

After the service, in the brightest of California suns, Cliff picked a wildflower he carried back with him like a prayer, which made me think he was "sensitive." Religious, flower picking, flute playing, bearded. This, outwardly, is how I saw him.

I met Cliff again in New York about six months after I moved there, on West Fourth Street in front of what is now Café Lanciani. I was working at the Sixty-third Street Y at the time for a series of workshops that would later become "The Writer's Voice," and he worked in the ASCAP building next door.

The first time we really got together we decided to make dinner at my house. The story of that dinner we've recounted many times since: it was the time we met James Taylor. Buying vegetables at a produce stand on Greenwich, this tall balding man overheard us debating about whether this particular green was cilantro or dill. "Dill," he said, leaning toward us. It took us a moment to realize who it was.

*I forgot it was that first dinner in New York when we saw James Taylor.*

And, too, it was the first time we really talked. After dinner we sat on the sagging couch I had inherited from my grandmother and I told him about Lauren, my first lover. Something changed between us. The veils of suspicion that seemed to keep us from clicking at Santa Cruz fell away. Cliff was suddenly clear to me. It was like that moment in life when you notice that at some point, imperceptibly, the fog of childhood has lifted. Rarely has this happened to me in my life, but somehow I knew that from this moment on Cliff would be an important person in my life.

We tried at one point to be lovers. Perhaps in our fifth year of friendship. It was a moment at which we were both single. (There have been many such moments in our fourteen years of friendship.)

We had gone to my parents' house in Freehold for the Fourth of July and had planned to fly back to the city in time for a party a friend was giving. From somewhere between Newark Airport and the Lincoln Tunnel, fireworks became visible above the skyline of Manhattan. The city was barely discernible in the graying twilight, distant and blurred by smog, as if a transparency had been put over the air. I leaned over Cliff, who was in the window seat, and we watched the dots of colored light pulse into the sky, then slowly disappear. Like afterimages on the eye, they seemed imagined.

*I remember necking on the bus then like teenagers. I remember not knowing where I wanted it to lead, and wanting to run.*

Later, we wove through East Village crowds to the party. "It's like the Middle East," Cliff said as we passed a new bar on St. Mark's place called Downtown Beirut. For days there had been explosions—firecrackers set off by boys on the street. Now it was extreme. The sky flashed with light, and there were deep, resonant booms every few steps. At some point I almost lost Cliff—we were both so dazed from the violence.

At the party was a woman I had recently broken up with, who was there with her new blond editor girlfriend, and I was jealous. I stole her away to the hallway of the floor above, where we looked at the haloed moon through the bars of the window, kissed and sighed, and talked about how bad we felt about what we were doing.

Cliff came home with me that night because it was late or we were drunk or my house was closer. He was living on Thompson Street at the time. We tried to make love. (In all honesty, I knew little at this point about making love to men. It would be another three years before I had my first and only serious boyfriend. He was Brazilian, an architect. The first time Cliff met him I was putting in a new lock on my apartment door. Cliff got hold of the measuring tape and said, "Let's see how tall we all are." He had somehow intuited in a matter of minutes Nahum's self-consciousness about his height.) Making love, I expected Cliff to do everything, like I'd seen in the movies. It didn't work. We were too nervous and awkward. I'm not sure what Cliff was feeling; we never talked about it.

Perhaps it was later the same week that I grabbed his arm before we walked out of the door to my building. "Kiss me," I said. "Again," I demanded. "Again." His kisses were sweet, more sensuous than I expected. The third time I said it, I could sense he felt uncomfortable. Then we were both embarrassed. The whole thing felt off.

I wanted Cliff to be the man I had always dreamed of. Men were never quite real to me. It seemed I was always too exacting in my desire for the fantasy. The boyfriends I had, from the first date onward, I had tried to turn into perfect husbands. I wanted, in some part of myself, to fulfill my fantasy with Cliff. I'm sorry now I couldn't let him just be Cliff kissing me.

There were years when we struggled with our sexual identities. Were we really gay or were we bi? How would our lives turn out? At one point in our friendship we talked about this almost as much as we talked about our writing. When Cliff came into his own and came out definitively as a gay man, I still harbored hopes that he would, nonetheless, be the father of my child.

Once we went up to the roof to read a story he'd written and came back with four kittens we had gathered up from this guy Beau who lived on the top floor. At one point they got loose and ran behind the stove of the old Ukrainian people next door. When we finally found them all, we brought them to my apartment and let them run around. One in particular got himself up on the bed and fell asleep. His sister, Josephine, tried to engage him in a fight. She hissed at him and tried to scratch him, but he wasn't moved. He just went about his business. Cliff and I agreed this was the one—which is how I got my cat, Eliot.

*Remember the Eliot song?*

*I feel kitty.*
*I feel kitty.*
*I feel kitty,*
*and witty*
*and gray!*

I grew up as a writer with Cliff. Soon after we met, we began talking shop. I found myself infinitely stimulated. I showed him my work; he showed me his. Once we tried writing found poetry. I remember both of us kneeling on either side of my single bed on Sixteenth Street flipping through books we had taken off the shelf. Cliff's friend Wayne had told him how to do it, and we decided to give it a try. My book was one on Galileo. I wrote a phrase we've quoted to each other since— "an invisible thread that keeps the moon from getting lost at its pinnacle"—which expresses in some way how I feel about the connection between us.

◼◼◼

September 17, 1989, the day my grandmother died, was a Thursday. I know this because Cliff works late on Thursday nights. I called him just about every hour to see when he would be free. Finally he just couldn't get away. He nearly cried with frustration.

The next day he took a bus to Freehold. My mother gave me the keys to her new red Thunderbird, and I went to pick him up at the station.

We drove to the orchards. I didn't want to go home. It was late September, and the trees were heavy with apples the color of my mother's Thunderbird. We parked the car on a muddy work road in the middle of the grove—there were No Trespassing signs posted all over— and walked in the drizzle under and between the trees. The apples were wet, dripping with mist, clustered and ready to be picked. We walked until we couldn't see the car. I don't remember what we said to each other. I remember only Cliff's new raincoat, this wonderful color of green, unbuttoned and opening as we walked. I remember, too, looking at the apples together in this private orchard just a few miles from my childhood home.

I would be sharing Cliff's grief only a year and half later when, it turned out, he would lose his brother, Ken, to AIDS.

Sometimes, in our years of friendship, Cliff got somewhere first and had to teach me what I needed to learn to get to where he was. With grief, I got there first. Who would have thought he was so close behind?

For the first year after my grandmother's death, Cliff was the only one I could let in. He was the only one I could bear to see. When his brother Ken died, I went back through the grief by going through it with him. "I felt exactly like that," I would say. "I know what you mean."

● ● ●

The year after his brother died, we went together to the gay parade. I had shown him a short story that morning sitting on a stoop on West Tenth Street. It was an incredibly humid day, late June. His response was lukewarm. This had angered me. I had wanted him to be more receptive. There was tension between us as we stood along the curb watching the floats and devils and boys in drag.

At exactly two o'clock, minutes after we arrived, the crowd grew silent. The bells of the church on Twelfth Street began to chime. It was the moment of silence for all those who had died of AIDS. Almost instantly, Cliff began to cry. It was the only time I've seen him cry like that, though so often, even at the lyrics of a song he liked, his eyes would fill with tears.

We held each other. There, in the middle of Fifth Avenue, Cliff cried in my arms. "Ken, Ken, Ken," I said over and over to myself as if to join with Cliff in bringing him, at least for the moment, back.

The silence seemed to clear a path from Washington Square Park to Columbus Circle. I could swear that at that moment I could see from one end of the parade to the other. There was, it seemed, a clear path from where we stood to *beyond somewhere,* and it was lined with me and Cliff and tens of thousand of other gay people, heads bowed in prayer.

II.

I'll start with Gabby's face—square; brown in summer; a small, square nose; not-huge brown eyes easily fascinated. I would never ordinarily think to describe it, so familiar is it to me, somewhere behind or beyond the verbal, in the realm of imprinting, of pure recognition.

Our common language, added to bit by bit over the years, is just as familiar, like the air you breathe. "I have the doom feeling today," I'll say. Or, "It was sublime. It was the definition of the sublime." We became friends when we were both fresh to New York, a time when perhaps there were many more feeling tentacles out in the world, and everything was more fluid. Since then there have been a thousand confidences; troubles told, untangled, and retangled; books shared; ideas puzzled over or enthusiastically explicated; unfinished manuscripts exchanged and pored over—the clanky noise of the café falling away, the waiter standing there trying to get our attention . . .

That we had known each other in school as well, only as acquaintances, gave our friendship a sense of depth, prehistory—as if we had met in another life. And it may as well have been another life—a college with no grades, situated at the top of a hill, on the edge of a redwood forest, overlooking the wide ocean; a sunny town and what seemed like half the California coastline—stunningly beautiful, rarefied, frightening; a place perhaps more than most set apart from the world. This is the country we both came from.

The Bach Society—which I called "Box Society"—was a miserable ensemble with sawing violins, but there was one occasion where Gabby and I played alone, with only a cellist, out in a meadow, prior to the yearly reading of *A Midsummer Night's Dream,* a college tradition. (This was a special occasion despite the fact that every day in Santa Cruz was like a midsummer night's dream.) We played well— you might even say it was our "moment" in the college's life that spring—and perhaps that performance foreshadowed the later, fuller collaboration.

*I remember that. It was late morning—the grass was still wet. Strawberries were laid out on tables under the scrub oak that shadowed the knoll. Cliff was this vague, finely tuned "other" beside me . . .*

Later, the day we ran into each other in New York: I was walking west on West Fourth—near Sheridan Square, not Café Lanciani—and Gabby and her friend Carolyn grabbed my arm as I passed them. We agreed that it certainly was a big coincidence and that we should get together. It was summer, and we stood in the warm shadow of Chemical Bank. Gabby looked at me intently—her hair was still long then, perhaps shoulder length, and perhaps she wore Birkenstocks; she hadn't yet taken on her sleeker New York persona. I went my way across

Seventh Avenue with the precarious notion that she might have a crush on me, which would be both flattering and confusing. I seemed to walk at once more lightly and more awkwardly as, way down the block behind me, from the buildings' shadows, I heard the two of them singing loudly, like high school girls, "She loves you, yeah, yeah, yeah."

*Is that true? I don't remember that. I do remember Cliff visiting Lauren and me at our sublet on West Eleventh Street one very hot August day . . .*

●○●

Our pretext for getting together was to play duets, but it never happened. We always just talked instead. The flutes never got out of their cases, and then I gave up bringing mine completely. Though the last time I had seen Gabby she was a biology major, it turned out that she had switched to English, and we had studied with some of the same professors, with a similar intensity, only at different times. Then, our third or fourth dinner, sitting in Gabby's tiny living room after stir-fried vegetables, I staring at her green-painted fireplace, Gabby began to tell me about Lauren, and then I told her about Dean.

Though we hadn't yet defined ourselves as gay—that would come years later for both of us—somehow I knew quite clearly just how defining was the experience of our first same-sex lovers. And I knew that I was talking to someone who *understood,* even if it was something I didn't fully understand myself. With the same kind of intuition, a feeling without naming, I knew then that Gabby and I would be friends.

There were two other key moments for me that first year.

I don't remember the setting for the first, only that at some point I realized, and remember remarking to Gabby, that she never forgot what she was about to say, even ten or fifteen minutes after I had interrupted her. "I really like that about you," I told her. For I knew then that whatever she was thinking at a given moment was important to her—that she believed strongly in her own preoccupations, intuitive leaps, half-formed perceptions. That is, she had interests. (What I didn't know yet was that this is what makes a writer. It would be several years before we each came to that self-definition as well.)

The second moment came during a lunch hour. Gabby and I worked around the corner from each other at our first miserable jobs in the city, and our early encounters included meeting for lunch in the park. I remember one day we were talking about our respective co-workers, and I said, tentatively, "Do you know how some people are really *dull?*"

Gabby could not possibly have known the rich history of this word for me, and its deep significance; it was the word my childhood friend Wayne and I had always used to describe anyone we didn't like. Yet Gabby, perhaps already exhibiting her brilliant gift as a reader of incomplete texts, nodded immediately and eagerly. "Yeah!" she said, with her particular enthusiasm. "I know *exactly* what you mean."

I thought then, perhaps more clearly than I had thought that night we discussed Lauren and Dean, that it was likely we would be good friends. And I gave her the highest compliment that Wayne and I could bestow on anyone: I said to myself, "Gabby's really *bright.*"

There are several imagined readers in my head when I'm writing—one laughing at a particular joke, another nodding at a good line—but Gabby is at the front of the internalized auditorium.

It's hard to imagine myself a writer without her there to read what I write. She is, in fact, an ideal reader, someone with a rare and uncanny gift of empathy, generosity, enthusiasm. She can look at a work in progress and imagine its completion, or see the whole in a single part.

*With Cliff's work I can see the whole. It's very satisfying, responding to his work. He's a gentler writer than I am, I think, and subtle. It's an amazing thing, this connection we have.*

There's a nonpublic, very intimate reading of my work that I get from Gabby, and which I crave since she moved to San Francisco. Far from holding back until I have something perfect and whole to show her, I find that I want her to see unfinished work. I want her to see the mistakes, the unpolished edges, the not quite resolved moments. For one thing, she might get a good idea for the piece that way; if I waited and showed her something more polished, she might miss the interesting flaws. She might only scratch her head and say, "There's something missing, but I can't tell what it is."

But beyond that, I want some further intimacy, someone to see my *own* interesting flaws. This is especially clear with autobiographical work, where coming to understand oneself is so obviously a part of the writing process. It would feel strange and repressed—it would be self-defeating—to edit out all the mistakes before anyone, even Gabby, were to see them.

Seeing Gabby lose her grandmother was, before I lost my brother, the closest death had ever come to me. My own grandparents had all died when I was little, and my parents hid their grief from me; as for the AIDS epidemic, before my brother, somehow I had never known anyone with the disease.

Working late, a series of phone calls that her grandmother was in intensive care, and then Gabby's voice once again, racked, barely a voice—"Cliff? . . . She died."

There's no way to punctuate or italicize it to convey how awful she sounded. It played like a tape in my head for weeks.

I remember how trapped I felt at work, how it seemed there was no way to define the situation as an emergency, so that I could leave early to be with her. I was on deadline and dealing with a difficult boss. "My best friend's grandmother died"—what did that mean? It seemed to me that if Gabby had been my wife or even a girlfriend, I might have been able to explain. I wished for that more tangible and conventional connection. As it was, running to a friend in trouble—"only" a friend—seemed the behavior of impulsive college kids, the opposite of responsible adulthood.

In fact, as I sat at the computer screen furiously trying to finish, Gabby's voice echoing in my brain, I felt twice removed from "emergency": there seemed no way to convey the importance of our relationship, or the importance to Gabby of the one she had lost—a grandmother, someone "secondary," not a mother, not a father or even a brother. How could I explain, there in the office, under the hard and fast glare of businesslike fluorescent lights, that Gabby had once confided in me how, as a child, she had called both her mother and her grandmother "Mom"?

It also occurs to me now that back then I wasn't out at work, which left me even more locked into the conventional. This is subtle but important: there's that precariousness of the closet, the back-of-the-mind tyranny of playing a role, which means conforming to all the rules. I had as yet staked no claim to the nontraditional, to alternative forms of kinship or obligation. If Gabby is a good friend, and I'm straight, then surely I must have a girlfriend, or I'm looking for one, and therefore Gabby must be somehow less important—again, secondary.

Anyway, my work should have been finished by now, or would be soon. Every half hour Gabby called, and I said, "Soon." But my neurotic boss appeared beside my computer with one revision after another, speaking excitedly, seeming to enjoy the overtime mood. This was a company newsletter, mind you, which she ran with the vehement, good-girl enthusiasm of the class valedictorian editing her high school newspaper. "We're almost done," I told Gabby once more, and here was my boss again, this time with a change in her hand that would undo nearly everything completed so far. In my confusion and frustration I resorted to the melodramatic. "I have to get out of here!" I growled. "There's been a death."

The next day, riding the bus out to Gabby's parents in New Jersey, I had the feeling of being pulled backward. Not into past unpleasantness, but into some unknown and frighteningly new future, like looking out the back of a train. I already knew—and tried not to know—that my brother was getting sick, and so the sensation was a premonition as much as it was sympathy for my friend, or worry over what to expect when I saw her. As it was, my brother was in the hospital with pneumonia only two months later.

I remember vividly that new, red Thunderbird Gabby was driving when she picked me up (and as if the Thunderbird were the bird of death, my brother bought one a few months before his final illness). We hugged nervously across the bucket seats, and I remarked that the last time she drove me anywhere was back in college, in her little Pinto, to a Bach Society rehearsal. I was at a loss for words. I couldn't read her face; everything had been so sudden. As Gabby drove past fields, she said, "Maybe we could go pick wildflowers." I replied, "If we came home with our arms full of flowers, then everyone would really know we had gone mad." I regretted resorting to our usual humor, but she laughed. "Ophelia," she said dryly.

So we settled on the apple farm, mostly just to walk. "Orchards would be comforting," Gabby said. "Don't you think?"

It was drizzling, and the orchard was totally deserted. The apples were very red on the trees, remarkable because some were not red and because the leaves were so green. We swished through the wet grass, and Gabby talked about what at the time I could only guess was grief. I didn't yet understand how you almost can't tell who has died, how it's like you yourself have breathed your last, and now you're just floating, waiting for something else to happen.

She said her grandmother's absence seemed to change virtually everything for her. Over the past two days her mother had been surprisingly clear about certain things: namely, the extent to which she herself had been unable to care for Gabby when she was little, and therefore, the extent to which Gabby's grandmother had filled the gap. But as an adult, too, Gabby had always seen her grandmother as someone to turn to.

On the other side of the orchard were huge pumpkins growing. It was the end of September. The largest ones were perhaps two feet across, not yet ripe, a whitish orange under the huge flat leaves, or speckled white and orange.

We labored down another dirt track, feeling lost. Finally, around a bend, there was the car again, red and staring at us with its extinguished headlights, through the rain. "It looks like it's trying not to be too conspicuous," Gabby observed. As if it were embarrassed somehow to be the exact color of apples that day, I thought, or as if it were trying to pass for a really huge apple. "Or it looks ready to pounce," I replied.

We considered stealing the apples we had picked, but decided that this, too, would be really crazy on such a day. Back at the farm stand, as we weighed our apples, I remarked on how deserted the orchard had been.

The woman at the counter stopped what she was doing. "Where did you get these apples?"

"There was a huge pumpkin patch," Gabby began.

"Pumpkins?"

Gabby and I looked at each other and nodded.

"That orchard isn't open today," the woman said testily. "You can't just go down any road. They may have been sprayed."

"My God, but we ate one!" Gabby cried.

The woman's expression grew suddenly conciliatory. "Oh no, don't worry." Smiling evenly, she handed us our bag of apples. "Just wash them. It won't kill you."

My eyes darted to Gabby. Why should my friend have to hear off-hand remarks about death on such a day? I almost wanted to hold my hands over her ears.

But she seemed unruffled. She took the apples and paid.

And perhaps I had an inkling then of something else pertaining to my brother—not only my own impending loss, but his imminent suffering. For I would soon need to learn how you cannot always protect someone who is in pain, and how, anyway, no one is quite as fragile or so much in need of protection as I once liked to believe.

Anyway, thinking back on it now, somehow I see all of that in this single moment in a little country market—in Gabby's calm and unblinking profile, as she took her change and I held the door for her, and she went forward into the rain.

*The taken-for-granted, the trusted and leaned-on, is the stuff of friendship—what's so hard to articulate and impossible to replace. Like the star perceptible only peripherally. And what happens when it suddenly disappears? Were we imagining it all along? Did it even exist? Did we exist to see it?*

*Not long after his brother's death, Cliff said, just before we got off the phone, for the first time in the ten years I had known him: "I love you, Gab." I understood then what he was seeing—that loss was possible, and happens. We both saw.*

L U C Y

J A N E

B L E D S O E

# The Night Danny Was Raped

The night Danny was raped, his rapist came to my lover's room.

I am eighteen years old, naked, and crammed in a closet. The odor of sweaty sneakers assaults my nose. Wool pants that smell like mildew hang in my face. A loose hanger, tangled in with the shoes on the floor, jabs dangerously close to my genitals. I think how much Danny will enjoy hearing about this scenario. Suppressing a giggle, I shift and a shoe slides off another and thuds to the floor. I freeze. The voices in the room outside the closet stop. Then I hear Angela's nervous laugh. She is the one who pushed me in here just moments ago when someone knocked on her dorm-room door. She is afraid not to answer her door, believing that the person on the outside will know that she is inside having sex. With another girl. She is afraid that even if I dress and greet the visitor with her, he will smell the sex in the room and know.

Angela is afraid. And her charm is her defense. She cultivates other people's affections like we are all plants on her farm. Her friends flock to her dorm room any time of day and night, and Angela is compelled to attend to each of them. If she does not, they will know. Now that I have knocked over a shoe, made noise, she will keep her visitor, Bob, the man who raped Danny, even longer to prove she is hiding nothing.

Bob is a yellow-blond white man, trying to convince Angela, my black girlfriend, to go to a movie with him. But really, he is trying to convince her to go to bed with him. "Come on, Ange, why *not?* What else you gonna do tonight?" I can picture his half smile, the expression on his face that shows he thinks he's getting something.

107

I am eighteen years old, a naked white girl, crammed in a closet on a snowy evening in New England. I am listening to my lover play along with this man coming on to her—or is she playing?—because she does not want anyone to think she is a lesbian.

I do not yet know that Bob raped Danny earlier this evening. But I do know that this intruder interrupted Angela's and my lovemaking. This man asked for my lover's attention and got it on demand.

The night Danny was raped, his rapist came to my lover's room while I sat in the closet, naked, and thought of my brothers, the first men in my life.

I am two years old. My family is vacationing in California and I toddle into the deep end of the motel swimming pool and begin to drown. Bubbles float to the surface as my fat little body rapidly sinks. Greg, my ten-year-old brother, dives into the pool. Despite the weight of his waterlogged Converse sneakers and blue jeans with the six-inch cuffs, he grabs me around the tummy, kicks to the surface, and swims to the pool's edge. I learn at age two that for the rest of my life my brother will protect me.

I am ten years old. I stand with the bat cocked expertly over my right shoulder, feet spread, and my eye on the ball in Charlie's fist. Charlie, my other brother, is twelve years old and the strongest pitcher in his league.

"Whatever you do," he tells me, "do not take your eye off the ball. Do not swing. Do not move. Not an inch."

Charlie winds up and pitches the hardball, overhand, at me with as much force as he can. It thuds into my left hip and the pain soars down my leg and up my side. I do not take my eye off the ball. I do not swing.

"You moved. Again."

Charlie pitches several more hardballs at my body until my left side throbs from the assaults. Finally satisfied, he says, "You won't be afraid of the ball anymore." And I am proud.

My brothers are the men in my life. I love them with all my heart. I date only their friends in high school. I measure all men against my brothers. I am not prepared to know Danny.

●—●—●

The night Danny was raped, his rapist came to my lover's room while I sat in the closet, naked, and thought of my brothers, the first men in my life, who caught me in an early act of lesbian separatism.

I am twelve years old, naked, and lying in the attic with my best friend, Nicole. Below me in the family room the men in my life watch the Super Bowl. I hear the pumped-up voices from the tube: "He's *down* on the ten-yard line" and "It's a long shot to the wide receiver." I hear the joy in my brothers' laughter as they shout at good and bad plays, and I recognize that their joy stems not just from the game, but from the maleness of the game. I am not a part of the football game and I do not care. I choose to ignore the men in my family; I choose to ignore football. They do not know I am choosing something other than them, but I know it. Up in the attic, above the family room, above the Super Bowl, I search Nicole's child's body and find a strength in her that kicks at my gut, more powerful than the arms of my brother when I am drowning, more explosively sensational to my body than any hardball. I sense the promise of everything I am looking for right there under my hands and in my mouth.

The attic has no floor, just long rafters across which we put a piece of plywood. On either side of the plywood are pockets of dust and below that the ceiling tiles of the family room. I like the feel of the cool plywood against my back as Nicole touches me. Later, still naked, something prods me to explore deeper in the attic and I crawl along one of those rafters with Nicole right behind me. My knee misses the rafter and plunges into the dust. I lose my balance altogether and fall off the rafter. I crash through the family room ceiling, up to my waist. I am gripping the rafter with my hands and Nicole holds me by the armpits. Below, the men in my family view my bare bum and dangling legs. I believe that they also view all the potency that I have discovered in

Nicole's body, my secret. There is silence except for the television. No one speaks of the naked little girl dangling above them. Nicole hauls me back up into the attic and my indiscretion is never mentioned, though the ceiling is quickly repaired.

For ten years, I loathe this memory.

●━●━●

The night Danny was raped, his rapist came to my lover's room while I sat in the closet, naked, and thought of my brothers, the first men in my life, who caught me in an early act of lesbian separatism, until Angela left with the rapist.

My muscles ache from my cramped position in Angela's closet as I hear her leave with Bob, the man who earlier in the evening raped Danny, though I do not know this now. I wonder what she expects of me: to stay in the closet until she returns, just in case? I kick open the door and stand to stretch my legs.

The door to Angela's dorm room cracks open. It is too late to cover my nakedness. But it is only Angela, who winks at me and whispers, "Sorry, sweetheart. What could I tell him? I'll see you later."

"Fuck you," I mutter. She pours into the room and carefully shuts the door behind her, then rushes over to kiss me. I am easily pacified. I am a slave to this woman's kisses. I will try to understand.

And I do. Somewhat. Angela is one of a tiny handful of black students on this small, very white liberal-arts campus. For her, coming out means alienating her peers, her small community of support. She cannot afford to do that. And I do have to concur that on a campus this small, you are out unless you prove that you are actively in, which is what Angela is trying to do.

I let her go with Bob and steel myself against the pain. Another hardball. I am well trained. I do not avert my eyes. I do not swing. I do not move.

I am eighteen years old and scared to death, though I will not admit this because I can take any hardball that comes my way. I am a white girl from Oregon on a very white, small New England campus, and I am drowning because I do not know how to drink cocktails and I do not own an evening gown. I do not yet consider myself an adult, though my classmates have been thinking of themselves that way for five years. I am a lesbian separatist by default, though I do not call myself this and never will. I understand loyalty, men to men and women to women, because that was how I was raised. I am shattered that my lover has walked out for the night with a man who I do not know at the time is Danny's rapist. But he is. And he asked for my lover's attention and got it. On demand.

●—●—●

The night Danny was raped, his rapist came to my lover's room while I sat in the closet, naked, and thought of my brothers, the first men in my life, who caught me in an early act of lesbian separatism, until Angela left with the rapist, and then I went to Danny's room, where he and I tried to make love.

The night is cold and clear. There is a foot of snow on the ground, and my breath makes dense clouds in the air. I arrive at Danny's dorm.

Danny seems delighted to see me. He is shriekier than usual, wired, and I wonder if I want to stay. But he launches into a story about a gay professor whom he saw in a bar in Boston and how the teacher wouldn't speak to him, and we die laughing at how this professor dates a female literature professor on campus to protect himself. I don't feel like telling Danny about the closet anymore. And I don't want to think about Bob and Angela. So I suggest that Danny and I do what we've talked about doing.

He balks, "You mean?"

"We don't have to," I say. It's not like I'm hot for him or anything.

"Let's!" Danny is suddenly ready. When we once talked about sleeping together, we had thought of it like a last hurrah, or maybe a final test, just to make sure we didn't really want heterosexuality after all. Later, I wonder why he agrees to this tonight. Perhaps he is hungry to be held. Perhaps I am too, though I do not admit this to myself.

Danny is a thin, nervous gay Jewish boy from New York. His fear of life is palpable; it's in the very paleness of his skin, the suddenness of his donkeylike laugh. Danny is my first gay male friend, and I love him for his love of gossip, for his easy vulnerability. I feel like a rock next to his ghost. I trust Danny because he seems powerless.

Danny and I touch one another and laugh at the oddness of the other's body. I run my fingers through the thick hair on his thin chest. I touch his bony hips, his floppy penis. His kisses are too sloppy. Wet with intent rather than passion.

By the way he touches my breasts I know he is slightly repulsed. My flesh feels like modeling clay under his hands.

I finally slap his hairy butt, he screeches, and we give up. After all, we tried.

Then, lying naked on his narrow dorm bed, he tells me about Bob.

Just a few hours earlier, the big blond boy came to his room on the pretext of borrowing some physics notes and shoved Danny onto his own bed. He stripped off Danny's corduroy pants and raped him. Danny tells me every detail, and he is shaking.

I listen. But. This is not easy vulnerability. This is raw exposure. I feel as if Danny is an antique goblet shattering in my hands. I am powerless, even more powerless than Danny, because I am holding the shards that could shred me to ribbons.

I am eighteen years old. I wonder. Who is this boy named Danny? He is not my brother.

Danny is unusually calm. He sits up and puts on his glasses. He walks hunched over, so I won't see his genitals, to get his pants and pulls them on. I grasp for my own clothes, suddenly desperate to cover my nakedness.

We are not talking now. My mind is careening. Angela just left with Danny's rapist, though I do not tell Danny this, and I do not know where they went. I feel trapped with Danny as if we were both caught in a shameful act. I do not tell Danny that I spent a lot of time shut in my lover's closet earlier this evening. It doesn't seem funny now. I do not tell him that his rapist is with my lover. My heart is reeling. Away from Danny.

I demand to know. "What are you going to *do?*" I understand action.

"I called the dean and told him," Danny tells me.

I feel myself plummet through the family-room ceiling again, hang there naked. How could Danny expose himself like that? I am amazed that Danny would ask for help so readily and almost angry at what I perceive as his privilege to do so.

I tell Danny that I hope Bob is expelled, because I think that is what Danny wants, and I leave.

●━●━●

The night Danny was raped, his rapist came to my lover's room while I sat in the closet, naked, and thought of my brothers, the first men in my life, who caught me in an early act of lesbian separatism, until Angela left with the rapist, and then I went to Danny's room, where he and I tried to make love, after which I walked back to my own room wondering if Angela was fucking Danny's rapist.

It is cold, clear, and I wear sneakers in the wet snow. I let my feet get very wet and very cold until they ache. The bare elm trees loom overhead. I feel as if Bob is lurking in the dark. I feel hunted by him, though it is not my body I am afraid for, but somehow my soul.

When I reach my room, I call Danny. I tell him, "Angela went off with Bob before I came over to your room."

Danny gasps dramatically, as if this is any old gossip, and I am relieved. We settle into the confines of our friendship as we've known it before tonight. I tell him about the closet and he dies laughing. We talk on the phone for two and a half hours. It is just like old times. When I finally hang up, the phone rings right away and it is Angela. She's been trying to call all night. Will I come over? I come. She says she did not fuck Bob. I do not and I do believe her.

I guess that Danny will roll his eyes if I tell him what Angela claims. But Danny and I do not speak of this evening ever again. In fact, we speak little in the spring that follows. We say we are busy. But the truth is that in spite of our two-and-a-half-hour phone talk that was just like old times, it really isn't like old times anymore. We know too much and we know too little. About each other. Danny graduates in May and I put him out of my mind.

Years later I learn that he is a very successful businessman in New York. This information surprises me because I do not see Danny as someone that powerful. And it threatens me because—although I can take it—I no longer trust people who wield hardballs. And I remember his easy access to the dean. I remember that Bob was expelled the following day.

Even so, one warm summer evening in Oregon I call directory assistance in New York and find his number. I dial eagerly. The voice on the machine is definitely Danny's. I leave a message, long and excited, and hang up. Danny never calls me back.

I tell myself, "He's a big shot now. Wouldn't you know he'd turn his back on his lesbian sister, merely a struggling writer."

But an ugly feeling burrows into my gut like an escaping rodent. I know that I had not allowed Danny to be anyone but my brother, and he certainly wasn't that, so to me Danny was never really anyone. At eighteen I had never known a boy who could need something from a girl. I had never known a man who would expose himself to the public, to a dean. I had never known a man who didn't associate the body with either shame or power. I was eighteen years old and I loved my brothers who protected me and taught me to be tough. They were my world of men. I realize now that there was a way that Danny's rapist, the man who wooed my lover, got more of my attention, and maybe even respect, than Danny. He got it on demand.

Today I am thirty-five years old. I miss Danny. I especially miss all the parts of him that I couldn't see and never knew. I pick up the phone and call New York's directory assistance again. The operator says there are now five people by that name living in Manhattan. She refuses to give me five numbers. I call directory assistance eleven times until I get an operator who agrees to give me all five numbers. Tonight I will begin dialing, looking for Danny.

# A Season of Turning Points

## Marsha

When Marsha returned to the living room she handed me a folded piece of paper with an almost casual sense of insignificance. But when she sat down, in a contradictory gesture, she shifted her eyes. "That was almost twenty years ago," she said, edginess hiding behind matter-of-factness. Her son Steven and I weren't sure what was going on.

I read the note, a discharge paper written by an emergency-room doctor. Marsha had been admitted for an overdose of Valium. "Subject was belligerent and uncooperative," the doctor had written. "Potentially harmful to self. Potentially harmful to others."

"I haven't seen that in years," Marsha said. She took the note away from me and tore it into pieces, depositing them inside a trash can next to the sofa, black plastic spilling over its sides, a flow of crinkly fake lava.

I was not prepared for the revelation. In the ten years that I'd known Marsha—the woman I'd often reacted to as if she were my own mother, in the same sort of complex alchemy of conflicting and confusing emotions (part awe, part fear, part love)—nothing in my experience of her had suggested this to me, that at one time she had been capable of taking her own life.

But then the surprise wore off. Of course it was possible. Marsha was a woman whose emotions clocked near the extremes. "I feel like a nerve turned inside out," she once said to me. In that way we were very much alike, though I usually kept the canister of my own volatile feelings capped and lidded.

*Mother substitute.*

Mine had shown me out the familial doorway. In the den one Easter Sunday I confronted Mom about our lack of communication, but she didn't want to hear what I had to say. "We can talk about the weather, your job, current events, but not your . . ." Her voice drizzled off. "I just can't accept this part of you." With Marsha that was never the case. She accepted people implicitly, explicitly rejected the notion of imposing her standards on others. If she'd decided to live her life primarily in the closet, to protect her children, she also admired my own choice to come out to my supervisor. I think it was her sense of the spiritual that explained this capacity for tolerance. Marsha always loved the glowing person inside and dismissed everything else—the body, its clothes, and the possessions it accumulated—as essentially unimportant.

She tore that discharge paper up on the first day of our reunion. I hadn't seen Marsha in over five years, hadn't communicated with her in over two. A few days before, I called her up and we planned the visit.

The sound of our voices erased the distancing effects of lost time and too many miles, and we picked right up where we'd last left off, bringing each other up to date. Her ex-lover Marion had moved back from Las Vegas to Pismo Beach with her husband, Raymond, where they'd once lived, and rented an apartment. Marsha had left her doctor boyfriend and moved into the same complex as Marion and Raymond. Her ex-husband had died of a heart attack. I was living in the same condominium in Los Angeles I had paid too much for in 1988. I was single now; Carlos had moved out six months previously.

Just before saying good-bye she asked, "Oh, did I tell you?"

"What?"

"Steven's gay."

"I always thought so," I said, pleased that my prediction had come true. "And so did my friends. Everyone I brought to the house always thought he'd turn out queer when he grew up."

Marsha and I were acquainted with each other primarily during the three years when we lived in Ventura, a coastal city seventy miles north of Los Angeles, where I began my first career job as a planner for the County Area Agency on Aging. I'd recently graduated with a master's degree from UCLA, and while I felt lucky to have found employment in my chosen field—1981 was Reagan's first year in office, and the cuts in social programs were just beginning to fall—I was reluctant to leave behind my friends and social life in Los Angeles.

Mostly I was worried that I wouldn't be able to find a lover. At twenty-five it seemed like the principal mission of my life. Part of me argued that small-town guys wouldn't be as jaded as the city boys back home, and therefore would make better "lover material," but another part maintained it'd be harder for me to find someone compatible. At the time there was no well-developed gay and lesbian community in Ventura, no organizations except for a small outpost of the Metropolitan Community Church, and no bars except for Thursday nights at a straight disco called the Library and a rather homely dive called the Wild Goose. Due to the limited selection of venues, I feared, most of the locals would be closet cases, not exactly my favorite political-mental-spiritual type.

Then there was the prickly issue of physical type. In Los Angeles I'd dated men of almost every hair and skin color. When I arrived in Ventura I found the sea of white faces, pink and steaming with suburban good cheer and health, freshly scrubbed and minty breathed, discouraging and limiting.

My job with the county was primarily about paper—writing reports and having them typed by the word-processing center. There were frequent deadlines, and Marion, the center's supervisor, was usually efficient and calm in the face of my alarm bells. We got along so well that one day I asked her out to lunch, intent on telling her I was gay. I wanted somebody in this county to know my real self (the waxen and incongruously cheerful "Alan" I'd introduced my new colleagues to seemed bogus, not the true ironic and introverted Alan my close friends knew and understood back home), and it felt natural to disclose myself to someone I instinctively believed would empathize with and not reject me.

When I told her, she raised her chin and brought a hand level with the top of the lunchroom table, narrowed her eyes and brightened her smile, and said, "I know. I'm that way too."

"How did you know?"

"I just knew. I figured that's the way you were, really, from almost the first time I met you."

"I wouldn't have made the same guess about you," I said.

She proceeded to tell me about herself, her lover, and their children.

Two days later a short woman stopped me in the hallway. "You're Alan, right? I'm Marsha."

Before I could issue a knowing gesture and a reply—that I understood she was Marion's lover, and that she worked for the county too, in the tax collector's office—she pressed herself close and motioned me not to say anything. Her index finger glided before me like a metronome.

"Yes," she said, reading the confused and knotted brow on my forehead. "Marion's Marsha. Soooo," she drawled out, "when are you coming over to the house?"

I hesitated.

"Are you doing anything special this weekend? Why don't you stop by for dinner?"

I was wrapped up and carried off. From that moment on there was no question I would now be a member of the family.

That Sunday, over plates of spaghetti with marinara sauce and bread puffs and green salad, they told me their love story, how they'd met twenty years previously in their mid-twenties, two bored non-orgasmic Jewish housewives living in side-by-side apartments in North Hollywood. They'd ditched their husbands and moved their kids in together—four between the two of them; Marion had a daughter and Marsha had three sons—and set up housekeeping. Passionately in love, all they wanted was to be with each other.

To survive they were forced to apply for state aid, although that didn't stop them from buying a home for their new family. "Nobody told us we weren't supposed to buy a house on welfare," Marsha said. Her head tilted back. "God! But we did!"

Somehow the subject turned explicitly to sex. We were curious. They'd never been frank with a gay man. I'd never talked openly with lesbians.

When Marsha told me about her first orgasm with Marion her arms reached for the ceiling. Her eyes shut themselves into tight bands of expression and her head moved from side to side.

"I didn't know an orgasm could be like that," she said. "There was just wave after wave—and her wave blended with my wave, and we just became, well, one big wave. I didn't know two human beings could be so connected like that, you know?"

I remember Marion saying how much it annoyed her that she'd spent years with a man who did nothing to please her, was incapable of pleasing her, and in return all she got or experienced was nothing. What astounded her was that she accepted this nothing, thought that nothing was all she ever deserved.

They were soul mates, they told me with conviction, and I believed them. At a gathering for psychics a few years back a woman had shouted at them as they were walking away, "They have one aura!"

They wanted to know about me, my first stirrings. I told them a story I'd recounted to most of my other friends: how I lost my virginity and learned how to masturbate, in that order.

My Catholic upbringing had left me so fearful of sex and concerned about committing a mortal sin and spending eternity in hell that I never masturbated as a teenager. Most mornings when I woke up I'd touch jockey briefs stiff with a yellowy gluelike substance. I had no idea what the gunk was, however, and sublimated any questions that might have led to an answer.

Fortunately, during my second year in college, all that changed. In the course of a single night I went from purely virginal boy to sex stud extraordinaire, initiating my love life with a ménage à trois with an older woman (Alexis, age twenty-three) and a younger man (Doug, age eighteen).

The three of us were hanging out together, singing songs and doodling on the piano, when we ended up in Alexis's room. Conveniently enough she had a single. After Doug left—for the most part leaving me unsatisfied because he refused to kiss—I stayed with Alexis. While inside her I experienced a strange intense contraction that she assured me was an orgasm.

Eventually we became lovers. After three months of daily liaisons I confessed to her that I'd never masturbated, not once in my life, that I'd never actually seen my own ejaculate. One time I withdrew just before coming and spilled myself on her belly. I was amazed to see all this glossy white gelatin, something I'd always assumed was yellow.

I asked her how it was done. She was astonished. "Well, I don't really know," she said. "I mean, I'm a girl. I suppose you just sort of jerk at it." To illustrate she made an up-and-down motion with her hand.

That day I went back to my dorm and, under cover of sheets and while the roommate was away, engaged in prodigious experimentation, testing all manner of finger positions. After forty-five minutes of strenuous effort I finally hit pay dirt. I've been an onanist ever since.

By the time I got to the punch line I was practically crying from laughter, and at every turn in the story Marsha and Marion exchanged looks and smiled, and urged me to proceed with the narrative. It felt good to know I could be myself. I had made new friends.

During this whole time I wondered what eleven-year-old Steven, sitting silent and small on the floor, was thinking. I did nothing to hide my gayness, nor did his two moms hide their relationship. Bright behind thick glasses, eager to join in and add his own contributions to the conversation, he also somehow seemed embarrassed by the outpouring of truth. He twisted his slender arms into noodles, peered between the baroque spaces molded into the back of a dining-room chair, and delivered smiles that were alternately shy and sardonic. I remember thinking that at his age I had acted just like him.

●━●━●

The drive from Los Angeles to Pismo Beach took more than four hours. Marsha's apartment was located in a complex of faded white bungalows, set down randomly as thrown dice, in a field of grass so green it looked artificial. When she first greeted me I noticed immediately that she'd lost weight—plus she was wearing a black wig, theatrically glossy and inward curving, with wide bangs that made her look girlish. When I looked down I also saw that she'd injured her left foot. The whole weekend she hobbled around the apartment in a shoelike cast held in place with blue Velcro straps.

Steven had undergone a remarkable transformation. The slight boy I'd watched reciting lines from the Torah at his bar mitzvah had filled out, taken to lifting weights, and somehow outgrown the need for glasses. I asked him what was going on in his life. He told me he was in junior college now and that he intended to transfer to a four-year school as soon as he received his associate arts degree. He and his lover of a year were living in Los Angeles, not too far from my place.

I first sighted Marion from Marsha's couch, waving to me from inside the frame of her living-room window, half smiling—amused, bemused, I couldn't tell which. Marsha told me that Marion and her husband, Raymond, were moving that weekend, from a one-bedroom to a two-bedroom apartment inside the same complex. "Just across the way, see there?" Marsha said. And of course the first thought that came to mind was, So, they've come full circle. Next-door neighbors once again.

Steven and I helped Marion and Raymond move. Afterward we returned to Marsha's. They stayed in their new place, sorting and organizing, and we didn't see them the rest of the weekend.

"It's like we've reversed roles," Marsha said from the kitchen. She filled a plastic tub with hot water and Epsom salts for her sore feet. "I've become like her and she's become like me. I was always the one on the edge, frazzled, not able to cope. She was always the cool one, even tempered, the one who had to calm me down." She carried the container back to the living room, unwrapped her feet, and placed them inside. "Now I've become more mellow and Marion's the one stressing out."

Yet only a little while later she had me pinned to the wall, arms and legs writhing like an insect's. Apparently I had upset Marion when I first arrived. "Look at him, he's just sitting there," Marion had said. Her arms shook, exasperated. "He's not responding, he's not reacting to you."

An old habit. While listening intently to someone my expressions usually drop away; I become quiet and focus an intense gaze on the other person. Marsha lectured me, suggesting that this behavior was rude. I protested, saying this was a fixed personality trait that couldn't be altered. She persisted with her criticisms, though, and I finally agreed I'd attempt to change and throw in the requisite interjections and head nods, although I knew the effort would be futile. I was annoyed but didn't tell her so, not wanting to risk triggering the temper I knew existed but had rarely seen, preferring instead the settlement of silence.

Beyond a wish to avoid confrontation, I don't know why I was always so moderate in her presence. Perhaps it was because she could be so insightful. Once I asked her to interpret a dream in which I was sipping tea with André Gide and Pearl Buck in a gold-gilded room filled with heavy French furniture. The fantasy Pearl Buck turned to me and said, "You're thick and thin in places."

The cryptic message puzzled as well as disturbed me, somehow seeming ominous. When I asked Marsha what she thought it could mean she said, "That you're out of balance. That you've lost your equilibrium." Her interpretation seemed exactly right.

I remembered that Marsha was interested in psychology, and so I'd brought along a book about personality types called *The Enneagram,* described by the author as a map of human nature first developed by the ancient Sufis. I read selections from the book and explained the basic theory. We speculated about which of the nine personality descriptions best fit Marsha, then Steven. In the end we concluded that we all had the same profile: creative, intuitive, depressive—"the artist."

These couplings seemed to fit. I had an interest in fiction writing, Steven in photography, and Marsha, most particularly, in people. She had that rare ability to seize meaning out of the chance encounters and odd moments of daily life. At one point she told us a story about sitting on a bus bench and asking the man next to her, "Did you ever wonder what the birds thought when they saw the first plane?"

We stayed up until four that morning. I asked Marsha why her relationship with Marion had broken up. She explained that Marion was never "that way" as much as she was, that she really wasn't satisfying Marion as a lover. Marsha said she was frustrated, too, that she couldn't live a more open lifestyle.

I asked Marsha if she considered herself to be a lesbian. She pulled back and thought about the question. I wasn't quite sure if she'd say yes, but she did, and told me and Steven a story about seeing fourteen-year-old Sophie Berkowitz's breasts for the first time in the locker room at Fairfax High.

Clearly this time in her life, about to turn fifty-five, was a season of turning points. The breakup with Marion had left her financially devastated, and was the principal reason she'd gotten involved with the doctor. A diabetic, in a couple of days she would have a hearing with an administrative-law judge on her application for disability.

The subject of suicide came up again. I was still aware of the torn pieces of paper lying at the bottom of the trash can. A few days previously Marsha had been shopping at Vons when she came across a makeup display case. In a moment of reflection she opened a package of Clairol hair coloring and turned the glass bottle around in the light. "I think I want to live," she thought. "Yeah, I think that's what I want."

On impulse Marsha said, "Oh, I don't feel like wearing this," and took off her wig. Her hair had thinned and aged into a gorgeous patina of blacks, dark reds, silvers, and grays, a long river of colors, blending and swirling—a look I much preferred over the monochromatic hairpiece.

I held that image in my head, of the wigless and beautiful Marsha, when a week later on the phone she told me of the circumstances surrounding her suicide attempt. There had been a showdown. Marion had given a speech to her husband that all she wanted was to be with Marsha. Then Marion's husband suddenly moved the whole family to Simi Valley. It was the separation that had provoked such despair in Marsha, enough for her to reach for that bottle of Valium.

The Sunday morning of my visit, Marsha was in the bathroom and Steven was still sleeping when the telephone rang. I let the machine answer. It was Paul, Marsha's middle son and the father of her two grandchildren, and the message he left started with, "Hi, Mom, it's me. I was just calling to let you know that I love you . . ."

I knew I'd never leave such a message with my own mother. Certainly I loved her, but when I said so those three little words sounded stilted and hollow, incomplete—obligatory language I felt compelled to mouth and pass along as real. In contrast, the sincerity I heard in Paul's voice struck me as completely genuine.

I was envious for an instant. Mom and I rarely communicated on the phone, corresponding once a month instead. I wondered what it would be like to have a relationship with my mother that was open and supportive and not clouded to the point where the present was obscured by past mistakes and regrets, something more akin to the relationship Marsha appeared to have with her own three sons.

That evening as I was about to leave for the return trip home the sky opened up and the rain started to pour. Steven had come up by train, and I offered to take him back with me to Los Angeles. "Call me as soon as you get in," Marsha said. "The both of you. I don't care how late." Before we left I hugged her. When I looked down I saw in her face both the wife and the mother, the friend and the lover, all those roles at once, turning and revealing themselves to me with each blink of her eye. "I love you, Alan," she said, and squeezed.

Once during morning break, while we were sipping Cokes in the employees' lunchroom, one of Marsha's co-workers approached us and asked her, "Is this your son?" The woman stared at Marsha, then at me, sure she was right. Certainly there were physical similarities. We were both dark complected and had brown hair and eyes. But there was something else. Hunched close together, there was an intimacy between us that to an observer could be mistaken for blood relation. Later Marsha told me that recollection of the incident had always tickled her. "It makes me smile too," I said.

# Mothers & Others, but Also Brothers

For most of my early childhood my mother and I had a bedtime ritual. She would sit on the edge of my bed rubbing my back. Then she'd lean forward and kiss my ear. The warmth of my mother's breath seeped into my brain like a balm, and consummated the day with a whispered ". . . there now." I wanted nothing more than that, the satisfaction of her words breathed into me. To be reassured, however falsely, lips pressed to ear, that no harm would come.

And if I stayed up beyond my mother's bedtime, as I did as I grew older, my father came in and kissed my mouth. It was a kiss that made me all too familiar with the insides of his cheeks and left my mouth clotted with bourbon. Every night alcohol paraded through his blood like bad religion. Some nights the bourbon's zeal erupted into riots, windows were smashed, cupboards kicked in. Mornings, I found rooms in ruin.

But I was not without stalwart male role models. I had three older brothers. They were trees in whose shade I grew strong. I grew like a tree, too, with possibilities branching unabashedly in every direction.

Richard was closest in age, only six years older. His pale skin, like mine, was flecked with brown, and his mouth smelled like root beer. Richard taught me not only to dig forts, to fish and to whittle, but to use my imagination in games, to create characters. I played "Speedy" to Richard's "Skyhawk." Gorgeous George, the good wrestler, to his villain, the Sheik. We made tommy guns out of blocks of wood, spray-painted silver. And when we snaked through ivy, we ensnared Nazis in ambush, liberated French villages.

Stephen told me stories, and showed me, as though teaching me to mold with clay, how to write my first words: *act,* then *fact,* and from there, *factory.* His shoes were large enough to fit the length of my lower arms, so I crawled around his bedroom in them, like a seal pup. Stephen paid me a nickel for half-hour back rubs. And when I lifted up his shirt, and touched the enormity of his back, his skin smelled like sleep, a rich broth of cream and potatoes.

Peter smelled the most like wood, a piece of oak split open, a pile of raked leaves. Peter waxed philosophical with me, often bedazzling my imagination. Sharing his belief, for example, that the universe was female, and nature, surely male. And once while we were watching a ewe in labor, he theorized that the pain of childbirth was mollified by a sense of expectation, making it "a good pain."

All three teased me, handled me, but never harmed me. With my brothers, trespassing boundaries was never an issue. Brothers were Lancelots, guardians, fellow travelers. They enjoyed my tomboyness. They were, in fact, agents of it. So partially out of gratitude, and partially out of awe, I fell in love with each of them.

I remember the exact moment I stopped playing, the exact moment when childhood snapped shut: I was twelve, sitting on a hill, looking down through a grove of buckeye trees with Dorothy, a playmate three years younger. She was pleading with me to choose from our assortment of fantasy games. The ground was littered with fallen buckeyes. I turned one over in my hands. The seed was moist, heavy, cleaved into globes like a dog's testicles.

"Spies?" she begged. "Tramps? Indian scouts?"

"I'm too old to play," I announced, trying on maturity like a hand-me-down.

Up until that moment, I had prided myself on being a tomboy. Tomboy meant that, among playmates, I was Alpha, aviator of the game's plot. Like my brothers before me, I could rev the game or land it, veer it in any direction, urge, as a film director might, deeper role-playing, a more satisfying scene. Tomboy meant I trusted the structure of tree limbs. Meant I knew the physics of flat stones against a taut skin of water. Meant I could slither into a hole in the dirt, a hollow in the brush. Meant I simply had to put my body into, onto, and through things.

But looking down that hill, I struggled with a new definition. Tomboy meant something sinister, what schoolmates in the city were beginning to call me: lez, Miss L, Miss H. Queer.

⊙⊙⊙

A convert to midcentury child psychology, my mother embraced the term *arrested development* as an explanation for deviancy, but also as a substitute, albeit a more sophisticated one, for *bad*.

When my devotions toward female teachers persisted into high school, my mother preached her belief that those crushes constituted a mere phase. Adults who never grew out of that stage could expect the same distant pity as persons suffering from dwarfism or mental retardation. I would grow out of that phase, she assured me, though her ministrations had the ring of commandments. I wanted to believe I would. I too began to perceive homosexuality as an emotional defect, damaged goods. Something inferior to the robust pageantry of normal longing.

At the same time I studied my mother's attractions for clues to the correct form of desire. During summers, the afternoon sun chased us behind the veil of venetian blinds, into the gloom of our house, to watch Merv and his weekly guest. Within the cool light of daytime TV I could turn my face to hers and examine her reactions. My mother's eyes danced to (irony of ironies) the antics of Peter Allen, the suave musings of Vincent Price, the absurd quips of Paul Lynde. No kidding. She loved these men, plain as day.

I suspect that I mimicked my mother's tastes until they were my own. Soon I too could zero in on that unmistakable something. I thought Lawrence Olivier and Rock Hudson were men with enormous sex appeal and, now I realize, not without that certain je ne sais quoi. Was I unknowingly drawn to gay men because of the model of my mother? Or because, as a budding Miss H, I was protected by them from the failure of heterosexual contact? Because gay men reminded me more of brothers than of fathers?

●●●

Until I came out, I might as well have been a gay man, for male was the only gender I could spot in the "pathology" of same-sex love. I read *Giovanni's Room,* saw *The Boys in the Band.* I eyed my mother's string of interior decorators. I listened for clues to my own stirrings in the swells and swirls of Tchaikovsky's music.

At sixteen his *Pathétique* consumed me. It was the first piece of music (non-Beatles, nonjazz) that I listened to as closely as I would a friend. Before this I had never been able to perceive the structure of a complex composition.

The symphony's form is as legible as a graph of the Dow on a bad day. Scales try to ascend, but succumb finally to decline. For a glowing moment it is Sisyphus nearing the top, before gravity bullies it back. The symphony is built like a mania trying to wriggle out of despair, like a life struggling to free itself from the inevitability of death. Like (or so the legend goes) the composer finally crushed by his own unspeakable perversion.

Did our music instructor suggest that this was homosexuality's anthem? Or did I only imagine he did? I was continually on guard. It seemed that everywhere I went, everything I read whispered about homosexuality, with the hiss of impending disaster. Lisping boys carried their loneliness through the American South, past ads for Nehi sodas, into dark, mysterious thickets. Some left home for dingy rooms in sea towns, to sleep with sailors who invariably dumped them. Some, like Capote, grew degenerate, whining incoherently on late-night talk shows. The homosexuality of men, while literate, seemed doomed to cataclysm.

●●●

I like to say the earth shook the day I met him. February 11, 1971, the day of the Sylmar quake. I moved to L.A. to go to art school, but I'd long stopped showing up for classes. I was spending my nights alone, watching TV in an apartment I shared with a woman I secretly wanted. I assumed I would spend the rest of my life like that, shrinking within a self-imposed quarantine.

That morning jolted me into quite a different world. My bed pitched like a runaway stagecoach. The old Frigidaire lurched like Frankenstein's monster into the center of the kitchen. When I pulled on my clothes and fled the building, I knew that nothing about my life would be the same. I drove toward the dorm, toward new friends, toward rescue. The sun set brighter that night, and I remember that the moon had an orange sheen, maybe from the dust the temblor stirred up.

We spent all of our time together after I moved into the dorm. I was first struck by his voice—earthy and masculine, but buoyant, playful, almost musical. He looked completely different from any man my age. He had short hair, a rabbinical beard, and wire-rim glasses. He wore baggy wool trousers. One leg had a plastic patch of a puppy ironed on the knee. And when he sat cross-legged on my bed and listened to my gospel records with his eyes closed, I could stare shamelessly at the length and curl of his eyelashes.

Bernard had a way of looking at things. He turned me on to pop art, on to the stunning beauty of ordinary, mass-produced objects. The grocery store was a latent museum, and all the shoppers collectors. The exalted realm of Art was democratized; the simple objects of the world were ripe for the picking.

One day, in the spirit of pop, we created a meal out of Pla-doh. White for the blubbery stripe that banked the chop. Yellow for the slab that sagged like an Oldenburg pickle atop a mound of peas. Each pea was a small wad of green, rolled into a perfect bead. And as we rolled and molded the clay with childlike abandon, our words falling easily between us, I could smell Bernard, or what I thought was Bernard—all the elements of a brother's scent: clay and salt, root beer and wood, cream and mashed potatoes.

I don't remember who ventured "I think I might be a homosexual" first. But regardless, our bond was sealed that day by those words. And for the first time, because we mirrored the same secret, we each stole a new glimpse of ourselves, each strutted a bit in the other's reflection, a cockiness that our hidden oddity might in fact make us "special." We developed a style of humor that lampooned the burlesque extremes of heterosexuality. Gender seemed an absurdity, and we had no scruples about mocking all its Mamie Van Dorens and Victor Matures. Years later I would recognize our joking as camp, the gay currency, the stuff upon which a worldview is crafted. I would also see, with the enhancement of hindsight, that the intimacy we were building would forge a lifetime partnership.

●●●

We found a house to rent in the northeast corner of the San Fernando Valley. Twenty years ago Sylmar was a hodgepodge community of students, bikers, and young families—tenants who enjoyed cheap rents after owners fled the quake's epicenter. At night, even months after the quake, dogs resumed pack behavior and could be seen trotting down darkened boulevards. Poodles, bulldogs, hounds, chihuahuas—all ganged together, drawn by the undertow that catastrophe sets in motion. Tumbleweeds roamed, too, on nights when the Santa Anas blew. The whole world, in fact, had a feral snarl to it. Only eighteen months before, the decade of flower power had fallen into dissolution when Manson's cult massacred Sharon Tate and her friends in a Southland canyon. Marvin Gaye sang, "Mercy, Mercy Me," and "What's Goin' On?" Up the freeway a mile or so, the rubble from a toppled overpass lay in ruins like a razed temple.

Mind you, all the upheaval was second nature to us. We were veterans of upheaval. Both had been bruised by a father's tantrums. Bernard's adolescence was shaken—not once but twice—by the loss of brothers to cancer. I had witnessed my father's sodden decline into suicide. And both understood how our secret desires, once exposed, would only provoke further havoc and loss. The notion of living on a fault line seemed to us as ordinary as, say, pretending to be straight.

Did I mention that Bernard and I were living together with another couple? They were a real couple, while we were still chaste, just good friends. Night after night they murmured behind their bedroom wall while we sat up in the living room listening to records. Their bodies seemed virile, sinewy; while mine, in its unrelenting virginity, had become as insubstantial as light on a movie screen. And Bernard's flesh, what was that to me? A hirsute amalgam of my own shadows?

One night Bernard and I both confessed that we had each recently masturbated. He said, "God, it's so ridiculous. We should have had sex with each other!" And so we decided, there and then, that yes, in fact, we'd better. Moments later we each bathed in anticipation of the great deflowering. During his shower, Bernard had doused his body hair with cream rinse. During mine—forget that I had masturbated the night before—the touch of my own soapy hand was new, as it slid lather along a female body just beginning to take form, just beginning to gather density and heat.

We emerged from the solitude of those showers, like Quakers from a silent prayer, grateful for the ease of each other's friendship, eager to taste what lay ahead: three nights rolling in the amber glow of a space heater, the obsolescence of my twin bed, the deepening of our intimacy.

And why not? I trusted Bernard more than anyone I knew. We were best friends and we were attracted to each other. It was perfect.

Except for one thing. The "shared secret" of our homosexuality, the disclosure that initially welded us together, suddenly loomed like a lunatic who had to be carefully subdued.

Nevertheless, no matter how we struggled to suppress it, once we started living as lovers Bernard's interest in men only got stronger. Our first summer was a nightmare of tanned pectorals, deltoids, and quadriceps. The seasonal display of masculine flesh confounded Bernard, and threatened to undermine our future. Of course, I was continually aroused by women, but felt more acutely the need to hold on to my first relationship as though it were my last. I could keep arousal safely shelved, could even ignore the portents of our breakup, because, quite simply, we were in love. As I watched him suffer his attractions to men I panicked and urged him to seek therapy. He went, half hoping he might change, half trying to keep what was good about us from shattering, like a fragile dowry, into a billion unrecognizable bits.

We stayed together three years, during which time we did everything a real couple does—laughed, worked, argued, had sex, went on diets. The pain of breaking apart was dampened by the inevitable exploration of same-sex love, pain my brother Peter might have reasoned "good."

It's a rare day Bernard and I don't speak to each other on the phone at least once. He, too, is my brother; more so my twin, though my hair has gone white while his recedes. We still laugh, argue, and diet together. We've grown in tandem as writers, sharing our discovery of favorite poems, helping each other to shape our works. The only thing we don't do is fondle each other, or share the kind of openheartedness fondling encourages. In many ways we are still a couple, a couple for whom a sexual impasse has meant anything but estrangement.

In the days when my lesbianism steeped me in a separatist community, Bernard would joke about being worried he'd inadvertently leave hairs in my house—evidence I'd been visited by a masculine presence. Needless to say, some of my girlfriends have been threatened by my commitment to Bernard, a man, the hirsute embodiment of patriarchy. Or more importantly, by my commitment to a relationship that continues to nourish our hearts and minds, that once was sexual, but worse, is steadfastly lifelong.

How can I explain to my mother that despite all her pleading with me to grow beyond my homosexuality, I've remained intractable, true to myself? Shall I show her the irony? How her secret adoration of gay masculinity formed me? Or how a woman's kisses pressed to my ear still reassure me beyond words? How can I tell her, without her thrilling to false hopes, that, having loved a man, having mated with a man, I know I could still?

I still find men attractive, and I still recall, with sexual excitement, my escapades into heterosexual sex. I especially enjoyed the encyclopedic range of sexual imagery to draw from. The gamut, from Bible to porno, an endless array. Not to mention the hundred cinematic kisses that left me breathless in the dark. Like Kim Novak and William Holden dancing to "Moonglow" in a July swelter.

Yet when a woman approaches I feel something older, less articulate. Something as absolutely hoped for as "there now." This is my polemic, justification for my nature. We all inevitably feel the pull toward some creature made luminous in the act of love. Is it toward the archetypal Mama? Or, if you're so inclined, Daddy? If all the world's faiths can sing the virtues of the Great Mother and Father, can these sex-inspired hallucinations be so pathological? Aren't all humans linked together by a need that predates adult development, when surrender was the mirror image of survival? When, at our most vulnerable, we were literally lifted up into the air toward the salvation of an adult body? Likewise, aren't our sucking lovers briefly infants? Their need for us is as primal as milk. Is it childish to employ our imaginations in the service of our pleasures? Is our development arrested, or are our natures finally realized?

Besides, look again. What once seemed *pathétique* is now sleek and predacious, like a spy snaking through ivy, a scout probing a new stand of trees. Like you surrounded by buckeyes as childhood snaps open. You, stepping over fallen columns, liberating French villages. While dogs howl beyond the woods, you undress and slip into the bath. The lather rolling in your hands makes its sucking sound. You will always find fascination in the flesh around the nipple, the back of the neck. Like Bernard will when Brian comes home tonight. Not for the sake of procreation, not for some higher purpose or polemic. Bernard, you, me, us all, our fingers branching, unabashed.

# Truth
# Serum

Every Tuesday at exactly three o'clock, the nurse would call my name
and lead me into the examining room, where I lay down on a padded
table. Comfortable? she always asked, and always I said yes without
conviction. I have no recollection of the woman's face, only her white,
immaculate back, and the click of the door as it closed behind her. I'd
be counting holes in the soundproof ceiling when Dr. Sward, my psy-
chotherapist, would bound into the room. The man possessed an inex-
haustible energy when it came to the task of psychic exploration, and I
think he hoped some of his enthusiasm would rub off on his reticent
clients. Dr. Sward prided himself on being a hale, contented fellow, a
man able to overcome adversity. A former smoker, he'd had an operation to remove part of his larynx, and his voice, or what remained of it,
was somnolent and gravelly. "Hello," he'd rasp. "Are we ready?" Dr.
Sward took a seat in the room's only chair—vinyl exhaled under his
weight—and removed a fountain pen and notepad from the breast
pocket of his blazer. Pen poised, he beamed a broad and expectant grin,
a lock of white hair falling onto his forehead.

Next entered Dr. Townsley, Dr. Sward's stout, mustachioed colleague, who swabbed my arm with alcohol and asked me to make a fist.
I barely felt the injection, but serum rode into my vein like an intra-
venous hot toddy, and a primal, womb-worthy comfort seemed to radi-
ate outward from the tip of the needle. Almost instantly my breathing
deepened into rich, intoxicating troughs of air. I steeped in a heedless
stew of sensation: release of rubber tied around my arm; small talk vol-
leying between the doctors; one shiny frond of a philodendron the

greenest thing on earth. With the sudden candor of a drunk, I wanted to tell the doctors how happy I felt, but before the words could form, I heard the sound of what I thought was a receptionist typing in another room. Her typing would quicken—faster, manic, superhuman—and invariably I would think to myself, A million words per minute! What nimble fingers! The keys must be shooting sparks from friction! And then I'd realize it wasn't the sound of typing after all, but something more miraculous—chattering watts of light showered down from a bulb on the ceiling. Stirred to the verge of tears, I wanted to shout, "Hold everything, doctors. I can hear light!" But my jaw went lax and my fist unclenched and I lost my grip on consciousness.

When I opened my eyes, the overhead lights were out. Dr. Townsley had gone, and Dr. Sward's voice emanated from somewhere near the wan glow of a table lamp. "How are you?" he asked.

I was eager to answer any question. I effervesced with things to say. I couldn't have lifted my head if I'd wanted to. "Good," I mumbled, trying to work the moisture back into my mouth. "Very good."

Dr. Sward believed that this experimental form of therapy would help me get to the root of my problem. His colleagues were having some success with the treatment, a combination of sodium pentathol, known during the Second World War as *truth serum,* and Ritalin, a mild amphetamine that, given to hyperactive children, helps them gather their scattered thoughts. The sodium pentathol, he'd explained, would cause me to pass out, and the Ritalin would revive me. This paradoxical cocktail numbs a patient's inhibitions while at the same time enhancing the person's capacity for insight, its effect vanishing without a trace in about forty minutes. He suggested the drugs after I told him that talking to him for the past six months had done nothing to reduce the frequency or intensity of my sexual fantasies involving men. *Frequency, intensity:* those were the terms we used, as though the clinical distance they imposed was in itself an achievement, a way of dividing me from the heat and draw of desire. The final decision was up to me; no treatment could make me change if I didn't have a strong desire to do so, but I might, he felt, be resistant, and the drugs could break down my unconscious defenses and hasten our progress.

"How are things at home?" asked Dr. Sward.

I'd been living with a woman for three years, a woman whom I loved, and with whom I had a sex life both playful and pleasurable. I met Bia in art school in 1970. Passing her dorm room, I'd watch her cut bits of black-and-white photographs out of *Time* magazine with an Exacto blade, and then paste the fragments into long, hieroglyphic columns, giving current events a cryptic twist. In a circle of lamplight, she worked with the meticulous intensity of a jeweler, her concentration unaffected by the jazz blaring from her stereo. We began to eat dinner together at a local restaurant called the Happy Steak, and it was there, amid the faux cowhide upholstery and Formica wood-grain tables, that we honed our love of the lowbrow, discussing at length the soup cans and crushed cars of contemporary art. Budding conceptualists, we were indifferent to the *taste* of the steak, but delighted by the *idea* that our dinners were impaled with a plastic cow, its flank branded *rare, medium,* or *well.* Instead of saying grace before we ate, we'd bow our heads, clasp our hands, and recite, "Cows are happy when they cry / So we kick them in the eye."

I'm not sure at what point friendship turned to love—our relationship remained platonic for nearly a year—but I'm sure we would have had sex much earlier if both of us hadn't harbored longings for people of the same gender. My secret crushes included Robert Conrad, whose television show, *The Wild Wild West,* had him stripped to the waist in almost every episode, his pectorals a lesson in advanced geometry, and Bill Medley of the Righteous Brothers, with whom I'd been smitten since junior high, romanticizing into satyrhood his long, lean, horsey face. Bia, it turned out, was crazy for Greta Garbo, piqued by her high cheekbones, moist eyes, and the world-weary manner that suggested a womanhood rich in glamorous disappointments. We confided these guilty attractions late one night during a marathon conversation. Once they were aired, our admissions seemed less shameful, less significant, and I began to feel that sleeping with Bia was inevitable; who better to sleep with than the keeper of your secrets? Besides, as a side effect of our heated discussions, her translucent skin and hazel eyes had begun to excite me.

The only word to describe our first sexual encounter is *premeditated.* We gave ourselves weeks to get used to the idea of sleeping with each other, to weigh the consequences—would physical intimacy jeopardize our friendship?—to prolong the delicious anticipation. Like a couple catering a large party, we tried to take into account every eventuality, every shift in the weather, every whim of appetite. Hers was the bed we'd use; it was the biggest, the most familiar; we'd sat on it for countless hours, smoking Marlboros, listening to jazz, watching TV with the sound turned down while improvising snappy patter. Intercourse, we decided, would be best in the late afternoon when the window shades turned Bia's room the color of butter. Afterward we'd shower together, and have a meal at the Happy Steak.

When the day we'd set aside finally arrived, we spent the morning at Descanso Gardens. Arms about each other, we were tender and nervous and telepathic, taking this path instead of that, staring at schools of darting koi, lingering before stands of cactus, awed by their bright, incongruous blossoms.

I had slept with only one person up to that point, a girl with whom I'd gone to high school. Jennifer whipped her long blond hair from side to side, a semaphore of the feminine. Her arms and legs were hard and tan, and she seemed, walking to class or sprawled on the lawn, all loose limbed and eager, a living invitation. Jennifer loved sex. Got it as often and with as many boys as she could. Her flirtations had about them an ingenuous joy, a stark curiosity. The sexual revolution was in full swing, and Jennifer's hedonism gave her a certain cachet.

The night before I left for college on the East Coast, I took her to a bar on the top floor of a high-rise in Hollywood. We shared fierce and slippery kisses in the elevator. As we toasted each other at a tiny table, the city glittered below us. Men looked at her with lust and at me with envy; her company quelled my sexual doubts. I knew we wouldn't sleep together that night—she had to drive back home to Malibu before her parents returned from a trip—and this freed me from the performance anxiety that surely would have swamped me had sex been imminent. I helped her off with her coat, leafed through her hair, and paid the bill, playing my masculine role to the hilt because I knew there was no pressure to follow through. I'd carry with me to college the memory of our date, a talisman to ward off the fear that I might never escape my desire for men.

Imagine my surprise when, two months later, Jennifer showed up at my Brooklyn dormitory wearing a skimpy white dress in the middle of winter, an overnight bag slung over her shoulder. We hadn't seen or written to each other since our date. She'd been visiting her cousins on Long Island and wanted to surprise me. "You're hilarious," she said when I suggested she stay in the guest room off the lobby. She flopped onto my bed. Kicked off her shoes. Fixed me in her bright green gaze. Flipped her hair to and fro like a flag.

We batted her overnight bag off the bed and it skidded across the floor. Articles of clothing arced through the air. I tried, with brusque adjustments of my hips, to disguise any tentativeness when I entered her. It's now or never, I remember thinking. Her vagina was silky, warm, and capacious. It struck me that my penis might be too small to fill her in the way she wanted, and just when I thought that this tightening knot of self-consciousness might make the act impossible, she let out a yelp of unabashed pleasure. I plunged in deeper, single-minded as a salmon swimming upstream. My hands swept the slope of Jennifer's shoulders, the rise of her breasts. I didn't realize it until afterward, but I sucked her neck the entire time, fastened by my lips to a bucking girl. Jennifer's climax was so protracted, her moans so operatic, her nails so sharp as they raked my back, that when she sat up and felt her neck, I thought she was checking her pulse. Suddenly, she rose and ran to the bathroom, a swath of bedsheet trailing in her wake. "I told you," she shrieked, her voice resounding off the tile walls. She appeared in the doorway, legs in a wide, defiant stance, nipples erect. "I told you no hickies!"

"No you didn't."

"I said it right at the beginning."

"Then I didn't hear you, Jennifer."

She held her hand to her neck, Cleopatra bitten by an asp. "What am I going to do?" Her voice was about to break. "What am I going to tell my cousins?"

It was preposterous; she had come to Brooklyn to seduce me, and now Jennifer was mortified by the small, sanguine badge of our abandon. I said I was sorry.

"'Sorry' isn't going to take it away."

"What about this?" I said, turning to show her the marks I could feel scored into my back.

"Oh, great," she said. "Let's compare war wounds." She bent down and scooped up her white dress; it lay on the floor like a monstrous corsage. "You men," she said bitterly.

Forgive me; I was flattered. Placed at last in a class from which I'd felt barred.

I lit a cigarette, watching as she stood before the window and dragged a brush through her hair, the strokes punishing, relentless, and I began to see that Jennifer was angry at herself for the rapacious nature of her needs, and that her future, overpopulated with lonely men, would be one long, unresolved argument between ardor and regret. Or was I seeing my own fate in her?

An icy sky dimmed above the city. Jennifer shook her head at an offer of dinner. Her face, framed by sheaths of yellow hair, was pinched with the reflex to flee. "So," she sighed. She slipped into her shoes, stared through me and toward the door. "Give me a call someday." Her tone was clipped and bitter. Standing in my bathrobe, at a loss for what to say, I touched her shoulder and she shrugged me away, managing a weak and fleeting smile before she shut the door behind her.

When I turned around, night veiled the Brooklyn skyline. I tried not to think how far I was from home. Touching was futile; men or women, what did it matter? I crawled back into bed—the residue of Jennifer's odor rose from the pillow like a puff of dust—and fell into a dreamless sleep.

It would be a long time before I had sex again. All the while I told myself, with a sad resolve, that lovemaking was not one of my natural skills; all mixed-up when it came to desire, I'd have to depend on something other than sex for satisfaction. Somewhere I'd read that Picasso spent a lifetime channeling his libido into painting (this explained his prodigious output), and I secretly hoped that my erotic energy would be sublimated into art. Deprivation for the sake of art—the idea made me feel noble. It's no coincidence that during this period my class projects became huge and ornate, and although I hadn't the slightest understanding of, say, the mathematical principles behind my three-dimensional model of the Golden Rectangle, my efforts were often singled out for discussion by instructors impressed with the obsessive detail that had begun to characterize my work. One night, after too much to drink, this obsessiveness led me to paint my dorm room cobalt blue and glue dozens of Styrofoam cups to the ceiling, thinking they looked like stalactites. It took three coats of white latex to rectify the situation. Woozy from fumes, I began to understand sublimation's wild, excessive underside. Soon after that night, restless and homesick, I transferred to the California Institute of the Arts, where I met Bia.

Bia was still a virgin when we made our plans to sleep with each other, a fact I took into account when I clipped my toenails, conditioned my pubic hair with cream rinse, and practically baptized myself with Brut before I walked into her room. My ablutions were not in vain; our sex was greedy, sweet-smelling teamwork. Spent as we were in the aftermath, we radiated fresh contentment. I rested my head on Bia's breast, grateful for my good luck and the buttery light. That afternoon we began to live together, devotion a knot we'd tied with our bodies.

As for our homosexual yearnings, once we became a couple, we didn't bring them up again out of affection and deference; like the foundation of a house, they remained present but unseen, the trust that prompted such confidences the basis of our relationship. Both of us, I think, wanted to believe that we were embarking on the grand adventure of heterosexuality, and that the fear of ostracism with which we had lived so much of our lives could be shucked off at last like a pair of tight shoes. We were relieved, those first few years of living together, to see our love reflected back from movies and billboards and books. Never taking for granted the privilege of public touching, we kissed in cars and markets and parks. But there persisted for me this unavoidable fact: regardless how gratifying I found sex with Bia, I wanted to have a man.

●●●

"Knock, knock. Is anybody there?" joked Dr. Sward. "I was asking what's new."

In the first few seconds of every session, consciousness was something I tried on for size like a huge droopy hat. Then I'd blurt a forbidden thought. *The Armenian who works the steam-press machine at the dry cleaners was wearing a T-shirt and I swear I could feel the fur on his forearms from across the room.* Usually, Dr. Sward greeted my disclosures with a bromide. Once, I told him that every masturbatory fantasy I'd ever had involved a man, and that I'd gotten to the point where I frankly didn't see how psychotherapy, no matter how probing, enhanced by drugs or not, could alter an impulse etched into my brain by years of unrelenting lust. Dr. Sward laughed his hearty laugh. I thought I heard him lean forward in his chair. He suggested I substitute the image of a woman for the image of a man the second before I ejaculated. I considered telling him that if I had to concentrate on his advice I'd never be able to come, but his casual tone made change seem so easy, like using a giant vaudeville hook to yank an awful act offstage.

Despite the fact that his advice was often facile, I continued to visit Dr. Sward once a week. He was sincere in his efforts to change me; I was the ambivalent party, riveted by the bodies of men, yet tired of grappling with secret lust. I blamed myself for the inability to reform, chalked it up to a failure of will, and would have tried just about anything that promised relief from confusion and shame. Determined to spend my life with Bia—she was my ally in art; there was no one with whom I had more fun—I thought it might be worth enduring my frustrations with therapy in order to ensure the longevity of our relationship. Perhaps there would come a point where my sexual impulses would be simplified, a straight line where there once had been all the twists and turns of a French curve. I knew few gay men, and to some extent still believed that homosexuals were doomed to a life of unhappiness; I never entirely exorcised the images of homosexuality that figured into the rumors and hearsay of my childhood, images of gloomy, clandestine encounters, trench coats, and candy the recurrent motifs. I suppose I understood that no behavioral modification, no psychological revelation would take away my desire for men, but in the end, I went back to Dr. Sward's office because—this is the hardest confession of all—I wanted to hear the light.

The terrible power of that sound. When I tried to describe it to Bia, I resorted to the phrase *the music of the spheres.* How lazy and inadequate! The universe seemed to be shuddering, seized by a vast, empathic spasm, crying out in a tremulous voice. I don't mean only visible stuff—chairs and cars and buildings and trees—but microcosmic tremblings, too—pollen and protons and cosmic dust. The sum of matter had been struck like a tuning fork, and one vital, cacophonous chord issued from a light bulb screwed into the ceiling of a room where I lay on a padded table and tried to revise my life. Compared with that sound, all the doctor's concern, all my apprehension, all the rules governing who touches whom were muffled to a feeble squeak. The glory of it left me breathless.

Now, I would never claim that the sound was a panacea, but it became an extremely beneficial aspect of therapy, given the way it trivialized my problems with its big aural blast. Dr. Sward believed that my desire for men could be broken down into a set of constituent griefs: lack of paternal love; envy toward other men for their sexual certainty; a need for identification confused with a drive for physical contact. And then, one day, the blare of light still ringing in my ears, I asked the doctor if heterosexual desire wasn't also a muddled, complex matter, fraught with the very same helplessness and hurt he attributed to my particular case. Didn't he, for example, ever seek his wife's maternal attentions, or envy her sexual receptivity, or yearn to burrow into her flesh, his nerves alert and bordering on anguish? Without a dose of desperation, or the aches and pains left over from one's past, what would sex between two people be? A pat on the back?

All the things I believed to be true pushed from behind like a harried crowd; it was the sodium pentathol talking. The silence that followed embarrassed us both. Worried that my challenge to his authority had upset him, I backpedaled a bit. "I'm just thinking out loud, you know, trying to fit the pieces together."

"Of course," said Dr. Sward. "Of course. But after all, we're not here to talk about me."

I saw Dr. Sward for another six months before I announced, emboldened by an especially heady dose of serum, that I felt it was time for me to terminate therapy. He offered no argument for my staying. In fact, he was surprisingly willing to see me leave, and I couldn't help but think my visits had become for him a source of professional, if not personal, disappointment. For the past year Dr. Sward had insisted that, since I lived with a woman and enjoyed with her a passionate sex life, I was, ipso facto, heterosexual—a conclusion that struck me as absurd, like thinking that when Charles Laughton plays Henry VIII he is actually king of England. During our final sessions, however, Dr. Sward seemed resigned to my conflict, more respectful of the obstinate, wayward power of human want.

"Would you say," he asked rather pensively at the end of our final session, "that the nature of your homosexual fantasies has changed at all during the course of our working together?"

"They've changed a little," I said to placate him, meaning they occurred with even greater frequency.

"Will you attempt a hetero- or homosexual life after you leave this office?"

"Don't know," I lied, sliding off the table and shaking his hand. We sighed and wished each other luck.

What I did know was that, as far as the outcome of sodium pentathol therapy was concerned, the one truth that mattered to me now was the electrifying strength of lust. Still, I made no effort to leave Bia for months after I quit seeing Dr. Sward. I was frightened of uncertainty, of exile to a shapeless fate, and the closer I came to a life without her, the more her company soothed me.

When I finally did tell her I wanted to move out and test my feelings for men, we were sitting side by side at Kennedy Airport, waiting to board a plane back to Los Angeles after a vacation. Destinations echoed over the loudspeaker. Travelers checked their boarding passes, gathered at gates. All that rush and flux, all those strangers embarking on journeys, made urgent and keen my sense of departure. I turned to Bia and, before I knew what I was doing, mumbled that there was something I had to say. I kept protesting my affection, my helplessness. I wanted desperately to take her hand, to hold her to me, but fought it down as a hypocritical impulse. She stared at me, uncomprehending, as though I were pleading in a foreign language. Then the dawning of fury and hurt as she understood.

Once on the plane, our steady, defeated weeping was disguised by the roar of the engines. Every time I turned to face her, at a loss for what to say, I glimpsed our reflections in the airplane window, vague and straying above the earth.

It wasn't until long after I'd moved out, after Bia found a woman and I found a man, that I mustered the courage to tell her what had happened in New York. We'd spent the afternoon at opposite ends of Manhattan, she uptown, having lunch with a friend, and me in SoHo, visiting galleries. Walking back to our midtown hotel, I cut through the West Village. It was hot and humid and overcast, the dark air charged with impending rain. Men congregated on the sidewalk or shared tables at outdoor cafés, their sleeves rolled up, shirts unbuttoned, talk and gestures intent. A few of them turned to watch me pass. Self-conscious as I was, I actually believed for a moment that they were straight men who thought I was gay, and I regretted wearing the gauzy Indian shirt I'd bought at an import shop, and which now felt as insubstantial as lingerie. I began to walk faster, as though I might outstrip the realization of what and where I was.

A salvo of thunder, a blanching flash of light, and there began a heavy, tepid rain. People ran for cover in doorways, gathered under awnings drummed by the rain. My shirt was drenched in seconds, patches of my bare skin seeping through the fabric like stains. I kept tugging the cloth away from my body, but the wet shirt clung and flesh bloomed through. Dressed yet exposed in the middle of the city, arms folded across my chest, I froze as though in an anxious dream. Then I dashed into the nearest doorway, where another man stood, waiting out the rain. He had a round, guileless face and brown hair beaded with drops of water. "You're positively soaked," he said. We eyed each other nervously, then peered up at the sluggish clouds. Though he was neither especially handsome nor interesting, his small talk—he knew where I could buy an umbrella, hoped he had closed his apartment windows—calmed me. His weathered neck, encircled by a gold chain, made me wonder how old he was and if he spent long hours in the sun on a balcony somewhere in the city, with friends perhaps, or the man with whom he lived, and I glimpsed, as if through the window of his skin, a life more solid and settled than my own. He was, I decided, a man who'd adapted to his own desires; I envied him his sexual certainty, and so bore out, although in reverse, one of Dr. Sward's theories. I would have had sex with that talkative, innocuous stranger in an instant, would have gladly given him the burden of releasing me from ambivalence. And just when it occurred to me that it might be possible to seduce him, just as I wrestled with a proposition, the rain let up, and he wished me luck, dashing down the street.

I walked aimlessly, for hours, till the pale sun made my shirt opaque.

That night, when Bia reached out in her sleep to touch me, she touched a man on the edge of action, shedding the skin of his former life. I tossed and turned. The hotel bed felt hard and unfamiliar. I didn't know then that Bia and I would remain lifelong friends, or that by never again falling in love with someone of the opposite sex, we'd preserve the exception of who we once were. I knew only that impatience outweighed my remorse. Over and over, I replayed my encounter with the man in the doorway; in fantasy, I lived on my own, and when he asked me if I had a place, I told him yes, I had a place.

# Tribute

*to Rodrigo Reyes\**

*the death of a brother
a sudden glimpse of a brother
an estranged brother
a once touched brother . . .*

Last night at the service, I kept thinking . . . Rodrigo loved his own kind, his own brown and male kind. Listening to the tributes made to him, it was clear that the hearts he touched the most deeply were his *carnalitos*. And each one, as lovely as the one preceding him, spoke about Rodrigo, "*Mi 'mano, mi papito, mi carnal, ese cabron . . .*," *con un cariño* wholly felt.

For a moment, I wondered if women had ever entered his heart in the same way. Perhaps his mother did when once as a young teenager he told her, "*Dejalo,*" referring to his father. "Leave him, *ama. Yo te cuido.* We don't need him." When Rodrigo told me that story from his sickbed, a different Rodrigo came into view, a man who was once a boy with a boy's earnestness to protect and defend his mother, with a boy's desire to conceive of a manhood outside of *abuso*. We were all *inocentes* once, and we carry that broken innocence into every meeting of every stranger, every potential *amante*.

---

*Rodrigo Reyes was a community organizer, theater director, actor, poet, and painter who made his life in the Gay Latino Mission District of San Francisco. He died of AIDS-related illness on January 19, 1992.

Was it the same visit he asked me, the barriers between us momentarily dissolving, as we met eye to eye, artist to artist, "Do you see that painting?" pointing to a living mass of color on the wall. "Yes," I answered. "That painting just passed through me," he said. "Rodrigo didn't paint that, it just happened. Rodrigo disappeared. Do you understand?" And a desire welled up in me to meet this man, to finally speak with a brother about my most private place, that place where the work possesses us and our pitiful egos take flight. "Yes," I answer. "I understand." He told me that all he wanted was a little more time, a little more time to repeat that moment, to be the servant of his art, and utterly humbled in the creation of it. There *is* no greater joy. And how I wanted him to live, too . . . for just that reason.

The gift of the dying is that they allow us to contemplate our own deaths, our own meanings . . . our own creations. I thank him for this. Me, with some time still to spare. This is the gift Rodrigo offers to all of us who survive him.

I wonder why and how we live in an era when dying is such a visceral part of our daily lives. Possibly, living in San Francisco and not San Salvador, we imagined we would be spared such a relentlessly intimate acquaintance with death, an intimacy seldom experienced except in times of war and natural disaster, but this is the era in which we live. Women dying in droves from cancer; gay men/colored folk dying of AIDS. I don't know what to make of it. It has barely begun to touch my life. Perhaps I have Rodrigo to thank again for this—initiating me to life with the knowledge of death.

Last night the homage given to Rodrigo convinced me how rare it is to be colored and queer and live to speak about it. In honoring Rodrigo, one young man said, "Rodrigo devoted his entire life to the community." And, I would like to add, he devoted his entire passion to his own brown brothers. He delighted in their beauty, their desire, their hope. He wanted them to be free, and righteously. I believe that in Rodrigo's final months and in his final words, he saw a much clearer road toward that freedom, and that it had something to do with the freedom of women, too. I believe he started to understand this not in his head, but in his gut, when he looked upon so much death and drugs and despair within his own community.

The last thing I did for Rodrigo, the last time I saw him, was cut his toenails. I marveled at it—how after all our heated debates, it had come down to this simple act. He was my brother, after all, and he needed his toenails cut. I confess I did not always feel recognized by Rodrigo as his sister. At times I felt that the sisters simply didn't matter to him. And in each rejection I saw the face of my own blood brother. Let us not kid ourselves, this *is* what we bring to our meetings as Latinos, *lesbianas, jotos, politicas*—all the wounds of family betrayals and abandonments. But I know—with or without his recognition—that (as artists and queers) we were intimately tied to each other's survival, knowledge, *y libertad.*

> He did make space for them, his brothers
> he did plant seeds,
>
> he did lay ground.
> And this is where the young ones pick up . . .

Adelante 'manitos!

January 23, 1992

STEVEN F.
KRUGER

# Webster
# Street

*for Judith L. Raiskin, Mary E. Wood, and Rebecca Mark*

At first the houses on Webster Street seemed off-limits to me, and rightly so. I understood that the two suburban buildings—the smaller one tucked up the driveway and behind the larger—formed a separate space for the women who lived there, a lesbian space. In fact, as I learned over the years, those two houses were part of a complicated network of lesbian lives that sprawled through the Bay Area, involving present and former students at the university, print workers, body workers, librarians, teachers, doctors, civil servants. My friends from Webster Street were students, as was I; our friendship began at school and for a while remained almost wholly linked to the university. It was years before I entered either of the two houses.

Julee and I began graduate school together in 1982, and, though we knew each other from the start, our friendship grew very gradually. That first year, beyond the vaguest of first impressions, I remember only that the two of us went together to see Paul Taylor, with tickets that Julee had somehow gotten, and that we once had coffee together with our Old English teacher (a terrifying experience for me since it meant an intimate conversation with two people I hardly knew). But few such unusual moments present themselves as I think back over the early years of our friendship; more important in establishing that friendship were the overlapping routines the two of us set up. We both chose usually to work in the basement of the library, and knowing that we could often find each other there made it all the more likely that we would not strike out for parts unknown. We started having lunch together at the Union with a group of fellow students, and we all worked hard at making the meal last as long as possible, lingering over shared coffee and cookies, then obsessively checking our mailboxes at the English department, anything to avoid returning to the library and our work. At a certain moment, Julee and I also began to take morning coffee breaks together, just the two of us.

Though I'm not sure either of us was conscious of doing so, we would often get our coffee (tea for Julee) at the most out-of-the-way place we could find, where it was unlikely (though never impossible) that others would join us. These breaks were our most consistent and intense time for talk, usually focused on our work (the upcoming oral exams; the latest snag, or excitement, in our research and writing). As we came to know each other better, we ventured as well into politics—Proposition 64 (the LaRouche-sponsored quarantining initiative), the English-only proposal—and sometimes we spoke more personally. Whether or not the content of these conversations was personal or academic, however, they were always *intimate*—close, energetic, funny, affectionate, sometimes difficult sharings of what was most pressing for each of us at that moment.

It was with Julee during our coffee breaks that I first began in a sustained way to talk about the AIDS crisis and what it meant, and might mean, for us both as individuals and members of the broader lesbian and gay community. We both read the sensationalistic excerpts from Randy Shilts's *And the Band Played On* printed in the *San Francisco Chronicle* and talked about the dangers of his account of "Patient Zero." We thought together about ACT UP when it existed for us only as the vague report of a newly formed activist group in New York. We both read Robert Ferro's novel *Second Son* so we could talk about it together, and we discussed both its moving depiction of a man living with AIDS and the problems we saw in that depiction. Julee talked about the illness and death of her friend David. And when our mutual teacher, and my dissertation adviser, Donald Howard, died, we mourned him together, remembering the ways in which he had helped and even loved us, but also the ways in which he, an enormously complicated man, had made our lives difficult.

◖◖◖

It may not in fact have been my first time inside the big house on Webster Street, but that's how I remember it. Two years before, Julee had apologized to me when she invited one of our mutual friends to the annual Webster Street lesbian/feminist Passover seder while not inviting me; as she explained then, the seder was for women. The following year, to my surprise, she did invite me, but I refused the invitation. I guess I still felt that the seder was for women and that I shouldn't intrude, despite my friendship with Julee. But the following year, when Julee invited me again, I accepted and went.

By this point, I knew not only Julee but several of the women who lived at Webster Street—Mary, Rebecca, Cathy. And I had met some of the others who would be attending the seder, particularly at events sponsored by the Graduate Women's Network, which Julee and another close friend, Mary F., were then involved in running. At such events, I had come to feel more and more comfortable with being one of the few men in the room, and though I was still nervous beforehand about the seder—would my knishes be a success? how might I be asked to participate in the ceremony, and would I embarrass myself in doing so?—I was looking forward to being with my friends, celebrating.

The seder began, as it began every year, with each participant speaking about a woman who had been important in her life. I spoke about my grandmother, then still alive, thinking back on the difficulties she had lived through, leaving behind her father and two brothers at the age of eight, arriving in New York alone with her mother, largely fending for herself while her mother worked long hours in a restaurant/bar. I hadn't really thought of my grandmother in a feminist context before, and I found it powerful to do so. The seder itself was a thorough refashioning of familiar rituals; Rebecca and the other women had rewritten the Haggadah in ways that allowed for a rethinking of Jewish traditions, a questioning of handed-down meanings and interpretations, a celebration of Jewishness without a covering over of what in fact has been oppressive within Judaism. At the Webster Street seder that year, and in following years, I felt connected to my Jewishness in a way I hadn't for a long time. (The knishes went quickly, and no one complained, so, though I may have made them too small, I guess they were a success.)

●━●━●

As graduate school approached its end, I began to feel more and more dissatisfied with the kind of work and writing I was doing. I still was intrigued by medieval literature, and the material I was uncovering about ancient and medieval theories of dreaming continued to interest me, but I felt more and more strongly a disjunction between this work— concentrating on mainstream voices of the Christian Middle Ages— and my own struggles as a queer Jew in the late twentieth century. It wasn't so much that I felt my work didn't reflect me; I knew in fact that it was in some important sense autobiographical (all the graduate students joked that our abstruse topics were *really* about us), but only in the most hidden, convoluted, and coded ways. I found myself wanting to write something that would do some significant work in the world I lived in, and not just excavate systems of meaning from the past.

My conversations with Julee solidified such a desire. Her work, infused with a strong feminism, seemed to point in a promising direction for my own. And Julee prodded me to confront more explicitly than I had some of the problems—particularly for a queer Jew—in studying a period so clearly anti-Semitic and homophobic as the Middle Ages. I found myself turning my attention, in the last section of my dissertation, to the dreams of a twelfth-century Jew (Hermann of Cologne) who converted to Christianity and who wrote an autobiography describing that conversion. In that final chapter, I began for the first time to look closely at medieval anti-Semitism, embarking on a kind of investigation that continues in my current work on the interconnections between late medieval homophobic and anti-Semitic discourses. Julee's encouragement also helped as I began, in my last year of graduate-school teaching, to incorporate literature about AIDS into my composition classes. That work too continues in my current teaching and writing.

In my last weeks in Palo Alto, as I got ready for a move to New York City and Julee was preparing to join Mary in Oregon, I think I spent more time in the small house on Webster Street than in my own apartment. I was helping Julee pack, but the two of us were also trying to spend as much time together as possible. At this point, I knew all the women who were living in the two Webster Street houses, and I knew women like Jesse who stopped by frequently. I was privy to people's love lives, and I could feel the various subtle tensions among the women who came and went amid Julee's accumulating boxes. I could see relationships shifting and reshaping themselves. I was, I guess, in those final weeks, a real part of the community.

Sometime near the end of that last school year, Julee and I made a kind of farewell journey to San Francisco together, walking the Mission and Castro, sitting and drinking coffee in Café Flore, visiting the bookstores. We had been in San Francisco together before, but always in a bigger group, and this last trip was special, each of us showing the other the places that we'd found important in our lives. We especially enjoyed doing the bookstores together, talking about books we'd read and would like to read. That day, in A Different Light, we began a "ritual" that we continue to practice, with Julee giving me a book by a lesbian author (that first time, it was Ellen Galford's *The Fires of Bride)* and me reciprocating with one by a gay man (Ethan Mordden's *Buddies,* which had helped keep me sane through my search for a job). I read *The Fires of Bride* on the plane ride to my new life in New York.

Julee and Mary now live across the country from me, while others of the women from Webster Street have moved to the South and Midwest; some still live in the Bay Area. Though we've scattered, we continue to see each other, if sporadically and briefly. Often our meetings come as part of some bigger gay event. In October 1992, Julee and I went together to the display of the Names Project quilt in Washington, D.C., and several of us met and marched together at the 1993 March on Washington. A year or two earlier, driving back to New York from a conference in Baltimore where four of us had gathered, we had a particularly memorable—long, intense, serious, funny—conversation about sex. That same weekend, Julee, Mary, Faye (a friend from post–Webster Street days), and I visited Ellis Island together. And we've met on other occasions in Los Angeles, San Francisco, New Orleans, Boston, Philadelphia, Eugene, Santa Barbara.

While there may no longer be a lesbian community centered in the houses on Webster Street—I don't actually know who lives there now—and the community that once was there has scattered, the connections among these women remain strong and my own link to them powerful. We all most recently were able to gather for a celebration of Mary and Julee's continuing commitment to each other on the occasion of their tenth anniversary, an event that had all the subversive and affirming energy of the old Webster Street seders. I expect we will all again gather this year to celebrate the birth of Mary and Julee's child.

I decided in the early eighties to go to the Bay Area for complicated reasons: to study, yes, but also to escape from the too familiar, from a life where I was ambivalently in and out of the closet, and to escape into (as I imagined) a new kind of life, a life of loving men in a way, with an intensity and freedom, that hadn't yet happened. (It was perhaps not a happy omen for my imagined *vita nuova* that I was also partly following a destructive relationship to San Francisco, hoping for its continuation when I should have rejoiced in its conclusion.) When I arrived in the West, though, escaping and beginning anew turned out not to be so easy. School and shyness got in the way, and I found myself not so distant from my former self as I had hoped three thousand miles might carry me. It took much longer than I then expected for me to join, without ambivalence, a community of gay men, though of course I found for myself some of the pleasures of Polk Street and the Castro and of more suburban cruising grounds.

Men have always made me nervous—at least since I realized in elementary school that I was often most attracted to the boys who most tormented me—and even in my early twenties I wasn't yet ready to commit myself to a community of men, gay and unthreatening though they might be. I was lucky, then, to find the women who came to constitute my lesbian community. That community helped provide me a place where I could think through questions about my own sexual identity; ultimately, I believe, being part of that community enabled me to move toward a fuller experience of relationships with other gay men. I don't mean, however, to imply that my relationships with lesbians were something that had to be "moved through" in order for me to arrive at a place of comfort with gay men. On the contrary, lesbian communities continue to be central to my life, both in the continuation of those connections formed years ago in California and in new connections made more recently in New York. Having just cotaught a course in lesbian and gay studies with Joan Nestle—an exhilarating, difficult, and pleasure-filled collaboration—I trust and hope that the lesbian presence in my life will only continue to deepen and grow.

# Golden
# Bars

Chris balanced on the small cut holds as he looked up the gray rock face into the California sun. He had just stepped off the narrow belay ledge we had been sharing one hundred fifty feet above the ground. The granite wall was smooth, almost vertical: these were the domes of Tuolumne Meadows, located in Yosemite National Park nine thousand feet above sea level, and one of my favorite rock-climbing areas in the United States.

Chris's tanned muscular calves were at the level of my face. Blue Lycra tights covered his knees, then encased his long tight thighs, small butt. He had taken off his shirt, revealing the perfect rock climber's body: lean and muscular, long limbed and broad shouldered. I also realized he had the body of the quintessential gay man. As I stared at his body, breathed in the smell of his sweat, I wanted to reach up and caress his legs, feel the strength of his calves. But I held on to the purple rope, belaying carefully, attentively, resisting my desire.

After all, I was consciously climbing with Chris to save myself from me, save myself from belay-ledge intimacy and the uncontrollable combination of adrenaline and hormones that had, time and again, led to what I called summit sex. It had happened with too many partners, both men and women. To save my lesbian identity, to save the relationship I was in, to save my ability to climb well and hard I had decided that the solution was to climb with gay men. Chris was to serve as the model.

Chris was unaware of my agenda. He thought we were just two gay people out to share our love of climbing in an open, gay-positive manner. We had met through the membership list of Stonewall Climbers, a newly formed gay and lesbian climbing organization. I had called at the last minute saying I would be in California, could he take off a few days to climb in Tuolumne? I loved Tuolumne, and the last time I had been there had been one of my best climbing seasons ever. I was only nineteen at the time, and had hitchhiked there from Colorado with my then boyfriend, Michael. We had a charmed summer, getting rides with friendly truckers, with mothers and their children in plush Winnebagos, and with the many French tourists who were cruising the West on a strong franc. We climbed every day, climbed hard, and when we returned to our tent at night we ate dinner and fell asleep to climb again the next day.

Sex had nothing to do with that summer, or my early life in climbing. My love was for climbing and for the perfect wall of cold hard rock. That affair began when I was fifteen, on a crumbling cliff in central Pennsylvania. It took only one climb and suddenly my life had a focus: here was something I could throw myself into body and soul. I loved the gear: my simple nylon harness, the aluminum carabiners that snapped shut so beautifully, the long coils of rope, and all the knots I had to learn to tie and untie with one hand, with my eyes closed. After high school I spent the summer sleeping in the parking lot in Eldorado Canyon in Boulder, dreaming and eating climbing. It wasn't a sport, it was a way of life.

Then I came out. Years of pent-up sexual energy emerged, and suddenly it mattered more who I climbed with than what I climbed. Women have always been hard to find in the climbing world, and many who were there had come because of boyfriends.

So I climbed mostly with straight men, most of whom were in search of a climbing girlfriend and simply couldn't accept that I was gay. Usually I was able to resist the belay-ledge kiss, but sometimes not, because climbing is such an odd and wonderfully intimate sport. You entrust your life to the person who holds your rope, you reveal your fears and strengths as you move up and through the crux of a climb, and you share the dreams that come while standing on a small ledge, looking down four hundred feet of vertical wall. The intimacy is physical, emotional, spiritual, and fueled by surges of adrenaline, often overwhelming. I love most of my partners in a fierce way, but also in a way that sometimes never translates off of the rock. I remember many post-climbing dinners, long tables of sweaty tired men and a few women eating pizza, drinking mugs of cheap beer, and swapping climbing stories. As the beer and hilarity of the evening progressed the stories always turn to love, or sex. It's a regular *As the Cliff Turns,* not only within an area, but across the country, and I would often laugh, until my laughter uncontrollably spun out of me. And sometimes, to my horror, I wouldn't be able to quiet that laughter as the boys pointed their stories, which seemed suddenly more like rumors, at the men who love boys. These men are usually public targets, men whose egos and activities on the rock had somehow offended other climbers. The language used in these tales—*bungholes* and *cocksuckers*—always takes me back to another homophobic milieu in my life: high school. If I did become silent in response to these jokes, no one would notice or understand, but the intimacy of the day had certainly been broken.

Homophobia in the climbing community is sometimes startling. Recently, there was a short blurb in the country's leading climbing magazine in which the editor exhorted all to practice safe sex, because, it was rumored, some of us had AIDS. The notice seemed odd, unnecessary. Climbers do believe that they are immune—to gravity, death, disease—but the real assumption here, I suspect, was that climbers are not gay.

So when Stonewall Climbers came into existence I celebrated: here was what I had been looking for, and now I would be able to climb with other dykes. But it wasn't that simple. At first I met lesbians who wanted to learn to climb, a very different creature from the hard-climbing dyke I had in mind (and heart). Yet when I finally did meet those hard-climbing dykes, my love of climbing and my love of women overflowed, entangled, so that I couldn't distinguish between the two, so that I couldn't climb without falling into at least a heavy crush. This wreaked havoc on my climbing, and on several relationships, not to mention the relationships that these women were in themselves. Climbing, which had previously been emotionally clean territory, was now completely complex.

In a rational, stoic mood, I decided that my two worlds shouldn't come together, that climbing and sex shouldn't and couldn't mix. And yet, I felt, I could keep the gay element and continue to climb hard, if I climbed only with gay men. It was gay men who were going to make it all possible, who were going to enable me to return to "clean" climbing.

Gay men had, after all, always been there for me. During breakups, crushes, struggles, and frustrations with the "lesbian community" I had always turned to my gay male friends for company, a good laugh, the assurance that being gay was good, that just a few women (and my lovers in particular) had it all wrong.

●—●—●

"This is run out," Chris said, noting the obvious: the protection on this route was thin.

I laughed, remembering that this was what made climbing in Tuolumne so exciting. Because natural protection was hard to come by, most of the routes are bolted, but those bolts are often far apart. At times, I had had to run it out as much as thirty feet between bolts. A worst-case scenario fall could have sent me as far as sixty feet. I like to protect more often than that, and clearly Chris did too: safe climbers, both of us.

"You can do it," I said. Though in fact I wasn't really sure of Chris's ability. This was only the third climb we were doing together. We had warmed up on two easier routes, rated 5.10 on a scale that runs from 5.0 to 5.14 (of which there are very few in this world). The last time I had been in Tuolumne 5.10 was considered difficult, but like all activities, climbing has been subject to inflation and 5.10 is now considered starting level for most climbers. I had led one of the climbs and he had led the other. We both seemed to be feeling limber, focused, and we were ready for something harder. I had picked Golden Bars, the last climb I had done in Tuolumne twelve years earlier. When I had gotten to the top of the climb my feet, squeezed tightly into EBs, the climbing shoes of that time, were screaming and all of my fingertips had split open from too many days of hanging on to slim sharp holds. I was bleeding, exhausted, elated, convinced I had done the hardest climb possible.

I remembered Michael at exactly the spot Chris was. He had stood for a long time silently examining the steepness, the lack of holds. And then he had moved up quickly, and just as quickly had fallen. He had pendulumed down, knocking into me. I dusted him off, kissed his chapped lips, and sent him back up.

"This doesn't let up," Chris said.

"I know. It's move after move."

"I'll give it a try. Watch me good."

"No problem. I got you."

I assumed Chris would believe me when I said I had him, which meant I would catch him if he fell. I realized I trusted Chris implicitly because he was gay, and I wondered if he trusted me for the same reason, and if perhaps we were being foolish in our trust. Being gay didn't assure we were good climbers, and our lives depended on that.

In recent years I had given up climbing with people I didn't know, or even picking up a partner at the cliffs. That's how I used to find all of my partners: hanging out at the base of the cliffs until someone asked me to climb. But rock climbing had grown too quickly, become too popular, and with that a certain community of trust had vanished. I had a few mishaps and decided it was simply too dangerous. I needed to know who I was climbing with.

I watched Chris move, stepping high, reaching for what looked like a decent hold.

"Shit," he yelled as I watched him slap the hold and then peel, his body tumbling down the rock directly at me, until he came to a sudden stop, caught by the rope, which I held tightly in my right hand. His thighs were back, inches from my face, and this time I did reach up, held him. "You OK?" I asked.

"Let me down."

I lowered him until he was back on the ledge beside me, standing inches from me, breathing heavily, bleeding from a scrape on his elbow. Most climbers would have wiped the blood with one hand, then smeared it on the rock, a token or warning to the those who came after. I watched as he stopped the flow with a corner of his T-shirt.

"Nice try," I said. "I guess this route hasn't gotten any easier."

"It's ridiculous," he said. "Your turn." He untied from the rope and handed it to me.

I looked up at the rock as I tied in, contemplating what gear I would need. I remembered how hard the climb had felt years ago. I turned to Chris, wanting a hug, a kiss, a word of encouragement. But I realized I was on my own: it was me and the rock, just the way I thought I wanted it to be. "Here goes," I said.

"Knock yourself out," he said.

"Hope not." I smiled.

I stepped high, clipping into the first bolt, then moved up, searching for the fingertip holds I would need to get me to the next bolt, the next piece of protection. The moves seemed obvious, the holds in place, but I wondered if it wasn't just an illusion, if some of the holds weren't as positive as they looked, or if the rock was steeper. "Watch me," I said as I stepped up, reached, and moved, my body brushing so close to the rock I could smell it sweat. I grabbed the thin edges, the tips of my fingers digging in, secure, while my feet played on slim ridges and crystal-sized bumps. I reached for a carabiner and runner as I neared the second bolt. Quickly I clipped in.

"Nice," Chris called.

I felt good, strong, moving with the rock, not against it. "Wild," I called down. "Watch me." I said it automatically, for comfort, or as a nervous tick.

"You're doing great. Just keep moving."

Yes, I had to keep moving. There weren't any real rests until the top. I hoped that my strength would hold out, that my mind wouldn't snap, that I would continue to look up rather than think about going down. I dipped my hands into my chalk bag and was off again, dancing with the rock, swaying gently from one hold to the next, stepping high, stretching, pulling. Soon, I had clipped all of the bolts and was moving toward the top. The rock gradually became less vertical, small cuts became ledges as I neared the summit, where I found two bolts to clip into, to take myself off belay.

"I'm off," I said, softly at first, and then louder, my voice traveling easily down the cliff in the clear dry air.

"Beautiful," Chris called up. I peered over the edge of the cliff and watched as he put on his shoes, chalked his hands, got ready to climb.

"Keep it tight," he said.

"No problem." I watched as Chris climbed boldly, aggressively. He was strong, beautiful, and I felt a certain pride when he pulled onto the top.

He sat next to me. "That was fantastic." He smiled.

I nodded, lost in my pleasure of doing the route, of having Chris follow so elegantly, of the perfection of climbing when everything feels so right. "This is heaven," I said. I slowly coiled the rope, looking down into the valley at Tenaya Lake and beyond into the Tuolumne wilderness. I lay down, my head resting on the rope as I looked up into the too-blue sky.

"Move over," Chris said. He lay down beside me, our heads sharing the rope. I could feel the heat rise between our sweaty bodies. I reached over and held his hand, wanting to acknowledge the connection between us. He gently squeezed in response.

"Thanks," I said.

"For what?" he asked. "You led the climb."

"Everything," I said. "Just being here." I wanted to say thank you for being a gay man, for being a climber, but I wasn't sure I could explain to him what I meant.

As my mind unwound from the concentration of the climb, my body went limp, and I dozed off. Minutes later I felt Chris get up, walk away, piss at a short distance. Then I felt his shadow cover me. "Move," I said. "I'm bronzing. I want a California tan."

He laughed. Then he bent over and kissed me, his tongue playing with my lips, searching to enter my mouth. It felt good, the logical extension of our climb, but I sat up. "No," I said, opening my eyes. "Don't ruin it."

He sat down next to me. "You don't sleep with men?" he asked.

"I don't sleep with climbing partners. I try not to."

"How ethical."

"Not really." I closed my eyes again, lay back down, containing my anger. I couldn't yell at him, tell him that he had ruined my plan—even worse, besmudged the name of gay climbing men worldwide.

I laughed softly.

"What's funny?" Chris asked.

Suddenly my logic was ridiculous and clear: I assumed that Chris, representing all gay men, would be moral, would be physically unattracted to women, would be able to operate with a sexual energy without being sexual. I was basing this on previous experience: my grad school days fuck-dancing with Paul at Louie's on the Upper West Side, or swapping stories of sexual adventure with Tom while walking home after work. We could move in and around our sexual energies, but always at the end of the evening, at the end of the walk, there was the quick dry kiss good-bye. Those kisses that were so very like the kisses Michael gave me on our belay ledges in Tuolumne twelve years ago: they were kisses of faith, that said, 'I believe in you,' not kisses of sex.

"Life," I said. "Gay life." Were we our own worst enemies, I wondered. "Sorry," I said, opening one eye.

"For what? I'm sorry."

I could tell he was serious, and also that he would never touch me again.

I sat up. "Let's do one more route."

Chris nodded.

"Your lead."

He nodded again.

# One
# of Us

Once upon a time, I knew no lesbians. Not one. Wasn't even sure what one would look like, or sound like, or act like, if I had happened to chance upon one. That seems odd now, sitting here with my lesbian partner and planning interviews with Blanche Boyd and Susie Bright and Urvashi Vaid and Chrystos. We're the publishers of *Metroline,* the queer newsmagazine for Connecticut and western Massachusetts, and there are lots of lesbians all through my life now: subjects of interviews, community activists, employees, members of our editorial board, neighbors, friends, my doctor. But there was a time, and not so very long ago, when I knew not one honest-to-goddess lesbian. And it wasn't as if I were some closeted homosexual who never went out.

This was back when I lived in Washington, D.C., a place considerably larger than Hartford, Connecticut, where we publish *Metroline,* and which had a much larger concentration of dykes than this city of two hundred thousand. But in Washington, I knew not one lesbian except Cleo, of course, and Cleo was straight. Let me tell you the story of my life without lesbians and how that came to change, and how, ultimately, that story begins with Cleo. It's a story, I think, that many gay men share, that maybe sheds some light on this strange kinship between homosexuals of opposite genders. Many gay men have known a Cleo, a straight woman who predates the coming of lesbians into their lives. Cleo prepared the way, she taught me a thing or two, she showed me the proverbial light: she gave me the wisdom that women don't have to be the stereotypical fag hags to be friends with gay men.

Cleo was a political consultant for the congressman I worked for in Washington, back in the days when I was just a boy, a lad, eager and fresh cheeked, just out of college, obscenely young at twenty-one. Cleo was a redheaded Irishwoman with ruddy cheeks and large hips, and who wore long dangling carrot-shaped earrings and never shaved her legs. Sitting with her on the Capitol lawn in summer, the other Hill staffers would arch their well-plucked eyebrows and sneer: "Must be a dyke," they'd say. My ears would perk up at such talk. This gay boy was eager for any gossip about sexual orientation on the Hill, and the idea that Cleo might be a lesbian intrigued me.

It intrigued me not only because I didn't know any lesbians, but because I wasn't sure what they looked like, what they sounded like, if they were, in fact, real. Sure, I'd seen photos, but none came by the boys' clubs I danced at, where male hormones hung so heavy in the air I could smell them on my shirt the next day. ("That's not smoke," I'd tell my roommate, "that's testosterone.") I'd been in Washington only a few months, and Cleo and I had struck up a friendship. I liked the fact that she didn't shave her legs, that she didn't talk about losing weight, that she didn't seem to mind that others were calling her a dyke. It was a rare sign of flouting the rules of gender on that stuffy, traditional, conservative Hill, a rare display of defying expectations—which, I realized even then, was something I did too, every time I had sex with a man.

Thinking back now, I'm reminded of a conversation I had, some years later, with Kate Bornstein, that fabulous playwright–performance artist who once had a penis and who now doesn't. I'd said to her, trying to make sense of it all: "You call yourself a lesbian transsexual. You were a straight man before the operation, so your orientation didn't change, just your gender." I was still an eager young man, a very eager young man, and I wanted to understand.

Kate and I were sipping orange tea on a cold spring day in Josie's Juice Joint in San Francisco. She had put down her cup and looked at me profoundly. Kindly. "No," she said, and today I understand that even using that pronoun, *she,* is misleading. "Just because I had a penis didn't make me a man," Kate told me. "Just because I had a vagina created between my legs doesn't make me a woman. What do those terms mean? *Man* and *woman*? They're artificial. The definition of *man* includes being attracted to woman. So how can you say you're a man when you suck dick? The definition of *gay man* includes being attracted to your own gender. Then what does that make me, when I find myself attracted to you? Or you, when you find yourself attracted to me?

I was dazzled. And that's what Cleo did, too: dazzled me, but in a less cognizant way. I was attracted to her lesbian qualities, even though I knew she slept with men. Once, when we were riding around in her battered old red pickup truck talking about social justice, we suddenly hit a rut and her tire went flat, and I panicked. Visions of my father hunched over a jack and straining to loosen lug nuts appeared in my head. "Every boy should know how to change a tire," he told me, and time after time I'd watch, carefully following each step of the process, only to let it all slip out of my head the moment he was through. And that day, sitting with Cleo in her pickup truck and realizing we had a flat, I felt helpless, worthless, a failure as a man. "I don't know how to change a tire," I started to say, but I managed to stutter only the first few words, for Cleo was out of the truck, still talking about abolishing the death penalty and how Reagan was killing babies in Nicaragua. She was hunched over, as my father had been in my mind, changing the damn thing herself. Not only was she doing it, but she didn't expect me to do it. It was her truck, after all.

Such a little thing. Such a little, life-changing, earth-shattering moment. "The definition of *woman*," I can hear Kate saying, had she been there, "includes changing tires." And yet Cleo was no dyke. She acknowledged, sitting afterward in a noisy café where I finally admitted I was a fag, that she'd slept with women, that she'd actually been in love with women before, but that she was, bottom-line, straight. I remember being disappointed. I knew no lesbians in this big city of ours, and I'd hoped she might be the first. But actually, it didn't matter. For what I learned from Cleo was similar to what I later learned from Kate: that genitals are about pleasure, not gender, and that orientation comes from the soul and the mind, not the gonads.

I wasn't physically attracted to Cleo, but I was in love with her, in a queer and wonderful way. What does that make me? A gay man in love with a straight woman because she reminds me of a lesbian. A man in love with a woman because she makes me realize that being who I am and not what a man is defined to be is a beautiful thing. And even more basic: a human being in love with another because our souls are similar, because our worldviews are the same, because we are, after all, *other*. A man who sucks other men's dicks and a woman who doesn't shave her legs.

It's odd that I didn't know any self-identified lesbians in D.C. I'm sure I must have known lots of closeted gay women who slept with other women on the Hill. But the only exposure I had to lesbians in Washington was at a Gay Pride Day celebration, when my then-boyfriend shook his head and wondered out loud why lesbians had to be so ugly, and our cadre of gay male friends had all nodded assent. It seemed odd to me then, and it seems odd to me now, that so many gay men just don't get it. Bear in mind, I knew not one lesbian then, but I had known Cleo, so I maybe had a step up on the other boys.

"They're not ugly," I'd said to my friends, including my know-it-all boyfriend. "They just don't have to do the lipstick thing and the stockings and the pumps. Men like those things. Not women."

"But lipstick makes women look prettier," one friend said, at an utter loss.

"Maybe," I said. "And maybe it'd make you look prettier, too. It doesn't have to do with gender."

They still didn't get it. We argued about shaving legs, and bras and mascara and being thin—all the things (straight) women do to look good as defined by men. Thing was, my friends didn't believe me when I said such attractiveness was defined by men; they believed, and emphatically so, that there was such a thing as an attractiveness absolute, that there was a universal classification as to what was attractive and what was not. Hairy legs on women were not attractive, they said. Lipstick was. It was useless to argue in the face of such entrenchment. Yet looking back today gives me new pause in this old argument, having spent a summer in Provincetown in which all my boyfriends shaved their legs (and their chests) and often went out wearing skirts, pumps, and lipstick. The benchmarks of attractiveness still. For men.

Bashing lesbians, and women in general, has always seemed to be an unfortunate rite of passage for some gay men as they break down their closet doors. "*Fish*," one friend in D.C. had said, scrunching up his face. What he was doing, really, was affirming that he could finally, after many years of secrecy, proclaim his sexual attraction to other men in public. He was affirming that he would no longer play the game straight men played in the locker rooms, when they talked about pussy and snatch and tits and fucking. "I had to pretend so long, and now I don't have to," my friend was, in reality, saying, and the real objects of his scorn were the straight men who'd oppressed him into toeing the line. But instead of bashing the straight boys, many gay men fall into the age-old sexist trap of using women as a means for men's ends—like my friend, who used the word *fish* and scrunched up his face, instead of saying, "Screw those straight assholes who demean women and expected me to follow along. Now I can be who I really am."

Maybe it was because of Cleo, but I don't recall falling into that trap. I can, however, remember consciously wishing my life included lesbians. But in Washington, that wasn't to be. I wasn't in the political movers-and-shakers crowd, the only place the two cultures seemed to intersect in the city. My only image of lesbians remained the inspiring independence of Cleo, and the dark, aching loneliness of a story my mother had once told me.

Now, this goes back to early childhood, to a time when my own orientation was just starting to nudge my psyche in strange and wonderful and frightening ways. There was a man on the nightly news, I don't remember who now, that I would watch on the small black-and-white TV in my room while I pressed my lips fiercely onto the hard lacquered wood of my bedpost, imagining it to be his torso. I was maybe seven at the time. There was a longing that I couldn't even name, didn't even consciously realize was there, but when my mother told me the story about the lesbian who put her hand on her knee, it resonated differently than she must have anticipated. Here's what my mother told me on that long-ago day when I was, at most, eight:

She had been just out of high school, living in New Jersey, and had taken a job as a stenographer in Manhattan. Every day she'd take the train into the city, and every day she worried about, as she called them, "those New York weirdos" approaching her. And one day, one of them did approach her, except it was a "weirdette": a woman, well dressed and pretty, sat down next to her on the bench while she waited for the train. She smiled at my mother and then shyly reached over and touched her knee. "Are those real nylons?" she asked, raising her eyes to meet my mother's. It was during World War II, and nylons were hard to come by. My mother had said yes, and the woman had left her hand on her knee just a second too long. "She was what they call a lesbian," my mother told me. "So I got up off that bench and ran and quit my job and never went back to New York."

I imagine my mother expected me to be outraged that such a creature would try to ravage her right there on that bench. I imagine she would be surprised to know that my reaction to her story was quite contrary to her expectations. Because what I felt for that long-ago lesbian, that faceless woman from the masses of New York some twenty years before, was empathy. Was compassion. Was kinship. I saw her as lonely, as reaching out for someone like herself, and over the years I bonded with her image, and wrote stories about her. As much as my experience with Cleo had prepared me for the reality of lesbians in my life, the image of my mother's mysterious encounter set the stage for the oneness I felt with dykes, even before I knew any real ones.

"Oh, she's one of us," said the first authentic lesbian I ever truly met, day four after I'd left Washington and moved to Hartford. It was the phrase I'd been waiting for, although I never knew it. *One of us.* She and I. Part of the same whole. We were talking about Cleo. They'd worked together on political campaigns.

"No," I corrected gently, frightened of screwing up my first lesbian acquaintance. "She's straight. I asked her."

"Well," said my new friend, smiling slyly, "I slept with her. She may not identify as a dyke, but she's one of us."

Of course, I'd known that all along. Cleo was one of us, and even more significantly, so was I. I was part of the *us* this woman, this lesbian, was referring to. It was with a rush of feeling that I realized this, and it was a strangely exhilarating experience to hear a woman call herself a dyke, talk about having sex with another woman, and say that she and I were part of *one of us.* And it had taken only four days. Here I was, meeting lesbians left and right in this small city, where I had come to get my master's degree, having decided that the power trip of Washington was an endless climb along a too-steep ladder that led only up and up, never to any landing. Here, in a community that could muster at best fifteen hundred people for its annual Gay Pride Day celebration—as many as probably walked in the sober contingent in D.C.'s parade—gay men and lesbians shared equal billing. Here, for there to be a critical mass that would matter, that would influence legislators and win votes, there had to be co-gender activism. But even the bars were mixed, and the social events were always stews of different genders and ages and races. There just weren't the numbers to allow for much specialization in this small, quiet, conservative, mostly closeted city.

Which isn't to imply that queers of all stripes existed in harmony. Far from it. Male bar owners still tried to discourage too many women from coming into their clubs. Lesbian bar owners kicked out drag queens. In the political groups, arguments about sexism and racism were not uncommon. And *Metroline,* the local newsmagazine that had debuted nearly twenty years before, consistently refused to add the word *lesbian* to its cover and had no interest in featuring stories about women, despite its editors' assertions that they "served the entire community." But such debates were at least occurring: I had heard nothing of the sort in D.C., and my own sexism had yet to be challenged.

When I started writing for *Metroline* and attempted, however timidly, to begin the process of outreach to lesbians, I was met with hostility, both from the established male readers and from the women's community. We did one story on breast cancer, and immediately we heard the cry "The dykes are taking over." Bar owners complained when we featured a woman on the cover, saying men didn't pick up the magazine unless they saw a man. And women scoffed at my attempts to write about them, refusing to return my calls. *Why should they trust me?* I reasoned. And yet it was frustrating.

And confounding. For I had come to see lesbians as part of my whole, as part of my perspective, my worldview, my heritage. It was the dawning of the 1990s, and the word *queer* meant more to me than "in your face" activism. Because I'd been queer before the word had become popular: my attraction to Cleo, my fascination with my mother's tale of attempted lesbian seduction, my appreciation of the term *one of us.* And here in Hartford, there were those women who, breaking tradition, identified (as I did) first around sexual orientation, and only later around gender. These queer women, these lesbians of the nineties, invited men to join the Lesbian Avengers. They marched with ACT UP. They demanded that men put breast cancer on their agendas as the women had put AIDS on theirs. Because we all were *one of us.* Like Cleo and me. And Kate Bornstein. Queer. Other. Men who suck dick and women who lick clit and men who have their penises cut off and women who don't shave their legs and men who don't talk about pussy in the locker room and women who touch other women's knees on benches in New York City.

When it became clear that the old regime at *Metroline* had no interest in pushing the publication past its once clearly defined boundaries, I looked for a partner to go in with me in offering to buy the business. I'm not sure how we were fortunate enough to find each other, how we both happened to connect at the right place, the right time, two queers with a vision, with a sensibility formed by being other and by seeing each other as "one of us," but we managed somehow. Surina Khan is a Pakistani lesbian, about as other as one can get in this society (and about as other as can be imagined even in Pakistan, where lesbians can still, by law, be publicly flogged). With the community's help, we bought *Metroline* in 1992 with a shared commitment to creating a co-gender, professional publication for Connecticut and western Massachusetts.

I'd made many lesbian friends by this point. I had accomplished my wish: lesbians were in my life. Going to my doctor for the first time, bending over and letting her see my dick, was a trip. I couldn't abide a straight man touching my balls, and who knows what dynamic I'd feel if it were a gay man or a straight woman. But I felt safe knowing I was under the care of a lesbian; call it irrational, call it whatever, but I can't imagine ever having anyone other than a dyke for a doctor. I remember long conversations on the telephone with my very first honest-to-goddess lesbian friend, Terri. We talked about dating, about relationships, about art and culture, about this thing we'd both found ourselves in: a community. A community of women and men bound by orientation and little else. But that was enough. In fact, it was more than enough. Licking clit and sucking dick are different, no doubt about that:

they carry different meanings, have different reverberations in the world. But on the phone, late at night, talking about them and about those with whom we would do them, they become inextricable, the same thing.

Getting to know Surina was a whole other process. We entered into our partnership assured of mutual trust and respect, of our firm belief in the concept of *one of us.* But I was still a man and she a woman: how would our business relationship develop? To be able to work together, I would have to get it: I'd have to discard whatever sexist bullshit I'd grown up with and accept a woman as my equal partner. If I were a straight man, if I were my brother, who looks like me and talks like me but who makes sexist comments and jokes about pussy, I would not get it. Had I been straight, my life, my relationship with women, would have been so different: Cleo wouldn't have mattered to me, I would never have met Kate Bornstein, I would never have had long talks into the night with Terri. But I am a gay man, and I'm a gay man who is queer. And Surina, too, is queer: "I'm a lesbian feminist fag hag," she once said, lovingly and proudly. We've stood together on the docks of Provincetown while I've cruised men; we've discussed the finer points of the emerging debates around lesbian sexuality; we've shared our exploits, or attempted exploits, with the opposite gender; I explained the cult of Bette Davis to her; and she finally filled me in on menstruation, the missing link in my understanding of human sexuality, something my parents never told me about and which never became a relevant issue to pursue as I grew up gay.

I've watched some of our male employees subtly bristle when she tells them what to do. For me, it wasn't difficult to accept that Surina was going to be able to do some things better than I could: advertising sales, for example. It was actually somewhat of a relief that I no longer had to do it all; it wasn't going to be up to me to change the tire. It was almost with a feeling of liberation that I entered into the partnership with Surina, a liberation from all those times I'd griped about my sister being allowed to remain warm and cozy under her blankets while my parents sent me out to shovel snow from the driveway. And understanding, finally, my sister's complaints when she had to clear the dishes from the table while I watched *Gilligan's Island.*

Working with a lesbian—sharing Surina's insights, her perspective as a woman, and her take on the world—has taught me that no matter how queer I am, no matter how other, there is always something new to comprehend. Watching those squirming male employees and Surina's persistence, and fairness and compassion, in dealing with them, has taught me a great deal about tolerance. After an initial skepticism, the community has responded to our joint effort with encouragement and cooperation—a sense that it can be done, that gay men and lesbians, that men and women, can work together.

What's amazed me the most, however, is the eternity of the boy-girl debate: How many men have been on the cover? How many women? We struggle for equal representation between the genders, as well as along racial and ethnic lines. But there are those men for whom two female covers in a row means that we've switched over, that we've sold out to the dykes, that we've become lesbian. "It was refreshing to see a man on your latest cover," one man wrote, "after all those lesbians." All those lesbians. Two in a row. Another reader derided us as *Metrolesbo* and the *Northampton Newsletter,* claiming we give preferential treatment to the one segment of our geographical territory that is predominantly lesbian. Another man wrote in to say we were "sacrificing" our "once-faithful gay male readership" because we'd "lost a sense of balance." Balance? My adrenaline was running, and I wanted to scream back at him across the letters page: "Balance? You want to talk balance? You want to add up all the male covers and the male articles for twenty years and then look at what we've done with women just this past year and then see how things balance out? We could run every issue and every cover for a full year with nothing but lesbian content and we'd still not have balance." For some gay men, talking about a co-gender movement is fine—until, that is, lesbians really have equal visibility. Then they say the women are taking over. So long as the male-to-female content ratio is always sixty-forty, these men will be satisfied. But once it's fifty-fifty, they go berserk.

That's not to say lesbians are immune to gender politics. Far from it. There are women who still refuse to pick up *Metroline,* even though our coverage is fifty-fifty male and female and we've removed the explicit sex ads from the main body of the publication and created a separate insert for them. Just the presence of the insert, the fact that we didn't do away with sex advertising altogether, is enough to steer some women away from us. But they are the extremes. There will always be women who do not support us because we aren't exclusively lesbian, and there will always be men who deride us for being too dykey. It comes with the territory.

I cheered when we finally got a letter that seemed to sum things up, that put it the way I would have, had I been a reader and not an owner of *Metroline*. "Tell those Neanderthals that the years of separate-but-equal treatment for gay men and lesbians are over," this man wrote. "Tell them that kind of thinking went the way of the *Miami Vice* look, Nancy Reagan's 'Just Say No' campaign, *Dynasty* house parties and Birkenstocks. The 1980s are over, the Queer '90s have begun. It's not about counting how many covers had women on them and how many had men, it's about the stories behind those covers. Blanche Boyd and Urvashi Vaid and Susie Bright are part of my community, and I'm a man."

"One of us," that first-ever lesbian in my life had said. Today, working with teenagers as a facilitator for Hartford's queer youth group, I see a shared sensibility among the boys and the girls, a bond of commonality that seems to transcend the obvious differences. They camp it up together; they wear the same clothes; they use the same language; they console each other after breakups; they tell the same coming-out stories; they call each other "one of us." That doesn't mean they don't bicker, or that the need for boys-only or girls-only space isn't still important, or that they're entirely free of gender misperceptions or sexism. But something's different—at least, it seems that way to me— different from those long-ago days when I had no lesbians in my life, except Cleo, and Cleo, of course, was straight.

JEWELLE
GOMEZ

# In the Wink of an Eye

## Black Lesbians & Gay Men Together

Saturdays were father's day for me during my teen years. Living separately, with only assigned weekends in which to play father/daughter, Duke and I made the shape of our relationship through tasks and conversation. I loved the sound of clinking change, cascades of silver—quarters, nickels, and dimes—my father's tips from the Regent, the corner bar where he worked as bartender. I lined them up neatly on his glass-topped desk, where he'd count them out and then grandly sweep a share off into my hand. He made a jolly ritual of this payment for my dusting his record collection. We discussed jazz and blues singers and his eclectic selection of books and magazines. These talks were as much a part of my education as any of the courses I took at school. Just as importantly, they taught me who my father was—a man of immense curiosity and charm, erudition and wit.

His sensuality was apparent in the easy way he wore his elegance, and the soft roll of his eyes; in the subtlety of his social observations and the belly-laugh timbre of his jokes. But he could be with women and not have to prove he was a "man." He had no difficulty looking any of us in the eye. I listen for him when I try to create male characters in my fiction and look for him in all of my friends—male and female.

I'm not certain if it's simply my getting older or that the times are changing. As the years pass, it becomes harder to find Duke in male friends. Each year the black men I know express more bitterness, less hope. There are many valid reasons, of course. Much is made of "manhood" in this culture, and the subtle ways that black men are told they will never be good enough are stunning. I see it every day. I've worked in administrative jobs for the past fifteen years of my life, yet it still continues to provoke a visceral pain inside me when I see the disdain directed toward black men delivering packages. No matter what age or state of dress, they are invisible to white people. This is certainly a question of class as well as race, but the "manness" of black men seems recognizable to whites only as a threat in this culture.

Working for an advertising company for many years, I developed a friendly familiarity with the regular messengers who were black. When a white co-worker heard one messenger inviting me to a musical event in which he was performing, she acted as if I'd been conversing with my typewriter table: not shocked, but confused. She appeared unable to imagine that this black messenger was also a man, that he had a life with aspirations and connections to something other than his bicycle and her packages. She also seemed incredulous that I, who'd been lifted up from what she seemed to perceive as the mire of blackness and blessed with a career, might feel connected to this messenger. She questioned me instantly, barely waiting for him to get out the door.

Today, more and more, that common bond between me and black men seems stretched thin. It is balanced less on personal interactions, like the wry wink the messenger returned to give me behind my co-worker's back, and more on vaguely remembered historical events. The sixties were a time when we had official titles—"Brother" and "Sister"—as if to negate all the other names slave owners had given us— mammy, uncle, Remus, Beulah. When I talk with heterosexual black men we speak of the Movement as if it were a shared adolescence that makes us siblings for life. But, like any vision of the past, it's never exactly the same in everyone's memory. And my assessment of the disadvantages of being a woman within the context of the civil-rights and black-power movements is certainly different from that of my brothers. None of them seem to remember Stokely Carmichael's heartily greeted pronouncement that "the only position for women in the Movement is prone." That's not a sentiment any revolutionary can endorse. Feminism has not taken away my pleasure at the hope which that period signified for me, yet it does require me to insist that both political consciousness and action be more comprehensive this time. In the nineties I demand that my brothers look past rhetoric and see me.

With our past in deep shadow, being continually reinterpreted by revolutionaries turned stockbrokers, it is increasingly difficult to find the shared contemporary experiences or opinions that might help me as a black woman work with black men to shape a bright future. There were always several groupings of black men with which I was never able to make serious connection. In college there were the strivers, those who I suspected would drop "the community" as soon as the right job came along. I could always recognize them by the elaborate efforts they made to keep their dashikis well pressed. Growing up in a tenement, living on welfare with my great-grandmother, I wanted crisp pleats and the right job as much as anyone, yet I thought their attitude reeked of escape rather than social consciousness.

Recently I heard a brother talking about finding a parking garage for his BWM as if that were a political triumph. He'd proudly maneuvered the baroque racism of corporate real estate in New York City, and I felt as though the beautiful sweat on the face of Fannie Lou Hamer had been rendered invisible. I knew he and I had taken different paths that were unlikely ever to meet. And on an East Coast campus I was visiting to do a reading, deliver a lecture, and meet with some of the writing students, the famous black male writer in residence didn't bother to show up. One of his female students told me not to take it personally; he never came to the readings women writers did.

When I heard, in the fall of 1991, that Spike Lee had begun his much publicized course on black film at Harvard by initially neglecting to include a single film by a black woman, I wasn't even surprised. In this case, as in the others, I felt as if an artificial construction—economics, academia—had rendered me superfluous to black male ego. I knew Duke would have been sorely disappointed in Duke, though. Just as he would with black men who feel duty bound on public streets to comment on women's body parts. Or those who call black women "out of their names," as we used to say. Or those who must trash other ethnic groups to feel like men. There's a level of solipsism pervading black male culture in the U.S. that Duke would never tolerate, and that I still find myself surprised to see.

Some of my heterosexual black male friends seem to have escaped or at least curbed the curse of culture and chromosomes. Clayton, a writer, has known me since I was in college, when he was struggling with his own career. Over the years he's offered the most consistent, uncondescending encouragement for my own writing, acting as an editor of my early clumsy efforts, while he wrote for the *New York Times*. He never appeared threatened by my attempts to catch up with him. Another good friend, Morgan, stuck by me in the deep emotional clinches that men aren't generally trained for: when my great-grandmother died, when I was out of work in New York City, when I couldn't figure out what to do next. He was managing a New York acting career, not the most lucrative undertaking for a black man in this country. But he offered himself and his family as a support system while I thrashed about trying not to drown.

I think that in the mid-1970s both Clayton and Morgan, unlike many of my other straight black friends, saw my coming out as a lesbian as a new aspect of me—perhaps a surprising revelation, but not an invasion by an alien being. They weren't afraid to like me even if our relationship wasn't about sex. These brothers took their title seriously. Their friendship kept my eyes open for the black gay brothers I knew had to be out there somewhere.

In the glitter-ball, disco world of the seventies, it was difficult to connect with them through the light shows and quadriphonic systems. But, as with Clayton and Morgan, it was through the intense personal aspirations—theater and writing—that I first caught the subtly gay winks of black men, thrown past unsuspecting heterosexuals, that let me know there was a community. The first people I remember trying to make social contact with as a lesbian were black gay men, actors who worked with me on a variety of productions in black theater. I would casually mention the name of a gay club like the Garage, and we'd glance at each other to check the response. Then, as with the wink from the messenger, we'd confirm our unity.

Until the mid-1980s the worlds of lesbians and gay men remained relatively separate. Except for the annual pride marches held around the country, we shared few cultural events, clubs, or political activities. But for black lesbians and gay men the world was not as easily divided. The history of oppression remained in our consciousness, even with some who were too young to really remember the Movement. And since we often were not accepted fully into the white gay world, we frequently socialized with each other. We hung together in the corner at the cast parties and invited each other over for holiday dinners, knowing the food would taste just like home.

When I went on the first national gay march on Washington in 1978, I had to be at the bus leaving Greenwich Village at 5 A.M. I slept on Rodney's couch, around the corner from the meeting place. We'd come out to each other years before when he was acting in a play I stage-managed. I was fascinated by his midwestern blackness and the way he paid attention when people talked to him, just like my father. I think he found my Bostonian manners and the rough ways of the theater a funny combination. We sat up talking most of the night, mainly about our lover relationships and what it was like to be black and gay in the New York theater world. It was a world of contradictions, where gay men and lesbians were fanatically closeted and heterosexuals were vying to see who could be the most iconoclastic and arty. When I left Rodney's house before dawn we hugged and kissed good-bye, and I remembered how much I'd missed black men since I'd stopped sleeping with them.

In reflecting on my friendships with black men in general and black gay men specifically, what is always at issue for me, whether conscious or not, is how these men view black women. That, of course, is an excellent indicator of how a man thinks of himself. And my great-grandmother always told me never to keep company with a man who doesn't think much of himself. That the sexual tension between men and women is largely eliminated between gay men and lesbians allows, I think, an opportunity for both to really see and think about each other, rather than reacting in socially prescribed ways. With straight friends like Morgan and Clayton, and later with gay friends like Rodney, I'm drawn to their ability to actually see me, not just see a woman as an object. They perceive my professionalism, intellect, and passion. And in turn they share their own attributes with me, rather than trying to use them to dominate me.

And then there's the unexpected pleasure of being able to view the object created by this culture—"woman"—alongside a man. It has been liberating to see another friend, Dan, let go of the strictures put on maleness and indulge in femaleness. We go through black magazines and scream at the brown-skinned cartoon fashion figures, because we know how far both of us are from that fake ideal—me with my size-sixteen figure and graying hair, him with hair everywhere. Dan dresses up in the very things that made me feel inadequate, the things I broke free of: heels, sequins, makeup. In doing so he has helped to create a space where we both can step back and see ourselves as separate from society's constructions of gender. From our perspective, the idealized glossy photographs as well as the other misleading clues about who women and men should be are reduced to their meaningless size.

Because neither of us would give up our blackness, even if it were possible, both of us can paint and primp, don the masks and laugh at whatever society imagines we both are. We share the wink behind the backs of both the straight and the black worlds. It's a special bond forged for me only with black gay men—a bond not broken in history by a slaver's lash or today by the disapproving sounds of air sucked through teeth.

For many years I've gone to concerts by the Lavender Light Black and People of All Color Gospel Choir. It's a lesbian and gay group that renders the songs of the gospel tradition in the most vibrant and moving ways I've experienced in years. What I see when I sit in the audience watching the black men I know—Charles, Lidell, others—is an abiding respect for our tradition and our survival. They sway in robes I'd recognize anywhere. Yet there is that extra movement, giving just a bit more to the spirit. And that extra bit signifies the insistence that the tradition can be carried on by all of us, not just heterosexuals or the black, closeted "choir queens." Charles and Lidell prefer to commune with their people and their God out in the open.

Although the sexual tension may not be there between us, what is allowed to flourish is the sensuality. When I'm with black men, we revel in the *feel* of being brothers and sisters. We talk that talk and walk that walk together. There is a sensuous texture to black life: the music, the use of words, the sensory pleasures of food, dance. We appreciate these things with each other. The commonality of our past and the linking of our future make the bond sensual and passionate, even when it's not sexual.

I spent an afternoon riding the train up from Washington, D.C., with the poet Essex Hemphill. We both were surprised at the opportunity to talk for a couple of hours without interruption. When the train pulled out, the conversation started with "Girrrrrl . . . " in that drawn-out way we can say and rolled out through the writing of Audre Lorde, Cheryl Clarke, and James Baldwin, the U.S. economy, the treachery of politicians, Luther Vandross, disco, white people in general and a few specific ones we knew, and broken hearts. We touched these things that have deep meaning for us in an unguarded way, using the familiar gestures and music of our fathers, mothers, and grandmothers. It was a synergy not so different from my intimate conversations with my best friend, Gwen, when we were in high school. And it felt much like those exhilarating moments when my father and I talked about books and music. Essex and I revealed ourselves to each other as writers, as a man and a woman, as brother and sister. We took each other in unreservedly. And we had barely begun before the train pulled into the station and we kissed good-bye.

And now AIDS. The first black friend I heard had died from HIV-related illness was Robert, an actor. He'd done a lot of television—*Kojak* and other series—and some small parts in films. But onstage he was a tall bundle of American/African energy, large eyes, dark, slightly wavy hair cut close, and mocha skin. In a play by Adrienne Kennedy (*A Movie Star Has to Star in Black and White*) at the Public Theatre, his character was on a hospital gurney during the entire performance. Even in that position he commanded the stage—an able partner to Gloria Foster, herself no small force on the boards. When Clayton called to tell me Bob was dead, it was so early in the epidemic we didn't even know what AIDS was and what we'd come to call it. It seemed like an isolated, terrifying disaster. He'd been luminescent, an embodiment of the brilliant talent we each hoped we ourselves possessed.

Since then the grim roll call has grown too long. And again we must draw together as black people. Until recently men of color were barred from participating in the testing programs that utilized experimental medications. And although women of color are the fastest-growing group in the U.S. contracting the AIDS virus, many of the symptoms that women specifically exhibit are just beginning to be accepted as indicators of AIDS. Thousands of people have already been left with inadequate health care. So that in the horror of the disease, just as in the horrors of war and poverty, African Americans as well as other people of color are left out in the open, unprovided for.

I was a speaker at the Gay Pride rally in Central Park when the New York section of the AIDS quilt was dedicated, and I walked the carefully laid-out rows where quilt workers had strategically placed the needed boxes of tissues. The beautifully crafted quilt panels went on for what seemed like acres, and my brothers were there—the photos, the Kente cloth, the snap-queen accessories embroidered in red, black, and green. And it seemed too cruel to try to squeeze our wondrous survival of the Middle Passage—slavery, Jim Crow, and benign neglect—into such small squares of fabric.

I think it is fitting that a womanly art—quilting—has come to embody a memorial instigated largely by gay men. When we try to discern what "gay" culture is, it is often found in the combination of things that highlight an irony or a difficult truth. When I watch the few media depictions of black lesbians or gay men, I'm disappointed with the flat acceptance of surface elements—campy mannerisms, colorful clothes, attitude—all of which fall quite short of that difficult truth.

When I look at TV's *In Living Color,* I may chuckle once or twice, but for the most part the black gay characters Blaine and Antoine completely miss the irony of the new vision being created. The writers seem easily satisfied with their own ability to startle viewers by showing black men in funny outfits who lisp, rather than drawing a real picture of a black drag queen, a truly outrageous and complex figure in our society. And never would the writers or the stars admit they might (if they ever took the chance) *like* these two characters they've created. Their casual contempt shows through. When my friend Dan makes over to look like Patti LaBelle, he's acknowledging layers of cultural references that only *begin* with the feathers. He's postulating many relationships to the ideas of maleness, femaleness, and blackness. He is a black man, and it is *not* an easy laugh.

When I see the AIDS Memorial Quilt, I perceive those layers of cultural reference, where they've come from, and how they are expanded when used in this new way. The quilt is the re-viewing of traditional crafts, imbuing them with more poignant meaning. And the relationship between black lesbians and gay men is also a similar re-viewing of an old relationship. It is sisters and brothers with the long line of traditions behind us—some of them good, some bad—reconnecting with different spices in the pot.

Such a new dish is not always easy to prepare. Often the bitter aftertaste of our pasts and heterosexual expectations is too heavy. Even black men can think they're John Wayne. And a few of us mistakenly imagine we're Miss Scarlett or, even more problematic, every man's mother. In some cases black gay men and lesbians have chosen to find no common ground and reject exploration of that which history has provided us. U.S. culture encourages that separation. Men huddled together in front of televised football or wrapping themselves in the pursuit of the perfect dance floor are each a different side of the same attempt to exclude women from male life. And lesbians, certainly more than our straight sisters, often find it easier to reject the rejecter than to continue to knock on a closed door. More than once I've found myself ready to walk away from black gay men who cling stubbornly to male arrogance and gleefully condescend to women. Where the connection seems most easily forged is in activities that provide first an opening and then a context for our caring. My reputation as an out lesbian writer and activist puts me in a fortunate position. Black gay men who know my work will assume the connection and the safety in our relationship.

Between me and other writers such as Essex Hemphill, Assoto Saint, and Colin Robinson, the writing provides us with a path to each other. Our passion for the use of words as a way to save our lives became an important frame of reference for trust and communication. We form a tenuous yet definite community. The great sadness is that now with the AIDS epidemic, too often loss is that reference point.

Recently I rode with four black men from New York to Philadelphia to attend a memorial service. On the trip we joked about how black people name children, agonized over what we were writing or working on, caught each other up on gossip. It could have been almost any family trip. At the church the black minister leading the service felt compelled (in the face of over a hundred gay people swelling his congregation) to emphasize God's forgiveness for our "sins." On the way back home, each of us commented on the minister's lapses. But we really were more interested in talking about our lost brother and all the family things that the minister clearly felt we had no right to. We laughed a lot on that drive back, as black people frequently do when faced with the unfaceable.

I was in college when my father was dying of cancer. On his hospital bed, Duke never lost his sense of humor or sense of humanity. He told me with a mischievous twinkle that his nurse, Walter, was the best in the hospital. The two of them kept up a stream of flirtatious patter right to the end. And my father never acted like that made either of them less a man. All that mattered was that he could still make connections with other people, and light up a room with his wit.

Twenty years later, riding home from the memorial service with my friends, I can see the same light. Duke may never have been able to envision such a ride or such company with me, but had he been there he would have laughed the loudest. And I wonder if his wit, like theirs, was one way to face the unfaceable. Cocooned in the smooth ride of the rental car, the sweet sound of their voices, the ribald laughter, the scent of after-shave lotion, I again heard the sensuous music of Billie Holiday and John Coltrane that I'd learned to love while tending my father's records. These men were comforting and familiar, like the expansive clink of my father's pocket change.

# Alex

I first met Alex at the Silver Pancake restaurant in Milton, Ontario, where she was a waitress. Half Greek, with dark hair, olive skin, and blue eyes, in a town full of beefy pink Scots Irish girls, she had a unique look that attracted and intimidated the men around her, myself included.

Alex had a smart mouth, and she was fast on her feet. The younger waitresses were a little in awe of her, because she was a hard worker and viewed her job as an essential source of income, not simply mall money. We hit it off right away. I drank my coffee iced, something I've discovered is deeply offensive to the snowbound Canadian psyche. I became known as the guy who asked for ice with his coffee. Alex always brought me a great deal of it. In her own way, she understood eccentricity.

She always asked about my writing, and she remembered the names of the friends I brought into the restaurant from the world beyond the town.

I asked about her family and her boyfriend. She was in a long-term relationship with a local bodybuilder named Gordon, whom I immediately nicknamed Rex because of his astonishing physique and his handsome face.

The local princesses giggled and stuck out their breasts when Rex was around, noting admiringly how "big" and "cute" he was.

"Sluts," Alex said dismissively, cocking a supercilious eyebrow in the direction of the girls as they flirted with Rex. "If that's what he wants, he's with the wrong woman."

The local boys looked up to Rex as well. He had lived in Milton all of his life, and drove a Zamboni ice tractor at the hockey games to clear it after each period. He worked for the town and made good money. Everyone knew him. Everyone knew Alex *belonged* to him. She was his woman.

Alex and I would walk home from the restaurant together after her shift was over, and before we even reached the end of Main Street, someone would have telephoned Rex with the news that his woman was making time with some guy, did he know? What was going on? Had they broken up?

"I don't like it," Rex told Alex over the telephone one night, shortly before he'd met me.

What the town thought, what his parents thought, was extremely important to Rex. Alex was his woman. There was talk.

Alex couldn't have cared less. She hated "talk."

Although she wasn't aware of exactly what she wanted from life, she knew that she didn't want what other girls wanted. Rex would be a good provider, she knew. His intentions were decent and honorable. He would buy a house (in Milton, of course), marry, raise a nice family, and start the whole correct cycle all over again.

The summer I met Alex was the summer I left my life in the city and moved to Milton to pursue a new one. The town has its dark side, though, as small towns with more churches than bars sometimes do. A few years before I moved there, a suspected gay teenager had been badly beaten outside one of the roadhouses on the edge of town. Milton is the home parish of the homophobic Canadian fundamentalist Ken Campbell, as well as the squatting ground of the rabidly right-wing anti-gay, antifeminist Family Coalition Party (a joke in the larger Canadian political arena but a loud, odious presence in rural areas like Milton).

I had wanted to feel safe, so I did not talk about my private life, and hoped that no one else would, either.

I was sharply divested of this illusion of anonymity one day when Blue, the owner of the Silver Pancake (with whom I had become friendly but not candid), took me aside "as a friend" and told me that the entire staff of the restaurant, and a good portion of the town, referred to me behind my back as "that queer."

Not, he assured me, in a *hostile* way, but I should be careful about whom I took into my confidence.

"How do they come up with this stuff?" I asked, genuinely fascinated. I hadn't counted on telepathy being one of the talents enjoyed by my neighbors.

"They never seen you with a girl," Blue explained patiently. "Plus, you got a mystery side. You talk different from them, too."

"I speak differently?" I said, baffled. "How?"

"Formal. Kinda polite. Nobody talks that way in Milton. And you got money, but you don't work a job."

"I am a *writer*," I said indignantly.

"I mean a real job," said Blue.

I was mortified. I looked up and suddenly, from where I was sitting, everyone's smile looked a little twisted. And there was my lovely Alex at the far end of the restaurant, raising her coffee pot as though toasting me. She was grinning.

I felt as though I might be sick. I excused myself and left the restaurant. That night I telephoned my friend Ron in Los Angeles. Ron was raised in the country outside New Lowell, a town that made Milton look like Paris. He is now a successful Los Angeles–based writer and director, but he still carried, somewhere deep inside, the flinty memory of small-town life.

"Face it," he said, not unkindly. "They are who they are, and you are who you are, and never the twain shall meet. They are never going to mistake you for a happily single straight man just hanging out in a small town waiting for the right woman to come along."

He paused, then said gently, "You really should have known that going in."

The next day, I felt cranky and betrayed. Like the townspeople in the Chevy Chase film *Funny Farm*, my new neighbors were not playing by the rules or acting the way small-town people were supposed to act. Someone was going to have to pick up the tab. That night in the restaurant, I glared at Alex, making her the focus of all my paranoia. She had betrayed me. She hadn't told me what was going on.

"What's your fuckin' problem?" she snapped.

"I think you know, Alex."

"What do I know?"

"About the rumors. That I'm gay."

Pause. "Listen. That wasn't me. That was the other girls."

"You could have told me," I said.

But by the time the conversation was over, she'd admitted that she had heard the talk and told the staff to mind their own fucking business. She didn't care anyway if I was or wasn't. And I believed her. That was my Alex. She always preferred to shoot from the hip.

I, however, couldn't bring myself to return the favor.

I concocted a story about a fiancée in the city who would have been terribly hurt to hear all the talk about her stalwart, manly future husband (I had even begun wearing work boots with the laces undone, and flannel shirts and green work pants, in an attempt to blend in). I even imported my friend Sad Ruth to play the part of the wronged wife-to-be.

Sad Ruth was a tortured Czech artist with a fine sense of the absurd, and an intense loathing for small towns. On the day she came to the Silver Pancake for lunch, we laughed behind our fingers as the entire restaurant staff, headed by a corpulent redheaded waitress named Juicy, trooped over to our table to meet my lovely future wife.

"Wayda go, bud," backslapped Boomer, the cook. "Heh-heh-heh!"

Most of the gossip stopped cold at that point. All the townspeople needed to hear was that I had a fiancée, and they revised their opinion completely. No proof required, just a warm female body ("Hot body!" opined Boomer) with all the parts intact and an engagement ring on her finger. (Sad Ruth had been previously engaged, but it hadn't worked out. She kept the diamond, smart girl.)

I had nipped the gossip in the bud, and made buffoons out of the gossips. But when Alex came over to meet "my woman," and told me that we made a nice couple, I felt less like a clever chameleon and more like a liar.

"Everyone needs someone," Alex said. "I hope you're very happy together."

"Thanks, Alex."

Splish-splash, pay no mind: it's just me, wading through the slime. I am an execrable coward and ought to commit hara-kiri immediately. Or move. Or be Young, Gay, and Proud—defiant in the face of the ravening mob. Instead, I reached for Sad Ruth's hand, exposing the pitiably small diamond her former future husband had procured for her.

"Show my friend Alex your ring, dear."

Months passed. Eventually, alas, my "engagement" to the lovely and talented Sad Ruth "came to an end."

Stress, I told Alex sadly. Ruth and I lived in different worlds.

Alex told me she'd seen it coming.

That afternoon, I told her I was gay. She told me she'd suspected it all along and thought it was "great." I told her about my fears, how alone I felt, but ultimately that I was uncomfortable with a friendship built on lies, and that our friendship mattered a great deal.

We walked home together that evening after her shift, from the top of Main Street all the way back to her apartment, for once not giving a shit whether or not Rexie and his pals were watching us.

In all fairness to Rex, he was a perfect gentleman to me after Alex told him I was gay. He was far more supportive and sensitive to me than I had anticipated. I had prejudged him a redneck before I'd even heard him out. Prejudice, I was discovering, sometimes cuts both ways.

Alex and Rex were a prominent local couple, and their endorsement of me as a friend was enough to assure my acceptability to even the most crimson of Milton's rednecks. Rex was a man's man, and Alex was more woman than any of them could handle. If Alex and Rex said I was cool, that was it. I was cool. But I still looked over my shoulder walking home at night.

"I don't care what they *think*, Alex," I told her. "I care about my physical safety. I care about my house and my dogs. I live across the street from a Catholic church, for God's sake."

"If those Christians have a problem with you being gay," growled Alex, "they can come and talk to me about it."

If a day passed without my either hearing from Alex or seeing her at the Silver Pancake, it was noted by both of us. We came to be able to recognize each other's voices on the telephone, and we spoke often, but not long, preferring to talk face-to-face.

I never grew tired of looking at Alex. Her physical beauty fascinated me in a way that I found curiously disorienting. I frequently caught myself exploring unformed daydreams about her as I watched her body move across the floor of the restaurant.

One night, I had a vivid dream that we were in a dark room with an open window and billowing white curtains. I realized that we were both naked, her perfect body gleaming like polished bronze in the moonlight. I smelled her perfume, Anaïs Anaïs. I felt the supple female muscles beneath her warm, flushed skin.

I was not translating her sexuality in my dream: this was indisputably a woman, a most alluring woman, the essence of the feminine, stripped of everything that I, as a gay man, have ever found sexually threatening about women. And I knew, in this dream, that I would give myself to this night-Alex willingly, in a way I never would have considered doing if I had been awake.

The next morning, I saw that I had torn the sheets off the bed, and my pillow had been flung to the far corner of my bedroom.

It took me months to tell Alex about that dream. She told me that she'd had a similar dream. She said she found me handsome, which, I confess, gave me as much pleasure as if the compliment had come from an attractive man. Returning to the warm, brother-sister currency of our friendship, we laughed about the dreams, and it became apparent to both of us that the erotic charge between us would thrive precisely because it would always remain below the surface.

Alex told me the stories of her family, and the stories of her life with Rex. I told her my own stories. Together we grappled with my love for Milton, a love she didn't understand at all, and with her desperate desire to be away from the town.

To Alex, Milton represented the death of every dream she'd ever had: no one ever got out, no one ever became anything. We became each other's center of gravity. I was her lifeline to the outside world; she was my protector as I established my identity within the town.

That winter, we had an early thaw. The mist rose up from the melted snow, and the gutters ran like white water. The night air was full of the dark scent of rain and waking earth from the surrounding fields.

Alex bought a fast car, and we burned up the roads around Milton late at night. She blasted the tape deck. Sometimes she played Whitney

Houston. Most often, she played Madonna, that patron saint of small-town girls dreaming of a way out.

She put the pedal to the floor.

"Freedom, man," she muttered, and we rocketed into the sweet country dark.

I loved riding shotgun as she swept along the winding country roads at night, scattering mist in front of the headlights. In the electric firelight of the dashboard, we told each other more secrets.

"Swear you won't tell?"

"I swear." And the stories came.

We passed stone houses full of early-to-bed farmers and their worthy wives. Dogs howled as we hurtled by. We passed ghastly prefab subdivisions on the edge of town.

"*Losers!*" we screamed, exhilarated by the car's speed and our complicity, each of us venting our sacrificial angers at the prim facades of the townhouses.

My anger was for the nameless, faceless people who had made me afraid for my safety in my adopted hometown. It was anger at the ugly minuet of polite tea-party homophobia, masking the darker potential for violence that bubbled discreetly beneath the white-picket facade.

Alex's anger was for the middle-class iron maiden poised to slowly squeeze her to death, impaling her on its dull, respectable spikes; anesthetizing her with mortgages and children and other people's narrow definitions of what it meant to be a woman—all before she turned twenty-one.

"This isn't me, man," she said sadly one night as we crested a hill and saw the town spread out before us like a glittering carpet of light. "It just isn't fuckin' me."

The days passed quickly. Alex grew despondent. I grew worried. She rarely had time to talk at the restaurant, and when she did, she had nothing to say. Rex refused to take her out of town to go dancing in the city, or really to even consider their life as something other than a drawn-out preamble to marriage. He didn't want to go anywhere.

"Everything's already here," Rex said, bewildered.

"Don't you have any dreams?" she asked him. "Don't you want to be anything exciting?"

"You don't know what you want, Alex," he told her bluntly. "That's always been your problem."

Alex came to me one day and told me something she thought I would understand. Two women had come into the Silver Pancake that day ("Classy ones," she said). She'd watched them, fascinated. The women appeared to Alex to be lovers, although she couldn't identify the nonverbal communication that had led her to believe this.

She tried to articulate what she'd felt, watching them. She tried to understand her strong physical attraction to their presence in her restaurant.

But what, she wondered, was it? Their love for each other? Their obvious affluence and independence? Or the fact that they were lesbians and wrote their own rules about how and where to act?

"I wanted those two women to like me," she said.

"Hmmm," I said.

"I don't know if I'm, like, *gay*," Alex said. "But I could tell that they found me attractive. And I liked that."

"Hmmm," I said again.

"What do you think?" she asked irritably. "Stop saying *hmmm!*"

"I don't know, Alex," I said. "I've never been a lesbian myself."

"Be serious," she snapped. "What if I'm bisexual?"

"Then you're one of the lucky ones," I said. "You get double the fun."

It was several days before I heard from Alex again.

She called me at home one night, sounding upset. She said she had to see me right away.

"We're going for a drive," she said.

We circled the town slowly as she told me that she was afraid she would eventually commit suicide. Life held nothing for her. No future, except as the wife of Rex and the fulfillment of her role as a woman by bearing his children.

She would always hold the same sort of low-income job she held now, if she was even allowed to work outside the home. Through me, she said, she had glimpsed a world of travel and excitement that she would never be a part of. She saw her life as a point of light speeding down a dark tunnel and disappearing as though it had never existed.

There wasn't a shred of self-pity in any of this. If there had been, it might have been less ominous. The terrifying fact of Alex's declaration was simply that: it was a declaration.

"You could move," I said.

"I'm afraid," she said.

"Alex," I said, "you don't need to kill yourself. What you need is to get out of Milton for a little while. The town will look very different from a different angle, I promise. Sometimes it's impossible to fix your life when it's right in your face."

She had never been anywhere except Portland, Maine, where she had family. The next day, she booked a two-week holiday package to the Dominican Republic.

Rex, not unexpectedly, was displeased. There would be talk, he wailed. What would his mother and father think about his girlfriend traveling alone to God knows where, to do God knew what? Her friends would talk, and so would his. What about her reputation? They might even call her a slut.

"Tough shit," said Alex.

As the departure date drew near, she became more and more excited. The day before she left, she hugged me.

"I love you honey," she said. "You give the best advice."

She came back two weeks later, a Sunday. I was in the Silver Pancake with her sisters, having brunch. I didn't notice Alex immediately. Alex no longer looked anything like Alex.

The woman standing by the banquette in the far corner of the restaurant, dressed in Levi's and a plain white T-shirt, was deeply tanned, her hair askew and sun streaked.

No makeup, no pouffy pleated jeans, no prissy jewelry, no stock-in-trade tokens of snippy femininity.

"Geez, Alex," I said after I hugged her. She even smelled like the sun. "What happened to you?"

She smiled an incandescent smile I had never seen before, and said, "This is the beginning of the rest of my life, honey."

In a matter of a week, Alex quit her job at the Silver Pancake, gave up her apartment in Milton, and gave Rex his walking papers.

She moved to Toronto, got another job at another restaurant, got a new apartment, and found herself a girlfriend: a striking Australian bodybuilder named Jan.

"I am so in love," Alex whooped one day over coffee. "I mean, I am just crazy in love with this woman! The way she touches me, the way she looks at me. I always wondered what was missing with men."

I asked her if she missed men at all.

She winked slyly. "There are things women can do that men could only dream of doing, honey."

The news eventually got back to Rex, who was in a bit of a twist: his woman had left him, not just for another woman but for another *bodybuilder*. He was devastated.

"Look at the bright side, Rex," I said. "You could always double-date. The two of you could cruise chicks."

Rex started dating a nurse's aide. Alex started bodybuilding.

A couple of years ago, Alex attended her first Pride Day parade, not just as part of the euphoric crowd, but as the star attraction of one of the more garish bar floats. Wearing little more than makeup and a brilliant smile, she worked that audience, girl. She had them clapping and snapping. The muscle boys all screamed *Alex! Alex! Alex!*

She and Jan have motorcycles, and an apartment in the heart of the Toronto gay ghetto off Church Street. Alex knows everyone, and they know her. Community celebrity is nothing new for Alex, but the lesbians and gay men who form her new world celebrate her for what she is.

It's always amusing to watch the reactions of straight couples when Alex and I walk downtown. The men slow down when they pass her. Their eyes glaze over, their jaws open slightly, and their breathing becomes audible. They are thinking of death by chocolate.

The women yank at their companion's arm as though it were a leash. They walk faster. They are thinking about olive-skinned, blue-eyed witches flying overhead, stealing husbands and souring milk. Or maybe they are taking stock of her glowing skin, her taut body, her short-cropped dark hair, and having a private response of their own.

Alex and I meet for lunch or dinner when I am in the city, which is often. She and Jan come out to my house in Milton for the two large parties I have each year, summer and Christmas. It doesn't seem fair, somehow, to ask Alex to leave her new life to return to the site of her old one too often.

Alex can't imagine what I'm still doing in Milton. She doesn't see Milton as a place for anyone gay—or even anyone interesting, for that matter. For my part, I have made a home for myself here. I have struck a satisfying balance between my fantasy of small-town life and its reality. My life and work are full of a variety of friends, both local and out of town. It's not Alex's life, but it's mine, and it works. So does hers in the city.

Alex and I were having dinner one night at Ciao, my favorite restaurant on Church Street. The meal was over, and we were sipping cappuccinos.

"I can't believe I ever thought of staying there," she said. "Couldn't you just see it? Pregnant all the time. I'd die." She shuddered. "My sisters always want me to come back to visit them, but I just can't."

"It's different when you're in a place because you want to be there," I said. "To me, Milton is beautiful. It's where I've made my home. There's good there as well as bad."

"Mostly bad," she said dryly.

"I met you there, didn't I? That's proof of the good."

"I left," she said archly. "You have to visit me in the big city now. This is where I should have been all along."

"You, my darling, make the city a richer place." I leaned over and kissed her. Her lips tasted of cinnamon and coffee. "Alex, you are my own sweet love. What would I do without you?"

"You'll never have to know," she said.

And she's right. I don't believe I ever will.

# Miss Thing

It was a two-hour drive to the treatment facility. An old man with a game leg picked me up at my doorstep. He didn't seem the least bit fazed by my tattoos, my razor-short haircut, or my Ray Bans, which, despite the overcast skies, I never took off. I don't remember what we talked about. Sobriety, most likely. But I do remember that these conversations stilled the incessant voices in my head that hissed at me to flip up the car doorknob and hurl myself out of the rapidly moving car.

Visually, the treatment facility was not at all what I expected. Once a nursing home, it was filled with plastic furniture and indoor-outdoor carpeting. The red brick buildings, attached by breezeways, were surrounded by a walkway. During my eleven-day stay I would come to intimately know each crack and tuft of grass in that walkway.

While waiting for my paperwork to be processed, I remember pacing about the small waiting room. I remember people staring at me as I incessantly got up, sat down, shoved my hands into the tattered pockets of my black leather jacket, and stared out the window at the asphalt parking lot. I know I never took off my sunglasses until I sat down in the psychiatrist's office. And, despite the July heat that periodically blasted through the automatic glass door entrance, I never removed my heavy jacket, preferring to gain comfort from the cool sweat that ran down my spine and under my unshaven armpits.

I believe it was the soft-spoken psychiatric resident who escorted me out the front door, across the grassy courtyard, and into an octagonal-shaped building. His escort, as gentle as a puppy's sniff, was a new and enticing sensation. It was the first time I was aware of another human being's concern for me. He was attentive to my every request; he watched my every move. He seemed to breathe as I breathed. I remember thinking that if this sense of safety and concern is what drew my older sister into her eleven institutionalizations, perhaps I would follow suit. Of course, I was quite aware that, unlike other prospective patients, I was getting VIP treatment. I assumed it was due to the razor blades.

I have no memory of my initial intake conversation with this man, although I am quite sure that I lied. I often do. But I am sure I skimmed my sadomasochism.

Eventually, the young resident stopped waiting and asked me to step back out into the plastic waiting room. We moved down the hallway, which, except for the brass nameplates on the doors, was completely barren. We stood again in the large rotunda filled with a harsh and barely detectable undersmell of urine—a fact I knew better than to mention to anyone, just in case I was the only one who smelled it. As our conversation lapsed and he turned to leave, the loneliness and fear that hounded me from the moment of my last relapse descended around me once again. I shoved my hands deeper into my jacket pockets and pulled the damp, padded lining close around my chest. Then I pulled up the left sleeve of my jacket and exposed my wrist. I pointed to the red mark, made by a magic marker, that I had put directly over my left wrist. The tiny dot assured me of swift, accurate aim should the voices get their way.

The rest I saved for the young psychiatrist. It was in his office that I told another human being of my cross-dressing, my masochistic self-mutilation gone awry—and Miss Thing.

I first spotted Miss Thing in a smoke-filled room of recovering gay and lesbian alcoholics. Like many rooms that I would come to know in the years that followed, it was littered with extras. Chairs were piled up in one corner, and computer parts, including reams of computer paper, lay forgotten in another. Scattered across the cigarette-burned carpet were coffee cans, which were used as ashtrays.

On that first day I walked halfway down the stairs leading into the room. Rather than fully enter and sit in the circle of chairs placed in the middle, I positioned myself partway down the short flight. I slid over next to the wrought-iron railing. From this position I could grip the railing and observe the action in the room.

It was into this room cluttered with people who like myself considered themselves extras in their own lives that Miss Thing stepped. I do not know if it is merely my wish or a fact that she was one of the dozen or so gay men who stepped around me on those stairs. If, in fact, this was what she did, I am sure she would have delicately picked her way down those stairs and, when she came to me, gently placed her hand on my shoulder and slipped by. Like a raindrop landing on the top of my head, an "Excuse me, baby" would have dropped from her lips. From my sitting position I'd have had a perfect view of her sweet bottom moving in the middle of her very practiced, sultry swagger. Miss L, who was Miss Thing's companion and roommate and like Miss Thing was also in her fifties, would have been right behind her.

For days I'd watch Miss Thing maneuver around that room. While waiting for the meeting to begin she'd entertain the small flock of young gay men who, like male dogs sniffing after a bitch, swarmed around her. From between the railings I'd watch her worry over this one's health, compliment that one's new haircut, or, after sliding her cigarette down to her fingertips, use some boy's back to write down her phone number on a piece of paper and slip it into his eager hand. Throughout these sessions she, with her darting eyes, continuously checked out all newcomers and gauged the impact of her conversations.

Perhaps is was this ability to mold a roomful of people to her person that initially drew me to Miss Thing. Or maybe it was the whorish femininity that undulated through her body that caught my eye. After all, I've always been a sucker for a whore. To this day I still don't know exactly why I was so quickly mesmerized by this petite and aging gay man. Or why, right before sliding her elbow through Miss L's extended arm and sauntering off, she gently pressed her phone number into the palm of my oh-so-eager hand.

All I know is that within a week, I became the soft spot in this aging drag queen's life.

Soon Miss Thing and I became inseparable. Like two teenagers, we'd spend all of our late-night hours chatting on the phone. Me? I'd bitch about my girlfriend. And Miss Thing? She'd just bitch about the entire fucking world and worry herself sick about her aging hillbilly mama.

When I wasn't at work, I was on my way to Miss Thing's apartment, which was actually a condo owned my Miss L. After Miss Thing's last binge, Miss L had brought her there. Once Miss Thing answered the door, she'd lead me up the narrow winding staircase to her apartment. Following behind, I tried to keep my eyes averted but was too fascinated by the swaying hips that moved gently before my eyes to keep myself from looking up.

Once in her sparsely furnished apartment, she'd direct me to the kitchen, where she gave me my first razor-short crew cut. If my hair didn't need attention, she'd point to the couch in her living room. After pouring me some of her bitter coffee or pulling an orange from her refrigerator, she'd walk back into the living room and arrange herself on the couch. She'd sit so close to me that her body would be touching mine. Sometimes she'd pull out her drag albums; other times she'd interrupt her leafing through old, faded photos of female impersonators and lead me into her bedroom. There she'd show me more formal portraits of herself. It was during one of these times in her bedroom that she pulled back her closet door, and there, next to the dull men's clothes that were her daily wardrobe, were her beaded and sequined gowns. One by one she'd pull them out, lay them on the bed, and, as she examined her "drags," as she called them, for tears or missing buttons, tell me about these dresses, which she treated like old and dear friends. Some were worn during her time with the Jewel Box Revue, a well-known drag entourage. Others, willed to her by old friends now dead, had not been with her all that long. I felt as though the spirits of these dead drag queens were nestled in the folds of those heavily brocaded dresses and that the faces of their original owners could be seen in the tear-shaped pearls that hung delicately among the reams of satin.

These drags, her photos, and her decades of memories became the center of our relationship. The Jewel Box became our primary point of reference. As we sat on that couch she'd tell me about many of her other memories. Sometimes she'd take me back to her tour of East Berlin, when she'd lost her wig while "carrying on" after a show with some German businessman. At other times she'd chatter on about her New

York escapades; once, while drunk, she practiced her talents as an electrolysist on some society matron who lay unsuspecting under her needle.

The details of her devastating childhood and her thirty years of drinking were usually mentioned when Miss Thing, leaving me with my face buried in her old albums, wandered off to the kitchen to get me yet another cup of her bitter coffee. While puttering in that kitchen she'd drop some detail about her life as a hillbilly sissy. Occasionally she'd toss in some drunken horror that had occurred during her hustling days—a career that, like drag, always led her back to booze.

Often, my time on her couch or under her scissors was interrupted by the phone or the doorbell ringing. Sometimes it would be one of the younger gay men who always hovered around her. But frequently it would be her older friends, gay men she'd know for years. There was Carlotta, a six-foot Texan drag queen, whom Miss Thing usually referred to as "the Bitch." Miss Thing had worked in his shows for years. And then there was Miss QT, who between bouts of shooting dope had worked in the theater for decades.

From the moment Miss Thing daintily slipped her phone number into the palm of my hand, she fed me. Mostly it was bitter coffee, dry oranges, or her famous chicken-and-onion sandwiches. At other times she'd "cook her tits off" for me, preparing meals in which I was invariably overfed. But Miss Thing also saw and then proceeded to feed a deeper appetite that was within me. From the moment we met, Miss Thing and later all her older friends told me I was just an old-time dyke like the ones who used to show up at her drag performances. She said I was just like these old-time dykes, who, with their high-femme girlfriends on their arms, used to flirt shamelessly with all the drags. "You must meet my friend Storme," Miss Thing used to say as she'd point to a faded photograph of a butch mulatto in a tuxedo. Storme would be standing on some stage with a line of drag queens at her back. Like me, she could have easily been mistaken for a man.

The ghosts of women like Storme or those butch women with their arms around their femmes began to hover near that couch. These women thought and felt like me; that is what Miss Thing told me. These nameless women, Miss Thing said, even looked like me. With

Miss Thing on my arm I was becoming one of those butch women who stay in those audiences flirting with drags. I was becoming a woman I had not thought I could even dare to be.

A sensuality that was palpable began to engulf my relationship with Miss Thing. During the months I would spend in that apartment I'd find myself walking into her bedroom and staring at those photos on her wall. Now when I showed up at her door, there were flowers in my hands. When we'd go out in public I would open all the doors for her. When I'd meet her at some sober gay and lesbian event where she was entertaining, I'd make sure I was dressed all in men's drag. And during her performances, it would be me she'd always choose from the audience to be her special dance partner. Up there on that stage, I could dance with a woman just like a man could. It was the butch in me that Miss Thing and her old friends had found and fed religiously.

Then, desperate for money, Miss Thing decided to reenter the world of professional drag. I drove her to her first night's performance. We traveled to the Stateline, a huge and ancient drag joint. When we arrived, the parking lot was empty. Loaded down with her drags, wig cases, and makeup bags, I used my butt to push open the heavy swinging doors that led inside the Stateline. Old green and white awnings covered the ceiling of the dimly lit cavernous space; white linen covered the round tables that stretched outward from the drag runway. The bartender waved to Miss Thing, who tossed a "Hey, baby" in his direction. In my white tuxedo, I carried Miss Thing's dresses to her backstage dressing room and then returned to the front to wait for her. She reemerged from backstage wearing her silver wig and full makeup. Wrapped around her was an old bathrobe I'd seen lying around her bedroom. The staff, many of whom knew Miss Thing as Ratina, served us a luscious meal. Miss Thing and I ate quietly in the deserted dining room.

By the time we tapped our linen napkins to our lips, the room had begun to slowly fill up with fifty-year-old men and their wives. I folded my napkin, placed it on the table, and stood up. I followed Miss Thing to her closet-sized dressing room. The sound of tinkling glasses and laughter began to filter in from out front. There, in her small, stuffy dressing room she slipped off her robe. She let it drop to the floor. All she wore then was a G-string. She slipped into her white sequined gown. "Help me zip this up, will you, baby?" she said with her back to me. I could hear Carlotta warming up the crowd. I took a few steps toward Miss Thing. I touched her soft skin. Her heavy perfume filled the room. "Hurry up," she snapped as I tucked her into her skin-tight dress. After rummaging through her jewelry case she turned toward me and slipped a rhinestone necklace around my neck. Then she pulled out a tube of lipstick, and with her left hand holding my face, she painted my lips. Then she handed me the tube of lipstick, quickly turned, and stepped out of the dressing room and onto the stage. I slipped the tube of lipstick into my dinner jacket and walked back to the table that had been reserved for me. From there I saw Miss Thing work the crowd just as she had that first day in that cluttered, smoked-filled room. There I was, an old-time dyke sitting in the audience watching all these old-time drags. Sometimes Miss Thing would blow me a kiss; other times she'd wink at me with those eyes caked with mascara.

Then, after what seemed an endless night, it was over. I drove Miss Thing back home. We had very little to say to one another. When I arrived at her home, I desperately wanted to trail behind up those winding stairs. But on this visit it wasn't her bitter coffee I hungered for but her long, lean body filled with a femaleness that I never had been allowed to desire. But, as always, I had to settle for a kiss upon her cheek, a "Call me, baby," and the sight of those sweet hips swaying as she slowly climbed the long and winding stairs.

Things changed. Our nighttime conversations became sluggish; her jokes about muff divers now fell on less generous ears. I grew tired of looking at those albums and hearing about those women. Perhaps I was beginning to understand that my listening could not remove the desperation that, like the pearls on her drags, threaded throughout her life. Or maybe I could no longer sustain my love affair with an illusion.

I called Miss Thing from the treatment center. "It's just not working anymore," I mumbled into the phone. She asked no questions, and merely said, "Sure, baby, I understand." I knew she didn't. Nor did I. We said our good-byes, the old flirtation ended by an icy distance that was now between us.

*Just not working for me right now.* I moved deeper into my writing, my cross-dressing, and my sadomasochism. I needed to reshape my life, which no longer seemed to sustain me. Miss Thing moved away from meetings and returned to the bars, her booze, and her drag.

Some time would pass before I showed up at the budget haircutting salon where Miss Thing finally ended up working. It took a few minutes before she saw me sitting on the bench and leaning over the rail, as always staring at her sweet and sassy ass. "Hey, baby," she said, and signaled to the femme receptionist to bump me to the top of her list. Once in her chair I knew better than to tell her how to cut my hair. After all, wasn't she the one who shaped me into who I am? For the next hour we updated each other on our respective lives. Still poor and in love with yet another woman, I continued with my writing. She was still worrying about her mama, drinking, and doing drag, was probably heading off to Pittsburgh, where Miss L, who'd moved there a while ago, had said he'd take her in again. Before I knew it, she'd put down her clippers and tilted my head up. There in the mirror in front of me was that old-time butch with the old-time crew cut. It was the woman that Miss Thing, before anyone else, had unearthed from somewhere deep in me.

Before I left the salon for what would be the last time, Miss Thing and I checked to make sure we had each other's phone numbers. It was a ritual we'd performed at least a hundred times. As I did the first time I met her, I safely tucked her number in the corner of my wallet. As always, I told her that I loved her. And, as always, she turned her cheek for me to kiss and said, "I love you too, baby." Then I stepped out the door into a world that cowers at the sight of me.

I never told Miss Thing that her coffee was bitter or that her jokes were as tasteless as her oranges. After all, it wasn't her food but her sweet ass that I really hungered for.

# Home Alone?

Unlike, I suspect, many of the essays in this anthology, mine is a sad, perplexing, and incomplete one: the story of a failed relationship between a gay man (me) and a lesbian (my sister). It is a story of incomprehension, love, and guilt. It does not have a happy ending. It does not have an ending at all. I sometimes think that if I could find the ending, even an unhappy one, I would have solved a central riddle of my life. My sister and I, perhaps like many lesbians and gay men, remain mysterious to each other, though wishing each other well.

My sister and I, though indisputably legitimate, were nonetheless born to quite different mothers. Mine was a virago, sarcastic and composed, contemptuous of convention and hungry for victory: a great role model for any gay boy. My sister's was an embodied challenge: quick, voluble, and hard where my sister was slow, considering, and soft. Even their unhappiness differed, my mother (like me) favoring the more theatrical displays of temperament, my sister a stoically minimal sadness. My eventual homosexuality, however much it may have infuriated my mother, nonetheless owes everything to her. I have been as demanding, witty, and gregarious in my life as she in hers. My sister, on the other hand, has been able to take less from my mother's example, even though she too is gay. Private and conventional, she has quietly repudiated not only our mother's brittle harshness, but also the new gay world. She has chosen, rather, like my father, a long unglamorous war of attrition rather than a series of brilliant, usually unsuccessful skirmishes with the world.

Given such contradictory upbringings, is it a surprise that my sister and I have much less in common than our shared sexuality would suggest? Or that *brother* and *sister,* those staples of gay-liberationist vocabulary, should be as fraught with contradiction as with uplift? Are we brother and sister in any but the most biological sense? Are we—even when we're together—"home alone?"

## Tree Rot

My-sister-the-lesbian is standing by the fireplace at my parents' house. Dressed in trim, flat-stomached slacks from Banana Republic, hands in the pockets, she looks from my angle (the back) like a cute adolescent boy. With her, looking too into the muttering fire, is my father, handsome and youthful even at seventy-two, his eyes kind and crinkled.

They are talking about tree rot. The topic, to my amazement, seems to hold their interest—but then what is "interesting" has always had a different meaning for them than for me. Every so often, one of them softly laughs, shaking his or her head at the perversities of tree rot, its ingenuity in penetrating the hardiest elm or oak, the difficulties of preventing its spread. They are contented, I think; though in my sister's low laugh, her casual fireside pose, there is something uneasy, something studied. The logs in the fireplace crack and splinter in soothing counterpoint to their own soft laughs, their avoided gazes.

I am in an easy chair looking over the top of my copy of *Great Expectations,* a protective device designed to keep me safely silent for a few hours; it's an old ploy I remember from my horny, unexaminable adolescence. As I look at my sister and father, so seemingly relaxed and mirthful, the very embodiment of a Dickensian Christmas—and indeed we are surrounded by the happy detritus of Noel even as I look—I am aware with a pang that I have almost never stood next to a holiday fire and talked with my father about tree rot. Or perhaps I have—I think we did once talk while getting the rust spots out of my car—but the talk never seems to go so well as it does with them. I'm always smiling too hard, laughing too quickly, nodding as if I really *understood* rust. I feel a mixture of envy at their easy rapport and gratitude that my sister, not me, is taking the heat of endless slow conversation with my father.

Half listening to them, I turn to *Great Expectations* from time to time, idly wondering if like Pip I am an orphan in this friendly familiar house, whether my own expectations have been realized, whether they were in any way "great." Somewhere out of view, forever moving, restless and unhappy, is my mother; slamming cabinet doors, dropping spoons in the metal sink, foraging for a hunk of cold cheddar in the icebox. We will have our own kind of conversation later, when the fire is out and the house is as cold as the cheese, and Julie and Dad have gone to bed. Then to me, her best and only audience, she'll tell the old story of her bitterness.

*Brother* and *sister.* Like all the words denoting primary kinships, they are among the oldest words in our language, and recall yet older ones: Latin *frater* and *soror,* Sanskrit *bhratri* and *srastri. Brother* is related to an ancient word that means "to bear." *Sister,* like so many things feminine, is of more obscure origin. Skeat, a famous linguistic scholar, suggests that *srastri* means "consoler." "He who bears" and "She who consoles": how much family life is contained in those etymologies!

But bears what? Consoles for what? If it is the family name I am to bear, how I have stumbled! Gay from the start, I have never threatened to marry or have children: in that sense, the line ends with me. Or is it responsibility I bear? For what? Taking care of my parents when they get old? I can barely take care of myself. Bearing perhaps my parents' hopes for me, for the generation they produced. I suppose I've done that better—if you think being a teacher at a community college and a ballet pianist is hopeful. Sometimes I think that what sons are to bear is simply guilt, forced by Oedipus to excel the father, by exogamy to forsake the mother—and forced to accept punishment for both betrayals. In my case I've gone Oedipus and exogamy one better by opting out of heterosexuality altogether, which is of course an even more infernal betrayal.

And consolation? Do we still think of little sisters as consolers? Certainly that was the fashion even a generation ago, when unmarried sisters stayed home and took care of ailing parents, were kind friends, amiable busybodies. Even now I see that my sister consoles my parents in some mysterious way for the various failures of their lives (which include, I suspect, me). And this despite the fact that they know, or must guess, that my sister is herself such a failure. Perhaps this is why she cannot bring herself to come out to them: because they would then lose the last reassurance that they really did succeed with us. She cannot bear to turn from a consoler into a distresser.

But neither can she console *me*. Not for me the naturalization of my homosexuality by being "accepted" or "forgiven" by a sister, and thus reincorporated into the biological family. Gay pride being for me inseparable from gay arrogance, I have refused precisely the consolation she might willingly have offered. That leaves both of us strangely at loose ends not only with our parents, but with each other—and probably with ourselves too.

## The Ventilator Cap

There is, it seems, something called a *ventilator cap* that goes in, on, or under a chimney. My father and sister have strong opinions on it. As they sit and talk, both relax. She becomes less wary and more serious: a sort of pal. He, from being silent and withdrawn, becomes curious and talkative. Julie builds architectural models for a living, and she has brought some home. Turning them over in his large gentle hands, my father expresses the purest delight in them, exclaiming, "I'll be damned" and "Would you believe that?" My sister bathes in the praise, embarrassed but happy. I, too, find the models beautiful, but my praise is inexact and clumsy. And, to tell the truth, I don't know what to say after I've said it, so I go upstairs to my old room.

Lying now on the sexless twin bed of my youth and overhearing the incessant friendly rumble between my sister and father about ventilation, I feel building up within me, unventilated, the delicious poison of my early homosexuality. After a week of family togetherness, sex burns in me like solitude. It was under the covers of this very bed that I hid my first dirty magazine—hid it so unadroitly that my mother found it (by my unconscious wish) the next day; demanded to know where I'd gotten it, what it meant, what neighborhood boys I had "fooled around with." It was to this room a few hours later that my father was dispatched by my furious mother to talk to me about my sexual apostasy. Knocking politely, he sat in embarrassed silence while I waited to be either beaten or disowned. What he eventually said was: "So you must feel about boys the way I do about women"—a statement, not an accusation. He uttered it so calmly that for an awful moment I thought he was going to *tell* me how he "felt about women," or worse, ask *me* how I "felt about boys." A blow would have been preferable. It was from this bed of shame that I was sent, a month later, to Dr. Willmacher, a genial homophobe who told me he had nothing against homosexuality, it was just "a piss-poor way to lead your life." It was in this room that I hardened my heart against my mother, deciding in an adolescent passion that I regret but do not renounce, that if a gay life was indeed my fate, I would embrace it without her blessing or her curse. A year later, I had erected walls of intellectual accomplishment that I must have known would keep us forever wary and apart. With my ostentatiously useless skills of ancient Greek and Renaissance polyphony, I became a self-creation—and a recognizably gay man.

## Sniffs and Whispers

My sister has an odd habit, copied from my father, of conversational sniffing. It's not snooty or disdainful—the opposite of the Margaret Dumont character in Marx Brothers movies—but like what a man does when he taps his fingers and considers a reply. Like many unconscious habits it betrays not nervousness but relaxation, for it allows the body for once to go its own way, unsupervised. It's a companionable way for them to fill silence, to talk without words. At worst, with enemies, it's a form of defense, a polite impassable barrier.

When my mother talks, on the other hand, it is in the intense whispers of conspiracy, full of piercing glances, unfinished sentences, abrupt sarcastic laughs, and dark hand hatchet chops to indicate the utter futility of some specious hope. Her barriers are different from my father's. At dinner, she turns three-quarters to the table's edge (and to my father), angrily tastes a mouthful of her own delicious cooking, finds it "bad," then stares up into the darkest corner of the ceiling. My father, beaming like some golem of benignity, pretends not to notice the outlandish rudeness. He smiles, praises, sniffs, and taps his fingers. Every tap, every sniff is an insult to my mother, an incarnation of my father's immovable politeness and inertia.

When my sister and I are visiting, we occupy our childhood places at table, like heraldic animals holding up the shield. Unlike one another in many ways, we are at one in pretending that the dinner is a charming social occasion, and not Thyestes' feast. But our methods are different. I long ago decided that what this obviously dysfunctional family needed was simple adulthood: that is, relentlessly correct behavior, general topics for dinner-table discussion, a feigned indifference to the Fury at the end of the table. ("How *is* Alecto?") This approach has never worked, but I stick to it. My sister, also characteristically, has tried to make peace with the situation. She retreats into an unconvincing girlishness—my mother's vision of girlishness. She laughs, giggles, chats, and (like many former anorexics) smacks her lips over the deliciousness of each pea. This performance delights my father, mollifies my mother—and infuriates me, to whom it looks like a cowardly capitulation to the tyranny of family, heterosexuality, the past. Even as my own theatrical representation of "an adult" goes ignored, I reprehend my sister's imitation of a child. Since my own life of deviance has been made possible only by an attitude of defiance, I can't believe she can *stand* to duck the wave. Then I look at my nodding father, an unheroic, unbelieving Saint George smiling down the dragon, and I realize that it works, in a way. Like him, my sister has laid an enduring foundation for her life, and the family's. My proud towers, like my mother's, can easily be toppled.

Once a year Julie and I "get together for a drink" before going home for Christmas. This ought to be easy enough to do, since she lives in Dallas, I in Houston. Instead, it is always a half-comic half-pathetic one-upping match in which we get to play out our fantasies of innocence.

Last year, for instance, Julie came to my apartment in Houston, having had business in the city that day. Out of cowardice, I had invited my friend Tom, an even-keeled, not too screaming faggot. The hors d'oeuvres set out, we waited with a drink for Julie's arrival. She showed up promptly—why not get it over with?—looking, as she always does, beautiful and extremely put together. She took in my cluttered apartment, my expectant friend, my mask of good fellowship in a glance, became effusive. Chortling and exclaiming over some new decoration she hadn't seen the last time she was here (one year ago? two?), she finally accepted a drink and sat down. She seemed to have two postures: an ostentatiously casual sprawl—see how happy I am to be here!—and a tense gathered crouch, as if to take urgent flight. Like a weird cross between my father and mother, she made conversation as dutifully as my father, as manically as my mother. I responded "as an adult," laughing periodically but not excessively, treating her as if she were another friend who had happened to stop by, offering for discussion various plays she might have seen (she'd seen none of them) or political disasters she might inveigh against (she refused to inveigh). I got so absorbed in my role in fact that I spilled the wine not only into her glass but over her hand and most of my sofa.

The capstone of conviviality was our ritual present exchange. Unwrapping mine, I found—that most helpless of last-minute gifts—a set of four coasters, nicely tooled in leather. Unfortunately, I had bought her almost exactly the same thing. And it was with a sort of dismal fascination that I watched her unwrap the present ("What stunning paper!"), wonder aloud at what the dull gift might be, and laugh merrily at the coincidence of our both having picked coasters. We were both so embarrassed that we laughed more than usual—and quickly finished off the bottle of wine. Soon after, we parted with much evidence of sincerity, fervidly looking forward to seeing each other again in a few weeks "back home."

The whole event was so palpable a failure, from my first one-upping phone call to the last one-upped hug, that I couldn't help but laugh with Tom afterward. Indeed, later that night I realized that the whole thing was like an awful date: bright conversation, too much wine, forced smiles—then a late-night postmortem with Tom.

## Projects

Meanwhile, back in Christmas-land, my father and sister are playing cards. I am lying upstairs on my bed staring at the ceiling. Every now and then a fragment of conversation from below can be heard: they seem to be talking—but can this be possible?— about *glues.* They both build things, which of course fall apart and have to be fixed back up. Far from resenting this entropic tendency, Julie and Dad take it in stride, even enjoy it. The "things" are really less important to them than the activity of acquiring, making, or repairing them. I am exactly the opposite. The illnesses of my car, my stereo, my computer seem willful and malicious; as with my own illnesses, I suspect them of deep meaning.

When I was a child, there was an ongoing campaign on the part of my mother (always butcher than either me or my father) to make me more interested in the fixing part of life. I was often sent down to the cellar to watch my father work on a "project." These projects often involved an astonishing number of preliminary steps: measuring, sorting, finding that you didn't have the right materials, then driving to the hardware store for long, unfocused hours of aisle drifting and discussions about plaster or wood screws. To my incredulity, Dad undertook these tasks out of pleasure.

My presence was irrelevant to the enterprises' success. Indeed, my father seemed to have a different definition of success than either my mother or I. His was a surprisingly unmasculine athletic organization of time and energy: not the finishing but the doing of the task was what he liked. I, on the other hand, was imperiously masculine in desiring completion, brilliance of execution, and acclamation. Consequently, I was tormented by boredom and guilt at his patience and dreaminess, as well as resentful of my mother's obvious bad faith in making me do what would have bored her stiff. It was one of those half-comic, half-tragic dilemmas of childhood: how was I supposed to act, whom was I supposed to please? Even *my* histrionic abilities were taxed by the difficulty of appearing interested in the details of preparation and labor. I knew I was supposed to show interest, but even that was a tricky proposition. I couldn't be too enthusiastic, because that would have smacked not of sonship, but of daughterhood. (My father wouldn't have cared, but my mother . . .) Nor, obviously, could I display open boredom, which would have been interpreted as a sign of open rebellion, to be put down. As a result, I spent many rainy Saturday afternoons closeted with my father in his dank workroom, watching miserably as he soldered.

My sister, on the other hand, was an early and eager companion of these galling expeditions and patient projects. Sometimes with a craft beyond my years I would seduce her into helping me hold some wire while my father soldered it. Her eyes glowing, she would accept the challenge, eager to please both me and him—basking in the praise of having done it well, eager to be included. If I played my cards right, her willing steady hand would replace mine altogether, and I could slip away unnoticed to my room and its collection of Oz books, where I could hope to read away a few hours before my mother noticed that I wasn't where I ought to be, descended on me, and marched me back to my place at Dad's side. ("Could you not watch with him one hour?") When we got there, my sister would be calmly sitting at his side, sorting nails or reading the instruction manual aloud, word by slow word. They would not have noticed I was gone.

One Christmas when we were teenagers, my sister and I both got "good" presents: a drill press for her, and for me a recording of *Coppélia*.

My mother had firm plans to make a boy of me, and a girl of my sister. In both projects, she succeeded beyond her expectations, if also beyond her hope. But although my being gay has infuriated her, she must also realize that in so doing I have fulfilled her wish. When I was a teenager, my mother was forever telling me that the time would come when I would have to leave home; that it would not be "natural" or "healthy" if I didn't want to; that she herself was positively looking forward to such a flight from the nest as proof that I'd grown up. I'm not sure she believed this talk herself, nor that she guessed how far I was going to fly. I myself could hardly have known that my decision to put an abrupt distance between me and my mother would be echoed by a whole generation of gay men: the first in modern times to eschew the consolation of mothers, sisters, fag hags in favor of the difficult but alluring companionship of men.

What about my sister all this while? Younger by four years, she was a docile tomboyish kid, good-humored and eager to please where I was sardonic and vengeful. Like so many sexually anomalous people who are intolerant of the sexual anomalies of others, my mother insisted that Julie follow the girlish path she herself had seldom trod. Dresses, cotillions, boyfriends were all confidently predicted and demanded. Doing it not by ear—for like me she had no ear at all for heterosexuality—but by dogged persistence, Julie went along with these schemes, hopeful that she would eventually catch on. It is the most heartbreaking, and the bravest, thing I know about her.

But was my mother's effort a failure with her, any more than it was with me? Yes and no. If her success must be construed in strictly heterosexual terms, then of course Julie has failed to become a "girl." On the other hand, she has been, of all the members of our family, the one who has best caught on to "marriage" and fidelity. She and her girlfriend, Deborah, have been together now for nearly twenty years—half her life almost! Once I asked my sister whether they were still seeing each other (a gay man's routine question, expecting the answer "No"). She looked puzzled, then said: "Oh, Deborah—we'll *always* be together." It was a moment of chagrin for me. Certainly their relationship, private to the point of invisibility, has succeeded in ways my many infidelities have not, but also in ways my parents' rocky marriage has not. If she was being groomed to be "a wife," then my sister's life has in part proved my mother's success as a groomer.

Brothers and sisters share parents, whether actual or metaphorical. That is, they can be children of the same remembered past, or of the same imagined future; are joined by nostalgia or revolutionary hope. My sister and I are neither. Both now middle-aged, my sister and I find ourselves increasingly puzzled by, if increasingly reconciled to, each other. I don't know if this is the result of wisdom or mere weariness. I do know that our shared homosexuality has not made love between us any easier. For just as our biological parents were quite different, so too are our symbolic ones: the ideals we each have formed over the twenty-five years of our adulthood. We have not only loved different things in the past, in other words, but asked different things of the future.

My life, for instance, has been largely shaped by the desire to create myself as a gay man. Gay liberation is the revolution I somehow always wanted to join. Put like that, such an enlistment seems faintly ridiculous, if typical of a twenty-year-old; but I still can't persuade myself that it was a mistake. My gay life has been tremendously satisfying—paradoxically, because it has made me so hungry for new experience. I have liked the defiance of marching in parades, talking about sex and hunting for it. I have thrived on the peculiar passe-partout of gay social life, which permits a moderately attractive man to meet people of all ages and classes whom he would never have met otherwise, to hear about gay life in London, Hong Kong, and Des Moines. Nowadays, even death has been made a gay preserve.

Julie's homosexuality is far more invisible. If it has satisfied a hunger of hers, it is that for security, not adventure. She lives, for example, in a Dallas neighborhood with no strong profile of gayness to it, though with plenty of single men and women. The apartment she has lived in for eighteen years is cheap and unglamorous. Although she claims to like her proximity to stores and movie theaters, she never mentions going to them. Her apartment is a fortress, an unimpingeably private space that few have entered. (I myself have been there only a handful of times.) She has divided her life between work and something I guess you'd have to call "play," but which seems (like my father's "projects") a scrupulous kind of labor. She plays bridge once a month with three female friends, of whom my sister has seldom said a word, let alone that they are (like her) lesbians. She drinks moderately and has given up smoking. I don't think she goes to a gym, or indeed to any public gathering if she can help it.

My life, by contrast, has been virtually public. I live in the heart of Montrose, the original gay ghetto in Houston. After fifteen years, I cannot imagine living anywhere else. Within half a mile there are six gay bars, four neighborhood restaurants, and three shops selling Calvin Klein underwear on one aisle and greeting cards on the other. I not only like but need to see other gay men on the street or getting into their cars or doing laundry. When I go to the gay gym, my neighbors wave as I head off to the Stairmaster. My identity is created day to day by such recognitions ("Hi, Chris!"), which in themselves mean nothing but miraculously add up to a self, a life. The ghetto has kept me alive by keeping me hungry for such public experiences. My ex-anorexic sister perhaps has to watch hunger more warily, to satisfy it more moderately, to force herself to eat at all.

By not coming out, Julie maintains the fragile fiction of her normality, but pays the price of seeming unfulfilled, unhappy, lonely. Is she, though? I do not know what would make her happy, what *does* make her happy. Sometimes, I feel obscurely to blame for the strange sobriety of her life, as if experience were a golden road I had scared her away from. At other times, I am angry at her for giving in so easily, for choosing instead the dun-colored path of sacrifice and duty. Sometimes, I think she's chosen right.

My sister is in many ways like a gay person of an earlier generation: neither closeted nor out, stubborn and proud, deliberately alone. Indeed, her highest goal, my barest minimum, is freedom from interference. Is she cowardly or courageous? I have no idea, but I have a picture.

## Summer Vacation

In the summer, I become all mouth: moist air, spicy food, hot cock all enter me unopposed. Lying on a beach, I vacate my own premises, empty myself of myself, forget my own name. Water and fire are the only things I need: by the time I go home, I am wrung out, as weak and ecstatic as an infant.

Every September, when it's no longer so hot, Julie and her girlfriend go to Arizona. There, they stay in the same house they have rented for the past eight years, a small spare building five miles from town surrounded by desert and distant mountains. They eat dinner every night in the one restaurant, then go home, where they watch TV or sleep. The dry, clean air neutralizes all odors of the world. Towels dry in ten minutes, hair in fifteen. No one comes near them for two weeks.

Is this heaven or hell, or merely, profoundly, earth?

CANDACE

LEE

VAN AUKEN

# Survivors

I grew up in a rural New England mill town. When you say "rural New England," people think of postcards of church steeples pointing solemnly toward blue, blue skies that arch over vistas of colorful autumn leaves. They imagine those nice people who model clothes in the L. L. Bean catalogs. They remember those oil paintings reproduced in *Yankee* magazine, where quaint clapboard farmhouses provide the focal point for landscapes of rolling, snow-covered hills.

I guess you could see things like that, here and there, in the area in which I grew up, but that's not how I remember it. I think of a family down the road from us—a mother, grandmother, and seven children—living in a two-room shack that had originally been built as a chicken coop. If I close my eyes I can still see those children, especially the girls, blue lipped, shivering at the bus stop, their faded dresses starched as stiff as paper, and just as thin. I remember their landlord, the man who owned the slaughterhouse. Collecting for the Red Cross, I pedaled my bicycle out the dirt lane to his farm, and after I explained why I had come, he took a five-dollar bill out of his pocket and threw it in a puddle. "There," he said. "You want charity? You can crawl in the mud for it." Those are the kinds of things I remember: poverty and ignorance, cruelty and smug intolerance.

I was not a native of the area in which I was raised, which meant that I was relentlessly persecuted from a tender age. My brother and I did not look like our neighbors, nor did we act like them. We grew up in a house containing more books than did all the village libraries put together, and our parents insisted that we speak grammatically passable English. This did not make us popular.

I am not talking here about a little teasing. I am talking about years and years of being beaten up—at school, on the school bus, and at the bus stop. I am talking about being attacked by six or ten people, being shoved down flights of concrete stairs, of eyeglasses being smashed, of kicks and karate chops, of hate notes signed by an entire class. It was brutal. It was like going to war every day with no gun and no ammunition. My brother and I became very good street fighters. We did not follow precisely the Marquis of Queensberry rules, but we learned that good, swift moves—brutal, savage maneuvers—might dissuade at least some of our attackers from getting too close.

We were not the only ones who were so tormented. There were a handful of Jewish children, a tongue-tied girl, an obese brother and sister, an effeminate boy, and a couple of kids who smelled bad. We were all pariahs, for whatever reasons, and because of the intensity of the hatred we suffered, we were not able to band together. Any one of us, alone, was a potential victim, but any two of us, even my brother and I, were like a target flashing a large and brightly demarcated bull's-eye.

We, the hated, did not get to know each other well, although on occasion, over the years, we exchanged furtive, sympathetic glances. It's not that we were not interested in one another. I spent minutes at a time, when I could, gazing at these children, my brothers and sisters in oppression, trying to understand what was so terribly wrong with us, why we were treated so cruelly.

I paid special attention to the effeminate boy, because my deepest, darkest secret—the one thing about me that my attackers never seemed quite clever enough to discern—was that I, even though I was a girl, was somehow just like him.

In that town, a poor community crushed and corrupted by the inexorable contraction of its inadequate mill-town economy, having a cunt was the only real measure of femininity. Of course the girls, by eleven or twelve, would learn to pad their breasts, tease and lacquer their hair skyward, and lard a thick layer of makeup over their faces, but that was just an announcement of availability. Life was too harsh for daintiness to be required of women. They were generally a coarse, tough lot, and my flagrant butchness didn't stand out.

But I knew. I knew I was different, and I knew that if anyone else suspected it, the abuse I would suffer would make my former persecution pale in comparison.

In my town, homosexuality was the deadliest sin. Bestiality, wife and child beating, incest, and rape were tolerated with a raunchy good humor that might have made a respectable nonresident blanch or wretch.

For instance, we had a town rapist whose identity was known to everyone. If a woman was stupid enough to be waylaid by him, well, to the town folks it was obvious that she got what she deserved. When one of the farming families won more than their share of blue ribbons at the county fair, it was explained, with a nudge and a wink, as the predictable result of how satisfied that family's cows were, given how dutifully the sons made sure the herd was well fucked.

I attended school with more than one product of father-daughter and brother-sister unions, and a couple of my schoolmates became pregnant by their fathers. These were not secrets. They were not spoken of in whispers. Delicacy was a luxury the townspeople could not afford, and so I knew just how every peccadillo was regarded.

One could break bread with a rapist, a cow fucker, or a man who beat his wife and kids. These activities were the stuff of jokes, but nothing to get too upset about. Homosexuality, which I never heard referred to by such a polite or positive term, was a predilection that deserved beating, rape, castration, and/or murder, as far as my neighbors were concerned.

In so hostile an atmosphere, I took the safest course. I did not, quite, admit to myself what I was, and I certainly did not act on it, until I was safely out of high school and out of town. I didn't wait a moment longer than I had to (within four months of graduation I had managed to sleep with my first woman), but while growing up I hid it even from myself, although I spent hours crying about this unnamed propensity.

Still, in that effeminate boy I saw myself. He provided the only hope I had that perhaps I was not utterly alone in my predicament. His existence was like a whisper in the wind, a small voice telling me that maybe, just maybe, I was not the only one. In that dark world of loneliness and terror, he provided my only hope. God might goof once, I reasoned, but if God had made two of us in one small town, maybe it wasn't an error at all. Maybe we were like albinos or double-pawed cats, unusual but not unique. Maybe, somewhere out there, there were more of us.

My fantasy was that there was someone, somewhere out in the world beyond my hometown, who could love me. The effeminate boy made me hopeful of this. I worried that even then, as he and I were being harangued and beaten, she was somewhere else, suffering similar punishments for being like us.

At night when I said my prayers, after I had prayed for my family and our pets, I would say a special prayer for this faceless girl, praying that she would have the strength to survive her childhood, praying that we would both survive and someday find one another. I knew that I had to be strong and savvy. I knew that I could not expect her to keep her end of the bargain if I did not keep mine.

As hard as my existence was, as much as I longed to put a chain around my neck, as my brother had, and try to end my life, I knew that I had to survive, that I had to not fail her, wherever she was and whatever she was going through.

On the school bus I did what little I could for the sissy boy. I longed to leap forward, an avenging Amazon, to do battle with his attackers, but I also knew that would only endanger both of us. So I would holler, "Leave him alone!" from the back of the bus, occasionally getting a few others to join me. It wasn't much, but it was what I could do.

By the time we were finishing junior high school, the effeminate boy, whom I'll call Ralph, had made a friend. His companion was a greasy, rat-faced fellow who I thought was hardly good enough for him. Still, his friend was tougher than he was, and better with his fists, and I was glad that Ralph had someone in this world to care about him.

They were known, of course, as the Class Couple, and everywhere they went, jeers followed. Although we were in the same grade in school, I was never in their classes, and so I saw them only in the hallways or on the school bus. I never saw them looking anything other than miserable. Ralph developed an impressive case of teenage acne, and I remember that whenever the taunts and catcalls got to him, his sores and pimples would take on a bright, bruised red-purple hue. This provided his tormentors with a convenient gauge, a visible thermometer of the success of their efforts.

There was only once, throughout our entire time in high school, that I ever saw Ralph smile. It was one day when I had ridden my bicycle down to the village, when I was pedaling by his house. In the backyard, his mother was holding some kind of garden party, and as I zoomed by I glimpsed the circle of older women on lawn chairs, talking and sipping lemonade. There, seated comfortably and chatting amiably, was Ralph. I was shocked to see him looking so relaxed, so at ease. His acne wasn't raging. His audience was gazing at him with admiration. Was he the wit of their gathering? Was he offering an amusing bon mot?

I screeched my bicycle to a halt and circled around. I had to look again. Had my eyes betrayed me? No, there he was, having a nice time. I envied him that. That he had found someplace, anyplace, where he could feel at home.

At school, of course, nothing had changed. It was only as we approached graduation that the level of abuse declined somewhat. One by one, our classmates turned their attention to the future. Some became pregnant. Many of them struggled with alcohol or drug addictions. A few died in car accidents—or by their own hands. Others accepted responsibility for pregnancies they had caused, dropping out of school or making plans to get a job in one of the remaining local mills.

To my surprise, I was named valedictorian. To my even greater surprise, this caused a marked change in my social standing. The clearer it became that I was to be valedictorian, the nicer everyone was to me. By the time the decision was officially announced, I found that my worst enemies, my most vile tormentors, were toadying up to me as though I were prom queen.

My years of social isolation had not prepared me for what seemed like an undeserved surge in popularity. With the unadorned honesty of one who is somewhat socially retarded, I asked them, "Why are you being nice to me?" Laughing, they assured me that of course they had just been teasing me for all those years. A little kidding for the "Most Likely to Succeed," that's all.

One or two confessed to feelings of jealousy. After all, everyone had always known that I would "make it out of there," a goal that was apparently everyone's most cherished hopeless fantasy.

I was uncomfortable about this change in status. I worried that it was all an elaborate joke, a setup for some new and fiendish embarrassment. As the spring semester of my senior year progressed, I learned to be gracious toward my new admirers. The first thing I learned as an ex-pariah was hypocrisy: I didn't trust their kindness, but I was damned if I would let them know it.

In that town, where less than half of those who started high school ever finished, graduation was a grand event. More than a week was spent practicing for the final ceremony, and since, as valedictorian, I would march alone at the head of the procession, I was spared most of the rehearsals in which the seniors were grilled in the fine art of marching up the center aisle in boy-girl pairs. I ignored the proceedings as much as I could, taking full advantage of my elevated status.

It was only by accident that I wandered into the gym on the morning they were assigning partners for the graduation procession. I was lounging on the bleachers when a to-do broke out after Ralph was paired up with one of the more popular girls.

"I'm not marching next to that faggot!" the girl exclaimed, and in moments, all the girls were swearing that they would not walk next to either member of the Class Couple. The teacher who was making the assignments had lost control of the situation, and the boys were hooting and suggesting loudly that Ralph and his friend should have to march together.

There was a moment when it looked as though the teacher was actually going to give in to this proposal, and I, enraged, leaped to my feet and shouted that if they were all that small-minded then I would be proud, I would be honored, to march at the head of the procession with one of those gentlemen on each arm.

"You can't do that!" someone yelled, and then a hush fell over the crowd. I was seized by a kind of terror, realizing what I had said, terrified that they would all, as one, fall on me and tear me to pieces. I could not even swallow. I had been hated only yesterday; how could I imagine that my own position was secure enough to do something so foolish?

"Well, all right, I'll march with him," one girl said. And then another. And then another. "Yeah, they're graduating, too," someone added. In moments, the crisis had passed. Ralph and his friend would be accorded their public heterosexual pairings.

Relieved, shaking, I fled the auditorium. I was shocked when people sought me out to thank me for having shamed the class into doing the right thing. It seemed as though the only ones who had nothing to say to me were the Class Couple.

Later, I felt proud of what I did. I had spent years as a victim, and that was my first experience of being brave, of not groveling in shame, of not merely trying to get by. I knew how to be an outcast, but I had no experience in being a leader, a role model. For me it provided an astounding insight into how people act—and react.

I would like to tell you that I went off to college and immediately turned into an out, proud gay leader, but that isn't what happened. I became a "practicing homosexual," but for years I lived in the closet. While I had learned to stick up for other people, I was only slowly learning to stick up for myself.

It was almost five years later, just months before my high school reunion, that I began the painful process of coming out into the community. It was only the week before I returned home for the gathering that I said, for the first time, out loud, that I was gay.

I was ambivalent about going to the reunion. My brother's wife was a member of my class, and she wanted someone to go with her. My mother said that I had turned out well and that I should not be shy about seeing my old classmates. Reluctantly, I agreed to go. I had wanted to wear blue jeans to demonstrate my disdain for the whole thing, but after a huge fight with my mother, I went out and bought an evening gown to make it up to her.

I did look good. I still knew how to do drag back then, and compared with my classmates, who were mostly broken down by the mills, their marriages, their frantic childbearing, I looked fine.

Survival is the best revenge, I'd heard, and I went back to demonstrate that I had survived. The few people I wanted to see weren't there, and my brother got roaring drunk and nasty. Otherwise, it was as anti-climactic and meaningless as most such gatherings can be.

My only surprise was running into Ralph, whose acne had long since abated and who had grown into a tall, handsome man. We greeted each other like long-lost friends, which I guess we were, although we exchanged more words that evening than we had in our entire childhoods.

We complimented each other on our appearances, and we noted, unkindly, the condition of each of our old tormentors. At one point later in the evening, after my brother and his wife had wandered off, he leaned across the table to thank me for what I had done, how I had stood up for him and his friend.

After all that time, his eyes were moist as he spoke of it. I, who no longer thought of my impulsive act as all that remarkable, was touched. How was his friend? I asked, to cover my embarrassment.

"Oh, I don't see him anymore," Ralph blurted. I nodded and we were silent for a moment.

What I wanted to say was that he, too, had helped me—just by being who he was, by being there—but I didn't have the nerve. If I had, perhaps we would have had a different conversation. Instead, we shared what we could. We talked about our lives in veiled terms. We shared without sharing.

When we ran out of things to say, we took to the dance floor. We were a striking couple, and we danced, chastely, divinely, enjoying ourselves immensely. It was a real celebration. Somehow, we had managed to survive our childhoods. Separately and together, we had survived.

# My Lover
# & My Wife

The worst moment of my life arrives on a sunny Monday morning in
New York. We're at JFK airport, Carmela and I. It's 7 A.M., and we've already drunk enough expensive lousy coffee to raise the *Titanic*. People
are hustling and bustling all around us, but I only have eyes for Carlos,
my beautiful Carlos, his broad shoulders rippling under his football jersey, his black hair slicked back like a matador.

"Well, *querida hermana*," he smiles, embracing Carmela, "I'll see
you in six months. Don't forget, in bad times, happy face."

"Give a big hug to *Mamacita* for me," she says.

And then Carlos turns to me.

"I'm going to miss you . . . a lot," he says. He makes me promise
not to cry and to take care of his sister. In my mind, I give him a phan-
tom kiss that this public place prevents. Then I quietly watch him walk
away, following his gold-colored shorts far into the drab crowd of
brown baggage and gray suits until he finally disappears through the
airport security gate. Only when he is gone do I begin to whimper.

"Ay, don't be a Mary Magdalen," Carmela says. "Let's go watch the
planes take off!"

Somehow the thought of watching Carlos's airplane take off into
the sky lifts my spirits. But the sight lines to the runway are blocked by
other planes, so we turn back into a shadowy corridor and watch
Carlos's flight number on a monitor as it jiggers up the screen and then
departs. For a moment I stand gaping blankly at the space on the screen
where his flight number has been. Carmela's voice snaps me out of my
stupor.

"*Ya*," she says. That's Spanish for "enough already." She puts her big denim-clad arm around my shoulders and leads me to the parking lot. A half hour later we're home, and I can still feel Carlos's presence in every room, hear him laughing and singing and telling jokes. When we reach the bedroom, Carmela and I climb into bed together for the first time in our two years of marriage.

And so I lost a lover and gained a wife.

To understand the impact of this statement you need to know a little about our family, which began the way so many traditional families do—with two people falling in love.

In this case—and I hesitate to make an issue of it because the difference seems insignificant to me now—the two people were men.

Carlos and I met at a college party on March 3, 1987. We celebrate that date as our anniversary, although in fact it's just the first night of our gay honeymoon. Our relationship started in earnest a few weeks later when he moved into my house and we began to slowly merge our lives together.

I assume that the way in which we became a couple was no different from the way in which other people—gay and straight— partner domestically. At first it was mechanical things—sharing a beer, a dresser drawer, and a credit card, and, of course, the same bed at the end of the day.

Then I found that I couldn't fall asleep at night at all without Carlos. Without Carlos, the bed felt sheer and barren, as if I might fall off without him there to hang on to. His muscular warmth and fragrance transported me to sweet dreams.

And finally I couldn't imagine *any* part of my life without Carlos. As weeks turned into months he instilled in me the discipline that I lacked; he coaxed, coerced, and sometimes even dragged me into a healthier lifestyle, putting me on an exercise regimen, getting me to keep my room clean and to dress in nice clothing instead of my usual torn blue jeans and faded T-shirt. It was as if he'd cast a lovely spell that made me—for want of a better term—a better person.

And best of all I remember the nights, especially those when nothing much at all happened. Those nights when we just climbed into bed together and made small talk. "How was your day?" "Did you hear about so-and-so?" "Did I ever tell you about the time . . . ?" After years of wondering if I'd ever have a family of my own, he became all the family I wanted.

Of course it wasn't all smooth as quicksilver. We had our fights, those conversations with flying plates that give gay life its spice. Ours usually came about through the clash of language and culture that results when a gringo and a Latino fall in love. I remember one blowout especially because it was the first time we disclosed our true feelings for one another. We were leaving the house to go to the gym one winter night when I reached into my pocket to make sure I had my key; our door locks automatically from the inside.

"Hold it," I said.

"Hold what?" he said, slamming the door.

"I left my key in the house," I said. "We'll have to use yours." But Carlos never takes his house key when he goes out; he was raised in a small village where he never had to do anything as paranoid as lock his front door.

So there we were, locked out of the car and the house, in the cold, with an almost burglar-proof domicile before us. But Carlos always knows what to do. In the downstairs bathroom there was a window facing the backyard. He broke one of the panes with a shovel, reached in, undid the latch, and climbed through.

Once the crisis was resolved the fight began—over whose fault it was that we had to break in. We underlined our main points with screams and slamming doors. I demanded he pay for the damage, so he pitched a piece of bric-a-brac through another windowpane. The glass spattered across the kitchen table and onto the floor. Meticulously, he patched up both holes and cleaned up the shards, then went upstairs and locked himself in our bedroom. I followed him and talked to him through the door as the muffled sound of his puppy-dog sobs melted my heart. I wound up taking the blame for both broken windows and the locked door, and when he finally let me into the bedroom, I stroked his brow until the tears subsided. Then I asked him why he got so carried away when we had a disagreement.

"Unfortunately, I *do* love you," was what he said.

I returned the sentiment that night, but how desperately I loved him back became abundantly clear when he had to leave for a week to visit his big sister in L.A. Without him guiding my life for seven days, I returned to my evil ways. Dirty and clean clothes piled up indiscriminately in our room; I neglected to shave, ate pizza every meal. I must have looked like a caveman when I picked him up at the airport a week later and, as we were returning home, confessed I would give anything not to go through such a lonely ordeal again.

"Really?" he said, his brown eyes lighting up.

Our favorite Gloria Estefan tape had been playing, so I sang, "Anything for you."

"Would you marry my sister?" he asked.

The spirit of the moment called for a hasty answer.

More than a moment's hesitation would have signaled indecision, and Carlos hates people to be wishy-washy.

My mind tuned out the Estefan tape and the noise of the traffic.

In the split second before my mouth formed its answer, two thoughts crossed my mind at something like the speed of light:

The vision of myself in a white wedding dress. Though on the outside I'm strictly a straight-appearing gay, my most intimate fantasy involves dressing up as a bride on my wedding day. I was being asked to marry a woman, so as far as I knew my *Modern Bride* fantasy was out the window.

The other thought was the fear of the concept of "submissive woman." I dreaded the treacly, tradition-bound, subservient person I imagined his bourgeois Latin American sister to be.

But I was willing to leap over these quibbles to make him happy.

"Sure," I said.

Suddenly the car was full of Gloria: "*Get on your feet! Get up, and make it happen.*"

"Baby, you are the best thing in my life," Carlos squealed, throwing his arms around me. There would be no fight today; rather, in a rare display of public affection, Carlos kissed me on the lips right there in the car. "It won't change anything between us, you know, because she's a lesbian," Carlos enthused. "But this way she'll finally get her green card, and it's sure going to make my mother and father happy. Soon as we get home I'm going to call them with the good news. After all the shit they've been through, they're going to be *so* happy."

●━●━●

Like most brilliant ideas that I approve of immediately, marrying Carmela turned out to be a bit more complicated an affair than I'd imagined at first.

Before I tell you about the complications, however, I should first say what appealed to me about the idea. First of all, as I mentioned earlier, I have always romanticized weddings. I love baby's-breath blossoms and prime rib and glitzy catering halls and all the other delicious things that go along with wedding days. By virtue of our being a gay couple, Carlos and I had been denied these pleasures. (Furthermore, he was dead set against any faux marriage that I dreamed of concocting for the two of us.) Now I was to have the kind of ceremony that both my sister and brother had enjoyed. As fringe benefits, Carlos would be my best man and my brother-in-law, and without a doubt he would stick around for the honeymoon after Carmela had gone to sleep by herself in the downstairs bedroom.

On the other hand, marrying Carmela meant that after years of groundwork I'd have to shoo myself back into the closet for at least a while. I had already told my brother and sister-in-law that I was gay. An ex-girlfriend had saved me additional effort by ratting me out with my sister and her husband. Meanwhile, I had been dropping hints the size of dirigibles on my mom and dad to soften them up for the eventual "Parents, guess what: I'm gay!" But because ours was to be an INS marriage, a union solely for the purpose of getting the Immigration and Naturalization Service to issue Carmela a green card, Carmela and I had to pretend to be a storybook couple. For the notoriously nosy and persnickety INS, it's not enough for you to like someone enough to go through the inconvenience of marrying them so they can get a green card. The INS has to believe that you love, live with, and, by implication, have sexual relations with your spouse. There was no telling how far they would go to sniff out fraud; there were rumors of after-midnight raids on visa applicants' homes to see if they were sleeping in the same bed. I was sure they would withdraw their offer of a green card and start thinking deportation for Carmela and criminal charges for me if they decided we were really a masquerading fag and dyke.

And fooling the INS was going to take some doing; Carlos had really understated the case when he told me Carmela was a lesbian. I'd expected a little inobtrusive lipstick lady from south of the border; Carmela turned out to be the butch from ten thousand fathoms. She thrived on denim and flannel, and liked her hair short, slicked back, and topped with a baseball cap, preferably brim back. With a beer in hand, she could sit on the front porch for hours, catcalling at any pretty woman who happened to walk by:

"*Ay, mamacita, que rico! Que barbaridad!*"

When I asked her why she behaved so much like a construction worker, she replied: "Because I'm a *real macho man!*"

My worst fears came damn near to being realized on the Sunday afternoon that Carmela submitted to the parental interview. My parents are traditional people, and they tend to think in terms such as *normal* and *ladylike*. In a foolish attempt to condescend to their old-fashioned ideas, I explained my parents' attitudes to Carmela. Carmela said she understood and would dress accordingly. To me, this meant a dress and makeup, but to her it meant a pantsuit and a fedora instead of jeans and a baseball cap. Regardless, things went well until after dinner, when Carmela raided the fridge, popped open a beer, and hiked her pants up to scratch her knees. I thought my mom was going to keel over at the sight of those hairy legs, but luckily, both Mom and Dad were so thunderstruck over the fact that I was actually getting married that they adored Carmela from the top of her Batman haircut to the soles of her high-top sneakers.

Of course the INS was a different story, and as time went by, I wondered aloud to Carlos how I was ever going to pass her off as my adoring wife.

"Don't worry," Carlos told me. "I can take care of my sister." The key, he explained, was to get her to stop drinking. Once she laid off the beer, some of the swagger left Carmela's walk, and her voice came up an octave. She didn't turn into a Madonna wanna-be, but at least she wasn't strutting around like Sylvester Stallone. To help bring out what Carlos saw as her submerged femininity, we took Carmela shopping for a wedding dress. At the department store, Carmela gazed wistfully at the black tuxedos, but she finally settled on a white brocade gown.

A few weeks before the wedding, I started to get cold feet. What if the justice of the peace—this was to be a civil ceremony—figured out we were queer and turned us over to the cops or something? What if Immigration *did* send agents to roust us out of bed at two in the morning? Carlos and I sleep in the nude, and Carmela has her own female bedmates.

And notwithstanding their unconditional acceptance of Carmela, my parents were shaping up as another kind of headache. Knowing we needed photos to present to the INS investigator, but wanting this ordeal to be as painless as possible, I consented to a small wedding reception at my parents' house for "immediate family only." I imagined beer, cold cuts, and a crumb cake with a plastic bride and groom. But in the excitement of the moment, and without first consulting me, the folks sent out invitations to the entire extended family—aunts and uncles, cousins, second cousins. Lying to my nuclear family was one thing; I had done that before. But lying to the whole clan? I wasn't sure I was up to such a grand subterfuge.

The night before the wedding, I asked Carmela if she felt nervous too.

"*Me pela las nalgas,*" she said, which, roughly translated, means, "It's no skin off my ass."

"Doesn't it bother you that we're not *really* going to be man and wife?"

To which Carmela replied: "Let's get this straight, and I mean it with all my heart: no matter what happens, in sickness or health, for richer or poorer, you will always be *my wife.*"

The ceremony went off without a hitch, largely because the magistrate was an old pro; he'd obviously seen it all before. He didn't bat an eye when, at the words "You may now kiss the bride," Carmela pressed her lips together tight enough to crush a diamond to prevent my tongue from even accidentally sliding into her mouth. I had my own near mishap when I turned to Carlos and zoomed in for a very un-best-man-like kiss on the lips, caught myself in midair, and veered off for a backslapping hug.

Afterward, all my friends and relatives were at the reception—my favorite aunt and uncle, the girl who used to live next door and her husband, my best friend from college and his wife—and yet in the midst of all these church-and-state–blessed couples I didn't feel shame at all; hell, I felt heroic. Laws, tradition, even our own upbringings conspired against us. But what strengths we had! Our union, at first arranged for immigration purposes, turned out to be a fount of love and friendship, strong enough to withstand even death and separation.

But celebrating was all that was on our minds as we returned home that night and changed back into queer drag. And despite Carlos's promise, things did change. Gaining a wife was the easy part of the transition. The hard part was becoming a family of three—with all the sacrifice that entails.

From that moment on we went everywhere as a threesome—the market, the movies, church on Sunday. Though Carmela was on the wagon and I get allergic smelling smoke, for Carlos's sake we hung out in the local gay bar. For Carmela's sake, Carlos and I suffered through endless innings of women's softball, and they both humored me when I just "had" to see the latest big-screen epic.

So we didn't have a lot of money! I could count on Carlos and Carmela for constant companionship, advice, a foot rub, an Alka-Seltzer when I was hung over, a dirty joke when I was depressed; we cleaned the house and cooked—anything from liver and onions to obscure but delectable Latin American dishes—as a family. And when the day was done, as a family we climbed into the big bed upstairs and watched Mexican soap operas and comedies until I fell asleep. Even with the television blaring, I snoozed peacefully knowing that they were beside me.

It was on such a night that the terrible call came through; even now, the thought of it makes me shiver: we had been guffawing at a Mexican comedy, and Carmela was laughing even as she picked up the receiver; Carlos and I had stayed with the program, but our attention was suddenly grabbed by Carmela's wrenching sobs.

"Whatsamatter?" Carlos shouted.

Tears were coming down her cheeks as she groaned, "*Se murio mi Papacito.*"

Then all I can remember is Carlos shouting, "*Mentira! Mentira!*" into the phone and me grabbing him and holding him as if I'd never let him go.

The next few days were a montage of long-distance phone calls, crying sessions, and hurried packing, followed by a chase to the airport. Someone had to go down to Central America for at least six months to comfort Mamacita and help her pick up the pieces of her life after Papacito's death. And because Carmela and I had to stay behind and play the love game, Carlos had to be the one to go.

It was a few months after Carlos departed that Carmela asked a question that really brought home the meaning of family for me. After Carlos left, we had begun sleeping together in the big bed—not only because I needed her to fill the lonely space on Carlos's side of the bed, but also so we'd feel close enough for verisimilitude in our INS interview. Sleeping in the same bed became such a habit that even after the INS interview—which we passed, thank God—we continued the practice, albeit chastely, as always. (We didn't need a bundling board; the fact that we slept in different worlds was enough of an impediment.) Consequently, we became quite the old married couple when we settled in at bedtime, she watching the evening news, I burying my nose in a book by the time the clock struck midnight. One night, as soon as the news was over, Carmela got out of bed, turned the television off, and asked me:

"Jimmy. Do you love me?"

"Yup," I said, hardly hearing her, so absorbed was I in my book.

But then she pushed the book down, looked into my eyes, and tried again:

"I don't mean do you love me because I'm Carlos's sister. I mean do you love *me*, Carmela, the person who's here in bed with you. Do you love *me* for myself?"

Here was something I hadn't considered at all. In all the late craziness, I hadn't thought one iota about Carmela's feelings. She was

Carlos's sister, and everything I'd done—lying to my parents, lying to the magistrate, lying to uncles and aunts and cousins—had been for Carlos.

But now, looking into Carmela's eyes, I realized that was wrong. Butch exterior and all, there was something more taking place inside Carmela's hard head. And a light went on inside my own hard head: Could it be that, in her gruff way, she was letting me know that *she loved me* and wanted to know if the feeling was mutual?

But how can a gay man love a lesbian? I can count the ways I couldn't love her: as a lover, as a sister or brother, as the mother of my children. She made an excellent friend, but I hadn't known her long enough to say if the friendship had developed into love on its own. And yet, as I examined my feelings, it really hit me: I did *love* Carmela, even if I couldn't say why. And then the why hit me too: because she was family; not blood, and yet thicker than blood. All the travails we'd been through in becoming a family had forged a new me, and, for better or worse, she was a part of that new me. Besides, she was just too irresistible not to love; funny, loyal, she had kept me sane all through the long months of Carlos's absence, and, with Carmela at my side, I felt that I could indeed go on until he came home to us.

And so I found the words: "Yes, Carmela, I *do* love *you*." The way her brown eyes lit up was all the affirmation I needed. It wasn't the best day of my life—that would come more than a year later when Carlos finally did find his way back home—but for all the warm family love it engendered in the meantime, it sure came in a solid second.

JOYCE
ZONANA

# A New Covenant

*Excuse me, Mirah, but does it seem quite
right to you that the women should sit
behind rails in a gallery apart?*

*George Eliot,* Daniel Deronda

Until my brother Victor's birth I was, as far as I can remember, bliss-
fully unconscious of gender. Although I was nearly five, I don't recall
any distinct awareness that I was a girl, or that being a girl made any
particular difference in how I was treated or how I could (or should)
behave. Victor's birth changed everything. Suddenly I knew that I was
one kind of child, that he was another, and that our places were by no
means the same. He was at the center; I was at the margin. His part was
to speak; mine was to be silent. He was to be cared for, while I, along
with my mother, was to do the caring. It wasn't a change I accepted
gracefully.

Perhaps I would have been equally disturbed by the birth of a
baby sister; it may well be that any new presence in our household
would have upset its precarious balance. Or it may be that five is inevitably the end of the age of innocence. Yet I am convinced that
Victor's maleness—not his infant being or my normal maturation—
was the real source of the changes I began to experience. For it was not
simply that I had to make room for a new arrival, nor that I had to give
up my connection with my mother. It was that I had to give up my

room entirely, to lose ground, to be displaced, to move from a well-lit center to a dim and fuzzy margin.

My designation as girl and my displacement were made palpable on the occasion of Victor's *bris,* less than two weeks after his birth. I was on the railed balcony of a crowded room somewhere in Brooklyn, beside many richly dressed, perfumed women; below us, at the center of the room, were a howling infant and a group of old men in dark clothes. I had a special dress for the day: pure white eyelet, starched and crisp, ruffled and flared. Someone—my mother?—had made it for me, and it was well designed and beautifully stitched, but it felt odd, uncomfortable, not quite mine. My female relatives admired me, making much of the dress, even as they told me how proud I should be of my little brother.

He was the one in the middle, screaming. I was on the edge, transfixed, unable to see or understand, yet wanting to join him, to leave the stiff, heavily made-up women with whom I was confined, to comfort him or share his pain. But we were separated by more than a railing; it was clear that this was an event for little boys, and that Victor's pain was a necessary part of the proceedings, part of why I was supposed to be proud of him. Instead of pride, I felt a mixture of empathy and envy, acutely aware that I could never be in his place. I didn't quite know what boys were, but I knew I wasn't one. I was the girl, the one in the dress, the silent witness. He was the one (I now know) with the penis, having it mutilated to symbolize his inclusion in the covenant community.

Today, nearly forty years later, Victor's still the one with the penis, I'm still the one in the dress. But we're also both the ones who are queer, the ones with busy lives, the ones who love to talk with and see each other. Victor's a gay journalist and activist; I'm a lesbian English professor and writer; to an extent that continually surprises us (though we're also always finding little remnants), we've left behind the roles assigned to us in the drama of the *bris,* having found places to stand where we are each equally at the center or at the margin, each alternately speaking or silent, each simultaneously nurturing and nurtured.

For the longest time, though, the stage set by gender prevented our meaningful contact. At my birth, the rabbi in Cairo had consoled my mother with the Arabic expression *maalesh.* The term is hard to translate; the best we've been able to come up with is "It's not the worst thing that can happen; better luck next time." That after two miscarriages my mother was ecstatic to have a child, and thrilled to have a girl (she named me Joyce in token of that emotion), was irrelevant to the rabbi. He knew: my mother and I might have our female bonding, our women's culture, our cooking and cleaning and sewing together, but we did not own our world; having a girl-child was not what Jewish motherhood was about. It was Victor, after all, who got the name meaning "triumphant." For it was his birth that satisfied the rabbi—and everyone else in the family. My mother had done her job, producing a boy to carry on her husband's name.

The Egyptian Jewish culture in which our parents grew up—and within which they raised us—was (and still is) intensely patriarchal. It is the men who count within this culture, the women who nurture and make the male lives possible. The hierarchy is made most obvious in Jewish ritual, the celebrations that center Jewish life. In our family, Passover was always the most special occasion: the Haggadah enjoins all Jews to act as if they had just come out of Egypt, and we were always proud to note that, in fact, we actually *had*. I loved the preparation of the Passover meal and the enactment of the seder, but I was always troubled by my marginal place within the ceremony. My father and the other assembled male elders would read prayers in Hebrew; the boys, including Victor, would ask the "four questions" and repeat in Arabic the words of a ritual unique to Sephardic Jews. My official part was simply, for one moment, to stand silently in another room, holding the tray that carried the ritual foods. This was the role for the eldest unmarried girl—a place I still occupy in the family, and which allows me, year after year, to hold the sacred tray. It's not a bad role; I'd just like to take on some of the speaking parts as well.

Gender division rules Egyptian Jewish culture, yet if our parents had been left to themselves, it is doubtful whether this division would have so strongly influenced the lives of my brother and me. Each of our parents was—and still is—a mild transgressor of norms. Felix, our father, is a gentle, unassuming man, given to depression and beset by a series of illnesses: skin cancer, a herniated disc, Parkinson's disease. Our mother, Nelly, is a strong, no-nonsense woman who believes that you can heal yourself by thinking positively. Felix likes good clothes and has a streak of the dandy in him; he has never in his life picked up a hammer or played a sport. Nelly has never worn makeup, hates shopping for clothes, and thinks I'm crazy to spend money on haircuts; she's the one who does all the house repairs and is an enthusiastic swimmer. Clearly these are people who more than made it possible for Victor and me to imagine alternatives to conventional gender roles. But imagining—or even living—alternative gender identities is not the same as escaping the structure of male power and privilege that governs Sephardic families. For all that Victor, Nelly, Felix, and I might have tried, we could not escape that structure—especially when an enforcer arrived in the form of my paternal grandmother.

I was seven and Victor two when "Nona," Felix's mother, came to live with us. As the third female in the household, she might have tipped the scale, moving the family toward a semblance of matriarchy, or at the very least female domination. Instead, what she brought with her from Cairo was a profound commitment to the power of the fathers, embodied in worship for the infant child who carried her dead husband's name. If the *bris* and the seder were ceremonial emblems of my marginality, my grandmother's arrival made it a literal, inescapably day-to-day experience. For her, baby Victor was the reason for all our being. Unlike my mother, she had no sentimental attachments to me: the perpetuation of patriarchy depended on Victor's survival, not mine.

I had to whisper while he slept, to be careful not to hurt him when we played, to save the best pieces of food for him when we ate. All of this might have been ordinary consideration for a small infant. Yet my grandmother made it plain that while her son was the head of the household, Victor, her *grand* son, was its center. The focus of our activity in the home was *his* survival and well-being. We, the women of the house, were charged with nurturing the grand son until he could assume his true role, as the head of a new household, a father continuing the work of his fathers—having sons of his own.

Who wouldn't have been furious? Perhaps a girl who was sure of the rewards of being a girl. But they weren't apparent to me, although, in an absurd irony, I had to mime "I Enjoy Being a Girl" in an elementary school performance. Instead of internalizing the message of the song, I consumed myself in fantasies of solitary escape: I would be a hobo, a gypsy, a sailor, a circus performer, a witch, a writer in a garret—anything to be free of the limits of a family that made me nothing but a servant or, as Virginia Woolf puts it, a mirror for men. While my mother and grandmother piled on the household chores—I would dust, wax, vacuum, make the beds, iron my father's handkerchiefs, and help with the shopping and cooking—I retreated further and further into fantasies of freedom and revenge.

After a while I didn't even notice that my brother was there, except to be jealous when he went to Hebrew school to learn the secrets of that language only men shared. I had begged my parents to send me too, but they claimed that learning Hebrew was unnecessary for girls, and, besides, they only had enough money to send one child. Later, at Victor's bar mitzvah—his "graduation" from Hebrew school during my first year of college—I would have the nervous breakdown that only barely expressed the pain I felt about my exclusion from so much that seemed to matter.

Evidently, Jewish rituals did not sit well with me. They were designed for boys or men. As a girl in a not quite Orthodox family, the only ceremony I could look forward to was a wedding. Since this seemed to be only a seal and enforcer of powerlessness (another white dress), I was having none of it. I was determined to live alone, to have a career, to be self-sufficient. And also, desperately, at the same time, I wanted to be a boy, so that I could have access to the kinds of love, attention, care, and inclusion I imagined Victor received.

My wish for the status and freedom of a boy was not exactly a wish to cross-dress, or to engage in what in America is typically male behavior. I wasn't butch, that is. But I did—within the Orthodox Egyptian Jewish context—take on male attributes: I studied hard, I was serious, I refused to concern myself with trivial female things like cooking and cleaning and sewing, clothes, makeup, and appearance, and I tried to place myself at the center, all the while feeling myself condemned to insignificance.

Going off to college had been a singularly charged struggle. During my senior year of high school, I had waged a deliberate, desperate campaign to obtain my parents' permission to attend an out-of-town school. I was graduating at the top of my class, and my teachers were encouraging me to aim high. But my parents were firm in their belief that going away to school was neither necessary nor prudent—for a girl. We had a perfectly good public school system in New York—the City University; I could go there if I wished. Girls did not need a fancy education, and they were at sexual risk if not at home. Money was also an issue. There wasn't much of it, and I understood that what there was would be put to better use for Victor's education.

I stormed and raged, calling on my teachers to help me to persuade my parents. Ultimately, they grudgingly relented, and I, filled with terror, guilt, and an utter lack of the social skills necessary for survival, went off to Radcliffe, the most forbidding school I could find. Somehow I made it through the first semester. But when I came home in March for Victor's bar mitzvah, all my defenses fell. My parents had organized a large party for Victor, and all the relatives had gathered for the occasion. There he was—in the center again—being publicly welcomed into the adult male Jewish community, while I found myself skulking along the edge.

I fell off. I dropped out of school and moved back home, doing what my parents had always wanted: I registered at Brooklyn College. But at the same time, I started having sex with a boy I had known in high school, acting out my rebellion against the expectations that I be a virgin awaiting marriage to an Egyptian Jewish man. The next year I moved out of my parents' house, taking a small, lovely apartment near Brooklyn College. My action provoked a family crisis: fainting fits by my grandmother, mourning by my parents, long lectures from an aunt who warned me that no decent man would want me now. Where was Victor? He now tells me that at the time he accepted the official family version of his sister: the disturbed, promiscuous girl-child gone astray. He, on the other hand, would be impassively normal, progressing through high school and on to college without missing a step. He chose to go to Dartmouth, a school that struck me as impossibly privileged and male. My resentment and desperation increased.

Yet it was while Victor was at Dartmouth that we began the slow rapprochement that brought us to friendship. I had spent some happy times in New England, and I decided that having a brother in New Hampshire provided a convenient, cheap way to get out of New York. I would hitch rides across Massachusetts and Vermont, reveling in the dangerous adventure of it. I was also—not incidentally—interested in redeeming my relationship to the Ivy League. Perhaps through Victor, I thought, I could be accepted, finding a place in this bastion of male privilege. It was 1970, and Dartmouth had just made the decision to slowly begin the process of admitting women. The issue was still being hotly debated on campus, and alumni and students were reluctant to see things change. It was the perfect backdrop for my fight.

On one of my visits to Hanover I had sex with Victor's best friend. Matthew was captain of the hockey team and a dance student, a "sensitive" heterosexual man who nevertheless made a practice of conquering women. We had spent the day hiking in the White Mountains, the boys showing me some of their special places, including a beautiful rock slab where we basked in the autumn sun. For a moment, it seemed like I could be one of them; and in the evening, I told Victor I was going to spend the night with Matthew. I went to his room, listened to *Tommy* on his elaborate sound system, and moved toward something like passion. In the morning, I slunk away, sure that it had meant nothing to Matthew, clear that I was simply another conquest.

I was aware even then that sleeping with Matthew was a desperate bid for acceptance and inclusion within their male community. Although, strictly speaking, it was an act of heterosexual intercourse, it grew out of my profound desire to be male, to be loved not as a girl, but as one of the boys. So, even when I was sleeping with men, I was being queer. And I was sleeping with men to prove that I was not queer. For I had by this time begun to experience what I had to face as my attraction to women; each time the feelings or behaviors surfaced I managed to shove them back down, but nevertheless, I knew quite clearly that they were present. I never spoke about any of this to Victor, and he never spoke to me about his own closeted but already self-acknowledged homosexuality to me. Yet surely we each must have had glimmers of the other's queerness. And part of our growing friendship must have been our developing awareness of our similarity, in this dimension if in no other.

In the summer of 1976, one year after Victor's graduation, I was working in a children's camp in Vermont. Victor came to see me for my birthday, a sort of inversion of my earlier New England trips. After dinner at a lakefront restaurant, Victor asked me when I was planning to have children. I said I didn't know, that I would when I could, how about him. And he said, quite calmly, that he was certain that he would never have children. I asked how he could be so sure. He said he was sure. Not that he didn't want to, but that he wouldn't. But he hoped that I would, so that someone would perpetuate our family genes, which, we both agreed, were pretty neat. Well, I said, I couldn't promise anything. If he wanted to perpetuate the Zonana clan, he would have to do it himself.

For months afterward, this conversation reverberated through my consciousness. I talked endlessly with friends about what it might mean. Was Victor trying to tell me something? Was he gay? I couldn't be sure, though certainly I couldn't remember his having had any girl-friends—though I probably would not have noticed if he had. Some-thing about Victor's manner, his certainty that he would never have children—the fact that he was speaking of neither chance nor choice as he negated the patriarchal imperative—convinced me. He must be gay, and he must want me to know. But I had no idea how to go further, how to make the discussion more explicit. Another year went by in silence.

This time it was Victor's birthday, and I was visiting him in Philadelphia, where I was about to move to begin graduate school. I had decided that the moment had arrived, I would have to speak with him candidly. So, sometime after a lavish dinner at the Astral Plane, I told him I had a question to ask him. He said, "Why do you want to ask it? Is it for you, is it for our parents, or is it for me?" I told him that it was for him and for me, for our friendship. And he said, "Yes, I'm gay." And I told him that I could certainly "deal with it," that I had myself had homoerotic attractions, and that I simply wanted us to be honest with one another. So we stayed up all night talking, and drove before dawn to the Jersey shore. We slept briefly on the beach in Wildwood be-fore the sun was too high, then spent the day wandering through Cape May, talking about what it was like to be gay—for him.

Victor now reminds me—not without some hurt and anger—that I didn't come out to him then, that I failed to express my full solidarity with him. He's right. It was easier to be accepting of Victor than of my-self. It was easier to let him risk speaking about his sexuality than to re-veal my own. I try to explain my failure by saying I didn't really know *for sure* that I was gay (and I didn't)—but the excuse sounds lame. At the time, my own sexuality felt like nothing more than a wound, and I feared uncovering it before my brother. It was easier to be the big sister, caring for the little boy. I knew it was my place to love him. I didn't know if he could love me.

Yet though Victor never knew it at the time, his open gayness helped to validate mine. Still, it would be another seven years before I fully chose to enter into a relationship with a woman. In my last attempt at heterosexuality, I had a two-year affair with a gay man, a friend who had once said to me, "Well, if Victor is as cute as you are, I'd love to meet him." In loving Jimmy, I had achieved what must have been my goal all along. I could at last *be* Victor—and be loved by someone like him. The experience finally allowed me to be—and love—myself.

When, in 1983, I entered into a committed relationship with a woman, I immediately told Victor. And the closeness that had begun during the Astral Plane conversation deepened. We now took to spending many days together, often on beaches, in California, New York, New Jersey, and Florida. We would walk and talk—about the family, about our careers and lovers, about being gay. But despite the genuine pleasure we took in one another's company, there remained some serious obstacles to full intimacy. For all my efforts to undo it, the old family structure still prevailed: he was the center and I was the margin; he was the one to be cared for, I was the nurturer; he was the one who spoke, I was the one who listened; he was still the boy and I was still the girl.

Being gay together didn't change the gender system that had us in its grip. Neither of us was entirely responsible for keeping this system in place, although we each had a part. I know that I was unable to think of myself as anything *but* marginal; and I suspect that until recently Victor did not consciously question his own centrality. When, in 1985, Victor learned that his lover was HIV-positive, he cried in my arms, and I urged him to travel with his partner to France to seek treatment. When Victor decided that he wanted to write about AIDS for the *Los Angeles Times,* I encouraged him to speak to his editor and make clear his commitment. When he moved recently to New York and was contemplating buying an apartment, I spoke with him on the phone every night for two weeks as he debated the merits of the Upper West Side, Greenwich Village, Lower East Side, brownstone or elevator building. Through it all, I was the good older sister—sincere in my love and engagement, yet also wondering why Victor never bothered to ask me how I was.

The frustrations I felt with Victor were a microcosm of the frustrations I experienced in the larger world; for all my accomplishments, I ultimately felt voiceless, silenced, and weak—a witness, not an actor, in a world ruled by men. So I turned, in my personal and professional life, to a separatist celebration of matriarchy. I did research on women writers and goddesses, I taught women's studies, I consciously celebrated the cooking and cleaning and sewing I had once rejected. I planted and cultivated an herb garden; I studies the phases of the moon; I conducted a women's seder; I learned to love my mother. But all the while, I longed for a balanced relationship with my brother; I chafed when he ignored me, and I remained angry at what I saw to be his unselfconscious enjoyment of his power.

My frustration came to a head two years ago during a phone call. I was in the midst of confused deliberations about whether to stay with or leave the woman with whom I had moved to New Orleans after three years together in Oklahoma. Although we had been together for four years, she seemed unable to make the permanent commitment I longed for. Alone in a new city, I needed to talk to someone—and I tried to talk with Victor, only to find that, after offering some conventional advice, he cavalierly and abruptly changed the subject—to himself. I was in terrible pain to begin with; when we got off the phone I was furious. And in an uncharacteristic fit of directed anger, I wrote a brief but forceful note—no editing—stating my experience of being ignored, and expressing my dismay that he seemed not to love me despite my constant support for him. I mailed it immediately, thoroughly disgusted with my brother, and wanting to shock and shake him.

To my astonishment, it worked. Two days later, Victor called. I could hear concern in his voice as he apologized for having hurt me. I recited my list of all the times he had ignored me, of his failure to become genuinely interested in my life. He insisted, "But I do love you, Joyce. You are important to me," while I complained that if he did, he never showed it. He went through a list of qualities for which he admired me and asked what he could do. I told him to listen—to me. I told him that I needed him now. He said, "I'll listen, Joyce. You just need to talk to me." And then, tentatively but clearly, we began a new kind of conversation, one in which I claimed the power to speak and in which he made a commitment to listen. Sometimes I have to remind Victor that he needs to be quiet for a moment, that *I* need to talk; but often, quite often, he freely asks about me.

These days, our conversation goes on almost daily. Victor's in Washington now, and I'm still in New Orleans, but we are, finally, in touch. We talk about everything: sex, love, work, money, family, clothes, food, exercise, therapy, politics, lesbian and gay culture. Victor's the one who told me about this anthology and who listened enthusiastically to this essay as it took shape; I'm the one who listens to his plans, offering feedback and support. When I recently needed surgery to remove an ovarian tumor, Victor immediately flew to New Orleans and spent three nights beside me in the hospital. On the last night, in pain and terrified because I was bleeding vaginally, I kept him awake with my crying. We didn't know whether I was hemorrhaging or whether it was my period, brought on by the surgery. A few days later, when Victor was back home, I was amazed to hear him ask if I was still bleeding; when I said no, he was relieved. "So it was your period," he said, calmly.

Nothing's perfect. There remain ways in which we irritate one another. Victor at times seems to me more self-centered than necessary, and I continue to be jealous of his greater economic freedom. We don't fully agree on how much we should comply with our parents' wishes to spend time with us; paradoxically, I'm the one who's more willing to go to Florida for Jewish holidays. But, more and more, we're now collaborators, partners in the project of empowering ourselves and others. No longer boy and girl, we're brother and sister, gay and lesbian, joined in a new relationship of reciprocity and love. Having removed the railing that divided us at the *bris,* we're engaged in destroying those railings wherever we find them. All it takes is a sister's scream. And a brother who's willing to listen.

PHILIP

GAMBONE

# The Kid I Already Have

## On Considering Fathering a Child with a Lesbian

It is early on a chilly spring morning, and I am waiting in the kitchen of my fellow teacher, Diane, while she gets her kids ready for the day. In a few minutes, Diane and I will be leaving for an important teachers' meeting at a private secondary school outside of Boston, but right now all her attention is on making sure that the children—four-year-old Wendy and one-year-old Andrew—finish their breakfast.

"Mmmm, isn't that *good*, Andrew?" she asks, spooning him another mouthful of oatmeal. Half of it drools out of his mouth, barely missing Diane's immaculate white linen jacket. "Oopsie," she says, and wipes Andrew's lips with a napkin. Despite the unflappable competency in her voice, I can hear a quiet note of frenzy. We are already running fifteen minutes late.

"That's a good girl," Diane tells Wendy, who is showing her mother an empty juice glass. "Time to put your jacket on now," she coaxes.

Then, as Diane hurries about the kitchen, stacking dishes in the sink, finding Wendy's backpack, giving final instructions to the Jamaican nanny who is taking care of Andrew this morning, I wander over to the refrigerator to look at the things Diane and her husband have posted on the door: artwork Wendy has done in nursery school, scribblings by Andrew, articles about childhood illnesses, emergency phone numbers for the baby-sitter.

It couldn't be more different from my own refrigerator door, a gay-themed collage assembled by my housemate Bruce, whose tastes run to magazine cutouts of drag queens, movie idols, and muscled Adonises modeling boxer shorts, bikinis, and biceps.

What, I wonder, would Diane think about *our* refrigerator door? Maybe she'd try to appreciate it as an example of "multicultural diversity," a major theme at the progressive school where we both teach. But I also suspect that Bruce's creation would leave my colleague feeling somewhat alienated and estranged, perhaps even irrelevant. I know that's how I'm feeling right now, standing here, confronting this refrigerator of theirs that's like a billboard advertising heterosexual family values. I think about all this: a life in which children figure so prominently, in which children seem such an unquestioned part of the fabric of day-to-day events. I think about it all and realize once again that I have made the right decision. Having kids of my own is just not for me.

●●●

Until quite recently, there really was no decision to be made. Having children was not an issue I had to deliberate about. Like most other gay men I know, I never assumed that fatherhood was an option for me. In fact, it seemed as if the only possibilities for being a gay man with children were: (1) getting married before you discovered your homosexuality; and (2) choosing to remain in the closet, pretending to be straight. It was as if, in the same way that many house cleaners regard washing windows, having children was something out-of-the-closet gay men just "didn't do."

But then I began to encounter gay men who were coming out of another closet—gay men who were publicly declaring that they indeed did want the opportunity to have a child, to raise a family, to be a father, and to do so outside of the context of a traditional marriage. At first, I wrote these men off. I thought they were deluding themselves, indulging in fantasies or nostalgia for their own lost childhoods. I assumed they had no idea of the responsibilities and compromises having children entails. "Get yourself a teddy bear" would have been my advice to them. But the more I listened to these men, the more I realized they were expressing carefully considered, adult convictions. At least some of them were. And I came to see—at least in an intellectual way—that being a gay man did not necessarily preclude me from having children, if that was what I really wanted.

About a year ago, a chain of circumstances left me considering a serious invitation to father a child with a lesbian with whom I'd become acquainted. For the first time in my life I had to take a personal, deliberate, and unequivocal stand on my being a father. In fact, in the space of a few months, two such proposals, from two lesbians—one a single woman, one in a coupled relationship—came my way. No longer was the issue of my having children something I could ignore or speculate about as a mere intellectual exercise. I had to make a decision that would have real and profound consequences for my life and the lives of others. Suddenly, all the old stories I had been telling myself as to why I, a gay man, didn't or couldn't have children were up for revision.

How I got to this juncture, and what I learned in the process of making the decision I did, is a story that begins the summer I lived with a lesbian mom and her two kids.

It was my boyfriend, Bill, who first came up with the idea of sharing a summer house with Ellen. Bill had first met her the previous summer when he and I were renting a house in Provincetown with three other gay men. I'd invited Ellen, who teaches at the same school that I do, to come down with her girlfriend for a weekend visit. Bill had taken to her immediately (they share a similar kind of chaotic domestic style) and even more so to Ellen's two daughters, then aged three and five. And so, when one of our original housemates decided he was not going to return for a second P-Town summer, Bill jumped at the chance to ask Ellen and the girls to become part of the new household. To our surprise, she said yes.

To say the least, our second summer in Provincetown was considerably different from the first, partially because we were already familiar with the house and the town, and partially because a lot more girls now became part of our scene. (One of the first things I learned, living with Ellen, was that it is okay, in some contexts, to refer to gay women as "girls.")

Of the four gay men in the house that second summer—Bill and I, my friend Bruce, and his boyfriend, Tom—none of us had interacted with so many lesbians before. The previous summer, we had, naively, prided ourselves on rubbing shoulders with lots of lesbians. They were, after all, everywhere: waitresses, shopkeepers, gallery owners, realtors, photographers, writers, bookstore entrepreneurs. Lesbians had been our neighbors, our casual acquaintances, hosts at a big fund-raiser for a gay and lesbian legal fund. They ran the gym, owned one of the cabarets in town, sold us stamps at the post office. We had danced next to them at after–tea dance at the Pied Piper and argued with them about why we couldn't get the 10 percent "lesbian discount" at one of the women's shops. But none of these interactions had prepared us for the experience of actually sharing a house with lesbians. A house and a bathroom.

The house we rented had one small bathroom with a door that didn't lock. No problem when it was just five gay men sharing the place, but the week we moved in with Ellen, we decided to make a two-sided sign: Boy Inside/Girl Inside. I remember decorating the sign with cut-out photographs from gay and lesbian magazines—beefcake boys on the boy's side, cheesecake girls on the girl's side; nothing pornographic, just a little erotic bathroom decoration inspired by Bruce's refrigerator decorating. At least that was the intention. But Ellen and her new girl-friend soon pointed out that the photographs of boys were far more sexy than the photographs of the girls. So much for a gay man deciding what would appeal to the lesbians in the house.

Ellen's daughters were an unavoidable presence in the household. They could be playful and silly one moment, cranky and demanding the next. While Ellen took on most of the responsibility for keeping them entertained, we four men did our share, too. There were trips to the playground, the beach, the store, and lots of around-the-house ac-tivities: coloring, cooking, storytelling.

Of the four of us, it was Bill who spent the most time with them. One of his favorite activities with them was playing dress-up. In fact, Bill was in dresses more often than the girls, who preferred bathing suits or going naked. By the middle of the summer, the girls had taken to calling him Aunt Trudy.

One day the five-year-old turned to him and, with troubled cu-riosity, asked, "Aunt Trudy, are you a girl?"

"No," Bill told her.

"So, are you a boy?"

"No."

"Well, what *are* you?" she insisted.

Carefully, as if he were imparting a very important piece of cultural information, Bill told her, "I'm a drag queen!"

We all wondered if Ellen's daughter would bring back stories of Aunt Trudy and drag queens when she returned to school in September.

In the evenings after dinner, we often spent long hours around the kitchen talking. The conversation frequently turned to gay topics, sometimes serious (gay politics, gay books), sometimes frivolous (guys we'd seen downtown)—though that distinction, between "serious" and "frivolous," has always seemed a pretty arbitrary one to me. When it's life you're talking about—this life that for so long could not be talked about at all—*every* observation seems important and necessary. But apparently, Ellen thought otherwise.

"All you boys ever talk about is sex," she teasingly chastised us one night.

We all looked at her as if she's just said, "All you boys ever breathe is air."

"So let's talk about something else," I suggested. "Let's talk about the situation in Russia."

"Yeah," Bruce concurred. "Let's talk about Russia. I hear there are lots of hot guys in Russia."

As in the previous year, we had many visitors that second summer. But this time, many more of them were lesbians, friends of Ellen and her girlfriend. Some would stay with us, becoming part of the household for the weekend; others were more casual visitors, dropping by for coffee or dinner.

Sylvie was a frequent visitor. She was one of Ellen's best friends and a kind of aunt to the two girls. I loved watching Sylvie play with them, taking them to the beach, decorating their faces with body paint, settling arguments and soothing hurt feelings. Nearing forty, Sylvie had decided that she wanted to have a child of her own. After considering her options, she had enrolled in an artificial-insemination—or, as I was to learn, *alternative*-insemination—program at the gay and lesbian health clinic in Boston. It had been over a year since she had first tried, but, after many monthly trips to the clinic, she still hadn't become pregnant.

One weekend, the subject of my perhaps helping to father her child came up. It was an offhand suggestion—I can't even remember which one of us first brought it up—really just a casual broaching of the subject. But, as we began to turn it over, the idea seemed to have a compelling logic to it: Sylvie's visits to the clinic were expensive, it wasn't working anyway, and Sylvie liked me (which meant, I suppose, that she also liked the genes I might contribute to this future son or daughter of hers). I was flattered, intrigued, and scared. I told her I'd be open to considering it.

Over the course of that weekend, Sylvie and I kept lightheartedly making references to "our" kid. It was a way, I now see, of my trying on the idea—the *drag,* if you will—of fatherhood. Indeed, in the same way that doing drag for the first time made me feel alternately self-conscious, awkward, giddy, politically incorrect, radically queer, and utterly masculine, letting me experience myself in a whole new way, so too did testing out the idea of fatherhood with Sylvie.

As Sylvie and I continued to talk, a memory came to me, of a time many years before when I had last seriously considered fatherhood.

*It is a summer afternoon and I am in my early twenties. Sprawled on my bed with the windows open and the curtains billowing in a slight breeze, I am reading Shakespeare's sonnets. It is not the first time I have read them—in high school I'd read a few, in college quite a few more—but this time I am making my way through a complete edition because I love the poetry and because I remember being told that many of them were addressed to a man ("a Renaissance convention," I was told), and because I find myself, at age twenty, attracted to a man. I come to Sonnet 3, in which the poet tells his friend he should sire a child: "Look in thy glass and tell the face thou viewest / Now is the time that face should form another." I do not read any further. I am in tears, uncontrollably weeping because as sure as I know I am a homosexual, I know that this means I will not have children.*

I grieved long and deeply that golden afternoon, a cathartic grief that left me, I'd thought, purged of any desire to have children. But now here was Sylvie, giving me the chance to reconsider, to rekindle that desire if I so wished.

Sylvie was about to take off for a summer trip to Europe (among other things, she was going to attend a clown conference in Copenhagen), so we left it that I'd "think about" the idea and when she returned we'd "talk more."

The summer went on. I began noticing Ellen's kids more, and found myself imagining having kids that age myself someday. I paid attention to their tantrums and happy times, their needs and quirks, to the way Ellen disciplined them, or failed to. I paid attention to all the anxieties I felt about children: their health, their safety, their fears. I watched Ellen, too—watched how tired she could get sometimes, how little time she seemed to have for herself. As July turned into August, I watched how we four men in the household were getting more tanned and more trim—the result of long days at the beach and a daily half-mile swim at the pool. By contrast, Ellen was pale and often bedraggled.

Toward the end of August, Sylvie returned from Europe with the happy news that her final visit to the clinic, just before she'd embarked for Europe, had done the job. She was pregnant and expecting in February. I was, to say the least, relieved.

A month before the baby was due, Bill and I received an invitation to a baby shower at the home of two of Sylvie's friends, a lesbian couple who had been two of our visitors in Provincetown during the summer.

It was the first baby shower I'd ever attended—an alternative baby shower, to be sure (almost all the guests were lesbians), but one that nevertheless made some concessions to the traditional rituals of such an event. There was plenty of food and drink, and a time set aside for Sylvie to open her presents and pass them around for the rest of us to admire. Our hosts, Gillian and Kim, helped her make a bonnet from the scraps of wrapping paper and ribbon, apparently another shower tradition. They had also set up a guess-the-date raffle board. Each guest paid a dollar to pick a day in February when he or she thought that Benjamin (ultrasound had revealed the baby's gender) would be born.

Never having attended a baby shower before, I was hard-pressed to know what to give as a gift. Gillian and Kim had sent out a list of suggestions—a share in a baby stroller, a month's worth of diaper service (these were ecologically correct lesbians who frowned on disposable diapers), a promise to baby-sit once a month. But none of these suggestions inspired me. Finally, I decided on a homemade gift. From the hundreds of photographs I had taken that second summer in Provincetown, I selected shots of Sylvie and Ellen and other people—including the four guys—people who I assumed would eventually figure in Benjamin's life. With these, I assembled a collage of his "family," at least that part of his family that I knew.

"Dear Ben," I wrote on a card that accompanied the mounted photo, "This is a collage of Mommie's life the summer before you were born. When you're older and look at these pictures, I hope you'll recognize lots of familiar faces. It was a very happy summer—because *you* were on the way, and because we all loved, and continue to love, your mother very much. And because we lived in a very special place called 'P-Town' that you will, undoubtedly, visit some day. When you do, may the sun and the sea and the sand smile on you as they did on us, may the spirit of the place bless you, and may love always surround you. Welcome to the world!" I signed it, "Uncle Phil."

Toward the end of the party, I found myself in the kitchen talking to Gillian and Kim. They were happy with the success of the party, and our conversation flowed easily: stories about our respective relationships, our jobs, our neighborhoods, our mutual affection for Sylvie. We talked about parenthood, too, about Sylvie's brave decision to become a single mother, about the commitment she had shown during all those months of discouraging news, about our feelings toward becoming parents. I probably mentioned to them that Sylvie and I had casually tossed around the idea of my donating sperm. Most likely I said something about how relieved I was when Sylvie did get pregnant, leaving me free of having to make that decision.

What did Kim and Gillian really hear me saying? In my offhand, jocular way, did I unwittingly hint to them that I was still open to the idea?

All I know is that a month later, Gillian called me to say: (a) Sylvie had delivered; (b) mother and baby were doing fine; (c) I'd won the baby lottery by guessing the correct delivery date, February 12; and (d) would I be interested in talking to them about the possibility of . . . ?

"I'd be the carrier," Gillian explained. "Kim and I are looking for someone not only to be the sperm donor, but someone who would also be open to part-time fathering."

I asked what *part-time* meant.

"Oh, it's open for discussion," Gillian said. "Something like once a week. Not fifty-fifty by any means. We haven't worked out all the details. What's really important is that there's a good fit." She giggled. "We want the child to have a relationship with the father."

Here it was again. For the second time in less than a year, I was being offered the opportunity to make a child with a lesbian. Only this time, the idea seemed more real, the proposal more direct. There were so many questions racing through my mind that I didn't even know where to start asking. Questions that under other circumstances would have been too personal or delicate now became crucial.

"Would part of the relationship be financial?" I asked.

"Not necessarily," Gillian said. Open-ended qualifiers—"not necessarily," "part-time," "not fifty-fifty by any means"—seemed to characterize both ends of our conversation.

"What about the issue of a son versus a daughter?"

"It's not an issue," Gillian said, "though honestly we'd prefer a daughter."

As we continued talking, I again felt those giddy, scared feelings I'd had when Sylvie broached the subject the summer before. The more questions I asked, the more I realized I was giving the impression of being seriously interested. That made me feel even more giddy and scared.

We ended our conversation by my promising—once again—to "think about it" and call them back.

As the weeks went by, my questions mounted up:

Is Gillian the woman I would choose to have a child with? Are Gillian and Kim the couple I would choose to have a child with? Would Gillian and Kim and I make the best trio of parents for a child? Did we know each other well enough?

What would it be like to be a father? What would it *feel* like? How would it alter my life? What kinds of freedom would I be giving up?

What would happen to my gay life? Even if I didn't have primary responsibility for raising the child, would I want to take on *any* responsibility?

Conversely, what if I wanted to be more involved, more than "not fifty-fifty by any means"?

Ten years down the road, how would I feel about having a child? (I admit I kept imagining it to be a boy.)

And how would this alter my relationship with Bill? He adores children and, after our summer with Ellen's daughters, had himself fantasized about our having a kid. But what about in this context? Would this solidify our relationship or come between it? Who would he be? A kind of second father? An uncle? It seemed as if there weren't even an adequate vocabulary to talk about all this.

Then there was my mother. Would my mother, whose four sons have yet to give her a single grandchild, and probably won't—a source of considerable sadness for her—be thrilled or aghast?

In the weeks that followed, I talked to a lot of people, throwing out the idea and outlining all the pros and cons as I saw them.

Everyone I talked to said it sounded as if I'd already made up my mind.

"I suppose so," I agreed, "but there's a tiny part of me that is still intrigued by the idea, that doesn't quite want to close off this option."

Why? my friends asked.

Why indeed? Is there a male equivalent to the biological clock, something deep inside that says to a man, "Now is the time that face should form another"? Or perhaps I liked the notion of helping to create a different model of family, a family based on intentional and brave choices, a family where the rules would be up to us to decide on. Or perhaps I felt too keenly Ellen's charge that "all you boys ever talk about is sex." Perhaps I wanted to convince myself that my life could be a lot more "serious" than Ellen seemed to think it was. Whatever the reasons, I couldn't quite let go of the idea. I couldn't quite say no.

Spring came and I still hadn't gotten back to Gillian and Kim. But now I had another excuse. With some other teachers from my school, I was about to leave on a two-week trip to Europe, chaperoning a group of fourteen-year-old Latin students around England to see Roman antiquities. (What would happen to trips to Europe if I had a kid? And what would it be like having a fourteen-year-old of my own?) The business of packing and attending to last-minute details had left me with "no time" to get in touch with Gillian and Kim. At the airport, just as we were about to leave, I dropped them a card explaining that I would call them when I got back.

One evening, about a week into the trip, while the other chaperons and I were enjoying a quiet meal in an English pub, I brought up the subject of Gillian and Kim's proposal. The other three chaperons, to whom I was out as a gay man, listened attentively to my story.

"What have you decided?" one of them asked.

I gave my standard answer—that I hadn't completely made up my mind, but I was leaning strongly against it. To my amazement, one of my colleagues said he hoped so because he thought it was unwise for Gillian, Kim, and me to even consider having children.

Stunned, I tried to follow his line of reasoning, which went something like this: As there were already far too many people in the world, it was really unwise—indeed, morally wrong—for the three of us to plan on bringing another child into the world.

But, I argued, as far as I knew they were planning on having only one child, they had the financial means to do so, and they were the kind of people who would raise their son or daughter to be a loving, caring, morally responsible citizen of the world. Just like, I emphasized, what we teachers were trying to do with the kids we worked with every day at school.

Then came the real shocker. My colleague said that because Kim and Gillian had "chosen" to be lesbians, they had "given up" their natural right to be mothers. In fact, he argued, it was "unnatural" for them to become mothers.

It was hard for me not to hear this as outright homophobia. I wanted to believe that I was missing some subtle, if flawed, line of reasoning. My colleague was a well-educated, liberal, open-minded person. How could he of all people be spouting such obvious prejudice? The rest of our conversation was tense and strained. There were times when I felt like announcing I'd made up my mind and that Gillian and I would indeed, damn it, have a kid. But I realized, of course, that I needed a better reason than spite to bring a child into the world.

◉◉◉

Soon after I returned from Europe, I called Gillian and Kim. I still hadn't fully made up my mind, but I figured talking to them might help me gain some perspective.

"That's OK," Gillian told me. "We've decided to take our time with this. I've recently gotten in touch with my ambivalence. We figure we need another eight months to a year to make a decision. Kim and I have talked about how we don't know how we'll feel about this child in ten years. There are a lot of unknowns."

Gillian mentioned the financial commitment of having a child and their qualms about whether that would mean a change in their style of living.

"We found ourselves already thinking about college costs," she told me. "It was a little overwhelming."

She mentioned, too, their fears about whether the agreement they would draw up with the father would hold up in a court of law.

"We've heard rumors about men who sue for custody. Those kinds of stories are pretty scary."

I felt myself wanting to assure her that I was not one of those kinds of men.

"So where are *you* in all this?" she asked.

I hesitated. "Well, yeah, I guess I've gotten in touch with my ambivalence, too," I said. "I guess I'm ninety-five percent saying no, and five percent giving you the option of asking me again later on."

◉◉◉

A year has gone by, and Gillian and Kim have not called. I think we all knew it would be that way. In that year, I've had more time to think about becoming a father. I am now as old as my parents were when they had their fourth and final son, my brother Richard. It seems too late for me to begin having a family, but I know this is just another excuse. The truth is—and here I bring it out of the closet—I don't *want* to have a child, not fifty-fifty, not once a week, not any way. And when I ask myself why, I keep coming up with this: because I love my life the way it is.

Bill, who would still like us to have a kid, says I play things too safe, that I've made my life too tidy, too organized, too comfortable.

"That's *part* of what my life is all about," I tell him, "and it works for me. That's how I get all my writing done." In fact, I can't imagine where I'd find the time to help raise a child and still pursue my career as a writer. How could I possibly do justice to both?

Sometimes I still think that I could, and should, get "bigger" than all these objections. Why couldn't I be both: a father and a writer? a father and a gay man? a father and a summer denizen of Provincetown? Presumably, other men manage it. Why couldn't I? Why not shake up my idea of who I am? Maybe, I tell myself, that's what living with a lesbian mom for a summer was really all about: shaking up my precious little notion of what it means to be gay.

I think of all these things, and still I know that I won't do it: I will not choose to become a father. And for the first time in my life, I see how clearly it has always been a matter of choice, and how much freedom, terrifying freedom, there is in making that choice. Yes, I bring it out of the closet: my life is about other things—writing, teaching, gay activism, putting together a "family" of friends, of dear comrades, as Walt Whitman once said. (And wasn't his choice, over a century ago, not to be a married man and a father, a brave one!)

What kept me from making the choice sooner was some idea I had that embracing parental responsibilities would give my life more legitimacy, that there was something deficient about my life as I was living it that needed fixing. In having to confront the actual possibility of bringing a son or daughter into the world, I saw how ingrained that idea was in my thinking, and how mistaken it was.

When I was first considering whether to write this essay, I wondered if I really had a story to tell. After all, the outcome—Gillian and Kim's and my decision not to have a child together—seemed so anticlimactic, seemed hardly an "outcome" at all. But then I realized that this kind of thinking only played into that notion that to have a child (or a grand-child, Mom) is "worthy" of a story, while not having children (or grand-children) is just a sad, maybe even embarrassing, footnote to some other story—is, in fact, no story at all. Indeed, for years we gay men and lesbians were told that we had no stories whatsoever that were worth telling, no lives worth writing about. And what damage that kind of re-pressive silence has done.

So I proclaim it: there *is* a story here, maybe several stories. Call it "The Bachelor's Story" or "The Man Who Chose Not to Be a Father." Call it "An Uncle to Benjamin Is Good Enough for Me." Or: "I Like My Refrigerator Door Just the Way It Is."

My relationships with Ellen and her girls, with Sylvie, with Gillian and Kim, even with Diane and her husband and their kids, have taught me a lot about myself. I've learned more clearly what some of my values are. I've seen, too, some of the fears and anxieties, prejudices and stereo-types I still harbor. I've learned where I'm willing to grow, and where I seem to have drawn a line and said, "Not beyond here." At my school, we tell the kids that learning never stops, that it's a lifetime activity. I believe that, and I've come to see that in learning, in being open to new discoveries about the world and about ourselves, we ultimately nurture the wondering child within us.

Perhaps the name of this story is "The Kid I Already Have."

# Neighbors

One thing about my old Longwood Avenue neighbor David Kidman: you didn't have to explain. Like the day I had my ears pierced and he asked if it hurt. "Not much more than when you've been wearing clip-ons for too long," I said, then paused to search for an analogy a man could understand. But "I know exactly," he grinned, and told me about this Halloween party he'd gone to in priest drag and spike heels and a pair of dangly earrings. "Plus there were a few other times..." He trailed off with a chuckle.

I was very lucky with the Longwood Avenue house. Found it through a lesbian real-estate agent, bought it from a gay man who was moving out of Los Angeles. I grew up in New York City, and I've known gay men most of my life, since before my own coming out, but on Longwood for the first time I was surrounded by them: in the duplex to the south lived David, who rented to Tom and Glynn; Ken lived in the duplex to the north.

David grew up on a farm in the Midwest, became a Lutheran minister, married, then fell in love with Ed, another Lutheran minister. He never looked back. He told wonderful stories of his adventures before and after coming out, which is probably why I wasn't completely surprised around six-thirty one morning to hear barking commands: "One-two, one-two! Faster! Faster! Come on!" I thought, You can't have sex that fast. But then, what did I know about gay men? After all, we'd heard all those wild stories from David. (I've always marveled that we are often as ignorant as heterosexuals in our knowledge of each other.) This wasn't the first time I'd heard any of our neighbors in the throes of passion—or whatever this was, because it sounded too grueling to be passionate. Our houses were separated by only the width of a driveway, and on warm nights—scent of mock orange to swoon over, windows open to catch a breeze—sound carried. No one ever mentioned it overtly the next day, of course, but there were times, at parties, or just schmoozing over our morning papers at the bottom of the driveway, that hints were dropped, jokes were made. Of course, like with David's early-morning trysts, you didn't want to say anything, wanted to wait until the information was offered.

So I waited, politely, until David felt ready to share his new relationship with us. One morning, after a few more barking episodes, I saw a burly guy bouncing down David's driveway. He didn't seem like David's type, and I bubbled with curiosity, but didn't say anything. Just as well. Turned out he wasn't David's type, he was Jake, of the soon to be trainer-to-the-stars Body by Jake, David's personal trainer.

Despite this stab at physical fitness, everything about David was soft—his voice, his manner, his body. More in keeping with my image of him was a message scrawled in thick marker on his bedroom wall: David Kidman Is the Sweetest Man in the World. "My contractor," David acknowledged, a mischievous smile playing on his face. We were in the bedroom because David was renovating his half of the duplex and giving me a tour. I wouldn't have been surprised had the message been left over from an old date. Being with David gave you permission to act like a kid, do something forbidden, experience a little freedom.

I can still hear his laugh—a rolling chuckle that built and burst into sound. When he spoke, a smile spilled through his syllables.

I wouldn't have been surprised to see a guy like Jake leaving Ken's duplex. In fact Rudy, Ken's steady at the time, could have matched Jake deltoid for deltoid. So could Ken himself. The moment he came home he shed his workday uniform of suit and tie for the briefest of running shorts, which showed off his hard body. When the neighbors got together—whether in someone's driveway or for dinner at Maurice's Snack 'n' Chat (Maurice was another neighbor, and her restaurant serves the best spoon bread and fried chicken in Los Angeles)—Ken's big contagious laugh broke out all over the place, midsentence, in response to something someone said, or to his own words.

My lover, Carole, and I had a dog then, Rocky, an Old Yeller type and an excellent watchdog. One night, we heard him barking furiously in the garage. We went outside and called him, but he wouldn't come, and he wouldn't stop barking. The longer this went on, the more sure we were that he'd cornered a burglar. Too afraid to face this on our own, we called in reinforcements: Ken and Rudy. Armored from long hours at the gym, they hardly needed weapons, looking like they could break a man in two with their bare hands, yet we gave each a baseball bat and stood back as they stalked cautiously toward the garage. Rocky's barking hadn't let up for a second. I envisioned a guy flat against the wall, or perhaps on the roof of one of the cars, pinned by our fierce protector. I had no idea what we'd do when we caught this intruder. That's what the men were there for. Broad and steel hard, they could take care of anything. As scared as I was, I loved the idea of them, fierce and strong, knights coming to our rescue.

Ken and Rudy tightened their grip on the bats, holding them at the ready. Ken nodded to me and I pushed the remote. The door clunked mechanically and slowly lifted. As it rose, Ken bent over to get a glimpse inside. We all did, the four of us inching downward as the door moved upward. Ken had stepped forward in anticipation, but instead of lunging and swinging his bat, Lancelot turned into Guinevere and let out a high-pitched screech.

There was Rocky, so frantic and intent he didn't even glance up from his prey: a possum huddled in terror under the VW. Ugliest animal you've ever seen, but still, Ken was supposed to save our lives. I comforted myself with the thought that had the intruder been human, Ken would have presented a more formidable, or at least deeper-pitched, front.

That wasn't the only Rocky episode requiring neighborly assistance. One night we were making dinner when Rocky came sniffing cautiously into the kitchen. He investigated every corner, then moved into the dining room. He slunk hesitantly, afraid, tail between his legs—very unusual behavior for him. He kept it up for so long that eventually Carole and I grew nervous. We knew no one could have slipped into the house; surely Rocky's reaction to that would have been barking. No, this was more ominous than a direct assault. Rocky was too sensitive to moods and feelings. We trusted him enough to know something was definitely amiss. I called Glynn, apologized for bothering him, and explained what was up with Rocky. He came right over.

Just having his strong presence in the house was reassuring. Glynn had a soothing calm about him. He squatted by the dog, stroking and talking to him in his soft Arkansas accent. Glynn looked at me: "Sometimes they sense things we can't see." Made perfect sense to me, since I'd never seen Rocky act this way and his behavior had to have some explanation, rational or not. Glynn, willing to explore the familiar as if it were the unknown, waited while I got Rocky's leash on, and together we led him around the house. We joked half-heartedly, neither of us willing to admit we were checking for ghosts. We went through every room, inspected every closet. Glynn let Rocky nose into every corner, sniff behind chairs and inside cabinets. He even walked us halfway down the block, as if to demonstrate to Rocky that everything was where it should be. The patience and tolerance Glynn showed reassured us and calmed the dog. By the time he left, whatever presence had been in the house had departed.

We don't usually choose our neighbors. We choose the apartment or house or whatever and move in hoping for the best. As gays and lesbians, unless we're moving into one of the few gay—and still fewer lesbian—neighborhoods, that often requires a lot of hope. And, for some, larger closets than any dwelling can provide.

*Neighbor* is a peculiar relationship, a mix of intimacy and distance. Neighbors are thrown together by proximity, luck, or possibly even fate. Like on Longwood. With men and women in the lesbian and gay community living separately as they did, I probably wouldn't have met David and Ken and Glynn if we hadn't been neighbors. We happened to hit it off and genuinely care about each other. And a great part of our bond was our homosexuality. We joked about butch/femme and role playing and about stereotypes because we knew we didn't fit any of them. We shared tools and the occasional cup of flour and pro-gay slates at election time, gossip about public figures rumored to be lesbian or gay. Without our making a big deal of it, our sexual orientation made us neighbors and then some.

Home became more than where I lived. It became these people, not just Carole and me and the dogs. Coming home meant not just sorting through the mail or checking the answering machine, but joking with Ken, spending five minutes at the bottom of the driveway talking to Glynn when we got the paper in the morning, David showing up in his bathrobe because he loved my coffee. This was all part of what I missed when we went away, what I wanted to come back to.

Maurice threw David a pity party when he lost his job at Nissan. Strictly no frills, in keeping with his new joblessness: she made chili, served cheap jug wine; we ate off paper plates. A friend gave him an unemployment kit: a deck of cards for solitaire, a bag of rubber bands so he'd have something to do with his hands, and a roll of dimes. We laughed and danced. David didn't seem worried at all.

I guess by then he already knew he was HIV-positive. (My first friend to be diagnosed.) When we found out, we offered to do whatever we could. Ken organized the neighbors, and we each prepared David's dinner one night a week. I remember him early on, sitting in our dining room telling us how he was going to beat this with a combination of diet and attitude. Later, when he was too weak to come out, we'd bring his food to him. I remember picking him up to take him to a doctor's appointment, helping him on with his pants, walking down the stairs with him, step by painful step. He laughed less; I couldn't remember his funny stories, only the writing on his wall: David Kidman Is the Sweetest Man in the World.

Carole and I moved off Longwood in 1988. David had already died. We all went to the funeral, and met his parents and sisters back at his house afterward. Glynn died in 1990. I talk to his lover, Tom, and we get together on occasion. I've seen Ken only a few times since we moved. Yet I still think of them as my neighbors.

Two years ago on a visit to New York City I drove over the Fifty-ninth Street Bridge at night. Carole and I were considering a move to Oregon at the time, and I looked at Manhattan glittering to my left and right and wondered what I would do in a small town. I thought how familiar, how home New York was. And then with a shock I had an overwhelming realization that the city was no longer home, that I no longer had a home. Because as much as New York was no longer home, L.A.—no matter how long I'm here or how much I like it—would never be home. And I felt sad and at the same time liberated by that thought. It meant I could go anywhere I wanted, because my home was within me, home was internal as well as external.

I think the seed for that realization was planted in my old Longwood neighborhood. Planted by Arlene, who took care of the dogs when we were out of town, whose dogs we fed when she was gone. By Ken, whose laugh I heard when he came home from work at night, who took over caring for a wild kitten we'd taken in. By David, who listened to me through a major breakup, and welcomed Carole when we started going out. What we built as neighbors prepared us for the times that were coming, that came, that are upon us now.

The house we live in today sits at the top of a steep driveway that dead-ends at the base of another hill. People live either at the bottom of our driveway or at the top of the hill, above us. I complain about the house that was built in the once empty field next to us, but still, this is the farthest I've ever been from any neighbor, and in spring and summer, when the walnut trees have leaves, you can hardly see that house. We rarely see the people who live near us; I hesitate to call them neighbors, even. And if I did, the word would have a different shape and meaning than the one I use for our Longwood neighbors.

I'd always liked the fact we no longer have neighbors, saw it as a blessing in this crowded city, our house as a secluded hideaway. But last week a friend of ours was robbed and mugged at gunpoint in her driveway. When I heard that, our isolation became a scary prospect. I thought of the pools of shadow that surround our little house here on the hill, no one close enough to come to our aid. I remembered Glynn walking me and Rocky through our Longwood house, guaranteeing its safety. I saw Ken and Rudy coming to our rescue against the burglar/ possum. Remembered Ken and David's distinctive laughs, and the accompanying comfort of their presence.

The older I get, the more things frighten me, the more I recognize potential for disaster in the simplest task. I think this comes not from encroaching feebleness—I'm only older, not old, after all—but because I sense how precious life is. I no longer know what's safe. I think of the dark places in the days. And I think of the shadows we walk through every day in our lives, and how as a community we become each other's neighbors, joined not by a common hedge or a shared driveway or a ride up in the elevator together, but by the fact that we inhabit the same psychic neighborhood. I remember David and Glynn—let them stand for all the others who are gone—and Glynn's lover, Tom, and Ken, who are still my neighbors even though we don't live anywhere near each other. And I think home isn't always safe, but there is a certain safety in community. There is too much against us out there in the world; we are neighbors through more than proximity. And however we do it— socially or through political activism or support groups or phone calls or reading each other's literature—we must help each other scout for ghosts and fight off intruders.

JUDITH P.
STELBOUM
&
ARNIE
KANTROWITZ

# Coming Out with Arnie/ A Date with Judith

## 1. Judith

Let me be very honest here. I was an intellectual, ignorant, middle-class snob. So the first day I walked into the basement of the Staten Island City Hall, which housed the English department of the newly formed Community College of Staten Island, in my Peck and Peck suit, I knew it was someplace that I did not belong. I had been forced to take this teaching job by my dissertation adviser, and it was an offer I could not refuse without antagonizing her. The spring term had just begun, and already I was wondering how soon I could hand in my resignation so that I wouldn't have to be around for the fall term. The students were not like any students I had known. They were working-class for the most part, and I was certain that without college their lives would have inevitably led them to a popular beauty school where they could learn to perm and color, or to the local gas station where they could tune up eight-cylinder Fords and Chevys. How could I talk to them about *Beowulf* and Chaucer?

My opinion of the English faculty was no better. While they were friendly toward me, I held them in contempt. They were not my ideal version of a college faculty. They talked like hippies. I had grown up in Brooklyn, but I had never been interested in the bohemian life and thought of people who lived in Greenwich Village as déclassé and pretentious.

The first time I saw Arnold Kantrowitz in the English department office, he was wearing a three-piece suit and had short, neatly combed hair and a well-kept goatee. He wore tortoiseshell glasses that he sprayed with Windex several times a day, and seemed compulsively driven to keep his papers in little neat piles on his desk.

Now almost thirty years later, much about Arnie's manner has changed, but the little neat stacks of student papers piled on his desk and the polishing of the glasses remain.

My training had taught me to consider him as a candidate for marriage, but my instincts told me that he was not a likely prospect to date. He appeared friendly but tense when we spoke. I guess I must have appeared the same way to him. We never spoke about anything personal at that time. How could I when I didn't know very much about my own personal life? Whenever I looked at Arnold across the huge open expanse of the basement office, I got the impression of someone who was trying to play the role of professor. I was not to realize how painful that pretense was until January 1968, when I was informed in hushed tones that Arnold had attempted suicide and was recovering in a hospital. I still did not know him well enough to visit, and certainly when he returned I never let on that I had heard what the real cause of his absence had been. Still I did not connect Arnold's anguish and closeted life with my own.

At first, I wanted only to survive the interminable semester and quickly get away from these people who were making me so uncomfortable. What must I have seemed like to them? I was thirty years old, did not have many friends, and had no social life to speak of. My father had just died, and I lived with my mother in our house in Brooklyn. I couldn't imagine living away from home on my own, as did all my colleagues in the department. I was waiting for my life to begin. A girl didn't move out of the house until she got married. But I was taking a long time in choosing whom to marry. I was focusing all of my efforts on graduate school. The availability of suitable males for an educated female seemed very slim. That's what I told myself, and everyone else who wanted to know why "a nice girl like you isn't married." Even though I had been in love with a woman for the past four years, we were both reluctant to admit that our relationship was lesbian, and we both still saw men.

## 2. Arnie

What can I say? The woman is supposed to be an English professor, yet she writes with sentence fragments. Incorrigible, but modish. I don't remember the first time I saw her. I'm sure it was in the dreary setting of our old department office, which was decorated in early olive drab filing cabinets with smart scratches and dents for accents. I remember only one of her dresses: some Russian camel-hair atrocity that was shaped like a stiff tent, which refused to have anything to do with her body except to hang from its shoulders. Along with her earlobe-length straightened hair that was wider at the bottom than the top, the outfit gave her the appearance of a trapezoid. She was so stiff it was hard to notice that she was a beautiful woman.

I was no model of relaxation myself. I remember I used to wear snug suits and shirts that had little tabs on the collar to hold the necktie up so that it formed a proud arc before it was snared by my understated tiepin. I always felt like I was being hanged. I was not a happy guy. I was on the wrong train to nowhere. It wasn't that I felt superior to my students. It was more like I was afraid of them. What would these gorgeous jocks do if they knew they had a pervert for a teacher? I was glad to have any job, having left my gig at an upstate college following my first suicide attempt. After seeing several job applications rejected when I referred to my recent "nervous collapse," I simply stopped mentioning that I had left that position before the school year was over, and soon I was dutifully toiling my way toward tenure at Staten Island Community College.

If Judith was giving attitude, I hardly had time to notice. Aside from marking papers, I was too busy bringing daffodils to Central Park to welcome 1967's "summer of love" and then trying suicide a second time during my own private winter of despair. Being alienated from the Establishment was very popular in those days, and along with other teachers who lived in the Village, I affected a blue denim work shirt when I was off duty. (I also affected a 4 A.M. cruising style to catch the men who were leaving the closing bars on Christopher Street.) So who had time for some asexual upper-class trapezoid who had studied in Wales and specialized in medieval poetry?

## 3. Judith

I was thirty-two years old before I moved into my own apartment in New York, where I was so lonely and unhappy that I agreed to marry the brother of the woman I loved. He had known me since high school, had been in love with me for a long time, and was ignorant of my true feelings for his sister. I saw this marriage as a way to stay close to her and make my family happy, so I married in May, but before the beginning of the fall term, I left him, deciding to have the marriage annulled. I knew that I would never be with a man again. I was on the verge of a totally new life, but I still had no idea what it was to be. A short while into therapy and a few trips to some appropriate bars quickly demonstrated why I had not found a suitable man to marry. I still get a thrill and an adrenaline rush when I walk into a lesbian bar. My only regret was that I had wasted so many of my young years with the wrong sex.

There was a hush in the large communal departmental office when I came in for my first day that fall term. I knew that people wanted to ask me about my summer vacation, and I decided to tell the truth. It was a difficult moment. I naturally sought out Arnold, who had adopted the name Arnie to go with the self-confidence he had gained by coming out of his closet. I wanted to come out to him first. When I told him that I thought I was a lesbian, he surprised me by saying that he had suspected this. I was shocked because, like everyone else who is closeted, I thought that no one knew. In my case, I was so hidden, even I didn't know.

During the next few months, as I began to explore my lesbian self, Arnie was there, encouraging and supportive, introducing me to people in the gay community, informing me about gay events. There was a deeper bond between us. The department was accepting of the new me. All those people toward whom I had felt such disdain were now becoming my best friends, and I was in the process of becoming a human being open to loving women. One of my straight colleagues introduced me to his wife's cousin, and I had my first lesbian love affair.

Arnie was, at that time, involved with the Gay Activists Alliance and living in a commune on Spring Street in Manhattan. I used to visit him and the other men to see how it could be possible for a community of homosexuals to live together. Arnie's life seemed ideal to me. His appearance had changed almost as radically as had mine. I was now dressed in pants, cowboy boots, and blazers. He was now losing weight and into bodybuilding. He let his hair grow into a ponytail and later shaved his head. His glasses, too, had changed. They were now little round red ones that contrasted beautifully with his long red mustache and sideburns. This was a great time for all of us. We went to parties where Arnie and I brought our respective lovers. We danced together. Everyone and everything was very open. My lover then was assistant to the president of our college, and she and I were often invited to his home for dinner with his wife and family. At one party Arnie came out to the president, who touched him on the cheek and wished him well.

## 4. Arnie

All the miserable repression changed with the coming of the seventies. I put my anguish behind me and discovered gay liberation. In short order, I demolished my closet door forever by coming out on a couple of national television shows, and I made my sexuality into a political issue by becoming the vice president of the Gay Activists Alliance, rushing breathlessly from meetings to demonstrations and breathlessly back to the classroom, where I came out boldly, angrily to every class on the first day of the semester. I was meeting live lesbians for the first time in my life, and my "gay-dar" (which, of course, is not genetic, but merely a matter of being sensitized to the subtlest of queer clues) was beginning to notice slight hints of an elegant butchness about Ms. Judith. (She never liked the more girlish "Judy.") Now I understood why she never looked at home in her clothes.

Small wonder, then, when she asked to speak to me that I wasn't totally surprised. I took her to a bench in the quadrangle of our somewhat less than fabulous new campus (architecture reminiscent of J.C. Penney), and she began to confide in me.

"I'm leaving my husband," she said. "The marriage is being annulled."

"After only two months?" I said, thrilled at the gossip but concerned for her welfare.

"It's really his sister I'm in love with, not him," she said softly, but clearly and firmly.

This would be wonderful for the daily TV soaps, I thought to myself, but they're not ready for it. Aloud, I said, "I'm glad you came to me. I know some people you could meet and some books you could read. That's why it's so important for us to come out, so the next generation won't have to go through what we did."

"I don't want to talk to everybody about it," she said. "Let people think what they want."

So I remained the only teacher out of the closet on our campus, in spite of the fact that there were about ten gay men and lesbians in the English department alone. I mellowed out in the following years and told my students about myself later in the semester, when it was less traumatic and more educational. But I remained the beacon for the gay ones, the men who weren't sure what they were and wanted to test it out on me, and the women who were contemplating suicide and couldn't find a lesbian to talk to. I taught the college's first gay studies course ("Homosexuals and Literature" [sic]), which had a small enrollment because most students did not want that title emblazoned on their transcripts; and I became the adviser to a short-lived gay and lesbian club, whose members spent most of their energy closing doors and pulling down window shades and being harassed for putting up posters. I was the one who spoke at the teach-in on New York City's gay-rights bill, and I always had to be the one to mention that some list of minority groups had omitted lesbians and gays. In short, I was the campus queer. If anyone had a question about the politically correct position on a gay issue, I was the one who was asked. I was more than a little miffed at my silently complacent colleagues, but whatever was wrong with her political-activism glands, Judith was my sister and my friend, and I loved and forgave her and prayed that she would see the lavender light.

## 5. Judith

Coming out is an ongoing process of growing awareness of one's identities. During this time, Arnie's life and mine took very different paths. I was lesbian, and everyone knew it—family, colleagues, friends—but I was not political. I thought that I was really just like everyone else (read *heterosexual women*), and although I taught the first women's studies course at the newly consolidated College of Staten Island, there was no specifically lesbian content in the course. I was not attempting to omit lesbian-oriented material; I just didn't think it was important. I also was unaware of the emerging writing of lesbian literature and theory. I spent those years trying to remain a feminist who was acceptable to my heterosexual friends in the women's movement. It was not important to align myself with other lesbians, with whom I felt I had little in common. Being a lesbian was no big deal. What people said about lesbians behind my back didn't matter. To call attention to my lesbianism, to force me to confront the real differences between heterosexual and lesbian women's lives, would have alienated Arnie and me completely.

I was chairperson of the English department. I had a lover, and we owned a small farm in upstate New York. I collected chicken eggs in Columbia County and sat on college promotion and budget meetings, rode my horse through the woods and hills of my country home, oblivious to the ways other lesbians had to live their lives.

Arnie, on the other hand, was writing about gay issues. During the years I was feminist and also lesbian, Arnie had defined himself as a gay political person. He insisted on coming out to all of his classes each term. When he would tell me the reactions of his students to his declarations, I knew it was something I would not have the courage to do. I could never reveal that part of my life to students. It was too personal, maybe even inappropriate for a professional academic. I must say that my feelings, at the time, about Arnie's undertaking were mixed. I admired his guts, but I couldn't understand the necessity for visibility. Why force people to see us as different? Why not just try to fit in and not make waves? He believed that we had to confront their homophobia for them and for us. I know that he must have been disappointed in me when I refused to claim my primary identity as lesbian. He would say that I was in such a good position to serve as a role model, an example. One of my students from the women's studies classes felt more comfortable discussing her problems about lesbianism with Arnie than she did with me. This really hurt, but I still believed that my being a lesbian was not a big deal. It was a fact of my life, not the whole of my life.

It was like the other important fact of my life: that I was Jewish. Arnie and I had that in common, too. We identified with being Jewish in an ethnic way, and we would go to plays and films about the Holocaust. If we had to choose which identity we would claim if they ever came to arrest us, we both agreed that we would be hard-pressed to decide between declaring ourselves gay and lesbian or Jewish first. But although being interested in Jewish issues was yet another link in our friendship, the real bonding, which we could not explain to our straight friends, came from the mystery and joy we found in discovering our sexuality.

Sometimes Arnie would come up to the country to visit, and we would sit and talk. My life must have seemed strange to him. He was a city boy who was bothered by the sounds of the woods at night, but who could sleep through fire engines, police sirens, and garbage trucks outside his window in Manhattan. He used to have an embarrassed laugh when the chickens would walk by. I still have a picture of him, in his city clothes, stepping deftly between the dung piles when we walked out into the pasture to see the horse. It was a wonder to him that anyone could be happy so far from the exciting activities that were to be found in the city. There were no movies, limited TV, and no local gay friends. Our worlds were so different then. Yet our friendship survived the disparity of our lifestyles. My lover and I were contemplating having a child, and I asked Arnie if he wanted to be the father. Just testing. Of course nothing ever came of it. Neither of us ever did become a parent, but Arnie remained a special person in my life.

## 6. Arnie

Judith blossomed nicely. That much I'll say for her. The trapezoid dress got thrown in the trash heap, and she started showing up in borderline masculine outfits, inspired by her Texan lover, a charming rodeo rider of a woman who brought out the cowboy that had lain dormant for so long in Judith's psyche. We were a four-year college now, but that didn't stop us. Now the freshmen were being taught by a self-confident woman in boots and hip-hugger jeans, with short curly hair, an easy smile, and fabulous skin. To the president's parties she wore a demure set of mechanic's coveralls, and a hunter green suit from Blooming-dale's boys' department was her pride and joy. I could never believe Judith in a skirt again, and whenever one reappeared for a special occasion, I hissed and booed because I knew that her real soul would always belong in pants.

What could the English department do with such an apparition but make her the chairperson? It wasn't too hard to take. She fixed racing-car motors, and her lover bought her a horse for her fortieth birthday, which she named Tywysog after something Welsh, and even when he threw her and banged up her jaw, she still loved him bravely and well. She regularly brought her huge malamute named Masha to the office, something like having a pet wolf for a fashion statement. I was a match for her, though, crocheting on the Staten Island ferry, and showing up for classes and meetings with my rhinestone-studded, artfully embroidered dungarees, my wrists and neck festooned with jewelry of dubious gender: cameos and necklaces and bracelets by the half dozen and a ring for every single finger. The ends of my mustache were aiming for my nipples, and I studied everyone through rose-colored glasses. None of that dowdy old Mr. Chips drag for me. No, sir.

We were free at last. Of course, I supported gay rights in my classes, and of course it caught up with me. My favorite incident happened when an angry middle-aged woman in my journal class complained to the dean that I was endorsing perversion. She didn't know that he was gay, too! He dutifully passed the message along to Professor Dyke, Chairwoman, who warned me not to offend the bigots, and all of us had a good laugh.

We were steady friends by then, and our lives touched at many points. When I grew all starry-eyed and infatuated, she didn't let me get through the doorway of the A Building before she said with eyebrows raised, "Arnold, are you in love?" and I nodded dreamily. When her romance broke up, her composure went with it, and she dripped hard tears onto the desk blotter in the office while I held her hand.

Eventually, I had to point out that she was putting away more Johnny Walker than was good for her, and she laid off. She pointed out that I could eat smaller portions, and I lost some weight. When my romance broke up, we spent more time together, putting gay politics aside.

It was Judith who got out of bed early on a Sunday morning to drive me to New Jersey on the first lap of my journey to my mother's funeral. Like most Americans in their leisure hours, we enjoyed watching Holocaust documentaries. I would visit her apartment, and we would play old Yiddish songs on the piano together while I eyed her collection of medieval crucifixes with discomfort. Could this be a self-hating Jew dressed up as a semi-open lesbian? Well, everything was so political in those days. I had to let her be whatever she was because, after all, I did love her.

## 7. Judith

In the early eighties life changed again for Arnie and for me. I broke up my long-term relationship, had to leave the farm I loved, and was devastated. I returned to college teaching feeling very depressed. Arnie and I had a long talk. He was supportive and comforting. Although he had never lived with anyone for as long as I had lived with my former lover, he had had several affairs and was thrown into despair when they ended, so he went to bars and had anonymous sex. I had modeled my life after the heterosexual monogamous marriages with which I was familiar. I couldn't do what Arnie did.

Life in the mid-eighties was certainly a lot less dramatic than it had been in the seventies. Most of our friends had settled down and were raising families. Arnie had found a lover and had moved in with him. He had long ago given up the colored glasses and ponytail and fancy jeans. There were no more all-night dancing parties at friends' lofts. I had found a new lover, and together we bought a house in Connecticut for weekend retreats from New York. I thought that this was the way it would continue until the retirement home beckoned: Arnie and I getting grayer and heavier, sitting in the office together, talking over a cup of coffee and relating stories of our respective weekends.

But Arnie kept on marching in Gay Pride parades. One June I told him that I would march with him, and I did. All the way from Central Park down Fifth Avenue, where I left the parade to shop at Saks. Neither of us has had any control over what has happened in recent history. Arnie has relived the Holocaust. There is no need to choose whether one will identify as Jewish or gay. The choice has already been taken out of our hands by AIDS. What was a moot Talmudic discussion has now become a reality. Arnie has suffered the loss of many of his closest friends, his chosen family. I can only watch passively, extend sympathy, and listen to the litany of names every week when he tells me, "You know who died this weekend? Remember, you met him at . . ."

I urged him to get tested himself. He told me that he didn't want to know. Months later, he went for the test and it was negative. Another miracle, I thought, as I held back the tears of relief. Maybe we would actually grow old together. Arnie's reaction was a mixture of happiness and guilt. Surely not unlike the concentration-camp victims' ambivalent feelings of the blessing of survival. For Arnie, this is a very dark, depressing time. We talk about how he tries to fight the numbing effect of the loss of so many people in his life. After all the years of fighting homophobia, AIDS has aroused all the violence and hatred of the pre-Stonewall days.

## 8. Arnie

Sex in the eighties became fraught with fear for me, so I rarely strayed from my relationship even though it was an open one. Judith clung to her monogamous lifestyle, yet I always wondered whether it was her true nature. Whatever else she was, the former trapezoid was obviously a sexual creature. She seemed to relate to everyone and everything with a slightly lustful leer, so when I visited her in her country home and we were alone together for days, it was all I could do, or so I thought, to protect my (slightly tarnished) virginity. I didn't want to ruin my gay credentials. And when she noted that her biological clock was ticking and suggested that we might have a child together, my first thought was: How? Actually, I wouldn't have minded our genes mixing. We probably would have produced one hell of a smart, good-looking kid. The problem was, what would we do with it then? We both heaved a sigh of relief when the idea was aborted.

Gay men, like most men, are plagued with the question of what lesbians do in bed. Everyone knows what gay men do. The pictures are rudely scrawled on most bathroom walls. But women—especially movement women—are very covert about their bedroom activities. My friend Jim used to guess that they "bumped doughnuts," but I never thought that sounded very dignified or satisfying. Judith, mercifully, is highly explicit about sex and leaves nothing to the imagination—not one finger or dildo or tongue—and I will never have to fall asleep pondering unanswered questions.

Although she always turned up her lip—so to speak—at the scruffy lesbians in the movement, she did attempt to join the Gay Pride march one June. We walked along under a brilliant sky, our identities open to the world. One of my former sex partners appeared from nowhere, inquiring what was behind the tab on my pants fly. "Possibilities," I purred, catching Judith's arched eyebrow out of the corner of my eye. Well, good taste isn't everything, I thought to myself. We started at Fifty-ninth Street and were heading all the way down to Greenwich Village, some miles away, but Judith checked out at Fiftieth Street, evidently to do some urgent shopping.

"Wasn't that a fine march?" she asked the next day.

"Judith," I said, "you didn't exactly march. You simply strolled from Bonwit Teller's to Saks Fifth Avenue. What a princess!"

"It was a good march," she said.

One step at a time, I thought. But she got there. By April 1993, she and Martha were proud participants in the great march on Washington, D.C. Judith says it was one of the best days of her life. It was good for me, too, but I was preoccupied with thoughts of absent friends who had been with me on earlier marches.

Life has changed a bit in recent years. I've never gone all the way back to ties and jackets. Now I teach in undramatic slacks and shirts, comfortable if not chic. But Judith is still at it. We met at the Metropolitan Opera House recently, and she looked terrific in Martha's father's tuxedo.

Judith and I both settled down at about the same time: ten years ago. Now my lover, Larry Mass, and I spend occasional weekends in Connecticut, where Judith and Martha have a lovely house. What with the epidemic and all, it's the safest form of fun.

## 9. Judith

My life, too, has changed. In January of 1991, I discovered lesbian literature. This must be similar to Herman Melville discovering Shakespeare at twenty-nine. Reading about my own experiences, thoughts, and feelings has changed my life. I feel like a born-again dyke. I have yet again come out. My primary identity is now solidly lesbian. I wanted to share my new enthusiasm with the students at the college. After a hiatus of almost fifteen years, I felt prepared to teach a class in women's studies again. This time, the focus of the course was on racism, homophobia, social and economic class, and other issues that prevent women from finding out who they are and what they want. The emphasis was on ways to construct our individual lives instead of believing myths that constrict our lives.

When Arnie and I had dinner after this self emerged, I told him that I wanted to really become involved with the lesbian community of writers. Again, Arnie was encouraging and actively supportive. He read my first writings and gave me constructive editorial advice. When we sat at a recent English department meeting and a new course offering was proposed, Arnie and I looked at each other, smiled, and simultaneously offered a course on lesbian and gay literature. Together we now serve as faculty advisers to the gay and lesbian student organization on campus. Sitting at the department meeting, I realized how lonely Arnie must have been all those years, without the vocal support of the other lesbians and gays in the department to come out and to speak up for our representation in the canon of literary studies. It's not that anyone would have opposed this. It's simply that no one, except Arnie, straight or gay, would have thought of a course about our sensibilities. It is this sensitivity and awareness that I now recognize as essential. I feel that, at last, I have caught up with Arnie in terms of the importance of defining ourselves, even at the cost of setting ourselves apart from others.

## 10. Arnie

After so many years of activism, I find myself only too happy to skip an occasional demonstration. So what happens? Judith's political consciousness comes out of hibernation! A year ago, she told me over dinner that she finally decided that her lesbian identity is no longer a peripheral issue. Now it is her central identity. She's reading lesbian theory so fast, you'd think it was going out of style. And she's become a writer, so I introduced her to my agent. Now we have manuscripts to edit and discuss and conferences to attend and networking to do. Recently, when a multicultural literature course was proposed along with the inevitable omission of gay and lesbian writing, I had Judith's support for my rewording of the course description, and when we mutually proposed a lesbian/gay literature course, we were a juggernaut that the department couldn't oppose. Now there are two advisers to shudder at the awkward acronym for the College of Staten Island Lesbian, Gay, and Bisexual Alliance. Now we can *tsk-tsk* together about our colleagues who think that lying behind the closet door is somehow more dignified. What a relief after a quarter of a century not to be alone. Now we are two.

# The Faggot
# as Animus

The man of my dreams is a faggot. This comes as an uneasy confession, for what am I if not a by-product of the lesbian days of rage? (Apologies to the Weather Underground, who brought us the original Days of Rage. For those interested in trivia, the Weather Underground were known as the Weathermen—proving once again that sexism and revolution are not necessarily mutually exclusive—until the women in their ranks, more than a few of them lesbians, suggested a name change.)

The lesbian days of rage, on the other hand, were brought to us by the Lesbian Police, who got to make the rules. I don't know why. They called it *politics*, which sounded considerably better than *rules*, when you think about it. Of course, the Lesbian Police never liked me as much as I liked them, but then I've always been a sucker for butches in uniform. Fortunately, the uniforms have changed somewhat over the years. Leather is more popular now than plaid flannel, but the Lesbian Police aren't, which proves nothing except that lesbians will tolerate a lot except being told how to fuck—one of the things the Lesbian Police did best. I've always been better at fucking than at politics, which is a lot about remembering rules and only sometimes about fucking. For one thing, you don't have to please as many people, which I've never been very good at. For another, no one expects fucking to change the world. Fucking is one of the few things I do very well (even my ex-lovers who give me credit for nothing else credit me with that). I am not nearly so accomplished at the day-to-day duties of relationships, or politics, which is what got me in trouble with the Lesbian Police in the first place. But I digress.

Fucking doesn't actually have much to do with the man of my dreams (I don't even dream of fucking women in my dreams, at least not often), but it has a great deal to do with how I discovered the faggot as animus. If it hadn't been for fucking, I likely wouldn't have fallen in love with the wrong woman and ended up following her to California, which is a very good place for psychoanalysis, fucking, and faggots. I suppose I should apologize for using the word *faggot*, but I won't. Besides, *gay* seems so flabby and out of date in the face of an epidemic that's already taken some of the best and brightest and most beautiful, and threatens to wipe the rest of us from the face of the earth as well— nothing to be very gay about there. (I personally have not felt very gay since the summer of 1983, when I had the great good sense to run away from Chicago winters into the arms of a woman whose exit line was that while the sex was great—back to fucking again—I was embarrassingly lacking in too many other areas to name; it took her six long years to discover them all. Remarkably, she even missed a few.)

She left just as I was pitching over the edge into a full-blown nervous breakdown, which had less to do with her than she likes to imagine and more than I like to admit. Of course, it was a while before I figured out I was probably nuts. (I'm a writer; depression is our disease of choice. I don't know why. Maybe Anne Sexton or Sylvia Plath or Ernest Hemingway, all of whom are dead from it, knows why by now, but none of them can say. William Styron and Kurt Vonnegut, who certainly are not dead, don't seem to know why either—and if they do, they're not saying. I am also the offspring of people so truly nuts that anything short of stark raving mad is considered sane.)

My psychiatrist, a card-carrying Jungian, was supposed to be interested in dreams, and mine have always been, as my best friend calls them, humdingers. (She's from the Midwest and still says things like *humdinger.*) Of course, what I didn't know at the time was that the doctor wasn't in much better shape than her patient, good old me (I just thought she was distracted), which proves that sanity is nothing if not tenuous. But I faithfully reported to the shrink how, not long after I crossed the California state line with my best friend, an ancient and very angry cat, and a smuggled house plant that I'd kept alive for five years and which promptly died two months later, I started dreaming about shit, dungeons, and catacombs. (In retrospect, this says quite a lot about the condition of my last serious relationship, and why I'm not anxious for another.)

Not long after I decided I was crazy but before I knew my psychiatrist was, the faggots started showing up in my dreams. Young. Old. Alone. In pairs. Sometimes small groups. But none wore a face I recognized or a name I knew. They showed me their rooms, fading but still nearly grand in the way old hotels, which I have always loved, are fading but not yet faded. They warned me away from paths and staircases and doors that I knew (*knew!*) led to the dungeons and shit and catacombs. Their message was always the same: *You don't want to go through that door.* When I didn't listen, it was back down to the shit, the dungeons, and the catacombs. Given that choice, I started listening. Who wouldn't? I didn't know they were the animus (I wouldn't learn about that until sometime later). And at the time, I was still concentrating on the standardized litmus test of sanity: What day of the week is it and who is the president of the United States? (Unfortunately, I've always been bad about days. On the other hand, I've always known who the president is; I wish I didn't, but I do.)

That was in 1989, which was a fairly eventful year: my first book was published, and the San Andreas Fault took a step west and taught San Francisco to shimmy. Ironically, no small number of otherwise sane people who live in this quake-racked region took personal responsibility, which seemed then—and does still—absolutely crazy to me. But maybe they grew up in a world where fissures are unknown, a world safer than any I've ever known.

The landscape of my childhood is cracked with dangerous fissures, some as deep as hell itself. One runs the length of the wood lot behind what used to be my grandfather's barn. Slightly less than a foot wide and deeper than anyone has ever been able to gauge, the crack stinks with sulfuric gases hanging on the thick early-evening air in summer. The stench of the fires of hell, my grandfather would declare whenever he was bored and had decided to terrorize any one or all of his many grandchildren as an afternoon's amusement. My grandfather hated children almost as much as he enjoyed terrifying them, and with any small amount of prodding would gladly turn back his thick gray sock and show us the brown mark on the outside of his left ankle. My grandmother declared it a common birthmark, but my grandfather insisted it was the devil's own thumbprint, left when he, as a boy, came too close to that fissure, which led straight to Satan's staircase. Grandpa's escapes from the devil's clutches changed each time he told the story—although not one of us had the courage to remind him of that—but always revolved around a trick far too clever to ever have been conjured by any ordinary child, especially the dullards he was cursed with as progeny. Too bad the old man was a liar. Too bad I didn't listen more closely; there have been times when I could've used one or two of those tricks.

My friend the Oracle, who is not a lesbian and definitely not crazy, has made no small reputation for herself in Jungian circles for, among other things, deciphering the importance of the myth of the Sumerian goddess Inanna, who tried to lay claim to hell. I know a great deal about hell, having spent much of 1989 and 1990 there myself. You lose a lot in hell, at least a lot of everything that matters. Inanna went there for greed; my own reasons are less clear. But we both got out with the help of best friends and magical faggots, which doesn't say much for lovers, who don't really give a good damn once you're there; at least Inanna's didn't or mine either. Inanna, by the way, banished her ex into a sort of netherworld exchange program; I can only wish mine there. But I digress.

The Oracle taught me about the faggot as animus. For the uninitiated, the *animus* is the positive force of maleness from forward-thrusting energy, which gets women out into the world. (At least I think that's what the Oracle said.) Some Jungians think this energy comes from the mother, which makes us not the women our mothers warned us about so much as the women they desperately wanted to be. My mother, a woman with the sentimental soul of a pastel artist, who has spent her life trapped in a small and savage world, would probably like to have been almost anything but what she is. So desperate to escape, my mother often floats away to another—I like to think, better—world of her own creation. The psychiatrists call it *dissociation;* I like *floating* better. It's what she does very well.

My mother actually has a fair amount of magic. So did her sister. So do I. (My grandmother likely had more than any of us, but then she was certifiably nuts, so it's hard to say.) My mother insists the magic comes from her great-great-grandmother, who was an Irish witch. (Mother says *midwife* because she doesn't want the neighbors to think she's a heretic, but we both know what she means.) Unfortunately, generations of mixed marriages to the earthbound have diluted the magic, until it's now good for little more than cheap parlor tricks: knowing when the phone's going to ring, telling the sex of unborn babies, an occasional visitation by a dead relative or two, a little mind reading. The usual stuff.

Fortunately for me, my great-great-great-grandma's grandma, whose name I will never know (more's the pity), had the great good sense to stay in Ireland birthing babies and digging potatoes and whatever else your average Irish witch did to keep busy, instead of coming to the New World and settling in Massachusetts, where witch burning was fast becoming the new pastime. (No small number of those women were disposed of in gruesomely inventive ways for a lot less than what my ancestors were doing, for a lot less than what we do today. For those interested in such things, the New World's torturers apparently didn't see the need to toss dead and sometimes not-so-dead faggots on the witching pyres, as had their Old World ancestors during the Inquisition. They were trying to make a point. Point made.) In fact, except for me, not one of my female ancestors ever set foot in Massachusetts, and I didn't linger. My strongest impression was of fur coats, which left me with the distinct suspicion that beneath all those cultured genteel exteriors still lie bloodthirsty Puritan souls.

I know where fur coats come from, thanks to my father, the killer. It's what he does very well. There are few men living or dead who could top my father's skills with a shotgun when he was in his prime. He has the trophies to prove it; I am one of them. I don't remember the first time I ever watched him skin anything, but I know where to make the cut, how the hide turns inside out, how the guts sound when they plop wet and dark onto a newspaper on the basement floor, how new death smells. For my sixth Christmas, my father gave me a night-light with a ballerina who twirled round and round on a tiny pink stage to a melody I've long since forgotten, and a BB gun. I still have the night-light; the music doesn't play anymore. My father still has the BB gun; it doesn't shoot straight anymore. When I was ten, he gave me a shotgun and taught me to shoot to kill and no excuse is good enough if you miss. He still has that shotgun, there in the big glass cabinet with all his others, where I left it years ago. I suppose he thinks I'll take it down again one day. "You could've been good," he tells me on my rare visits home. He doesn't understand that it would be too hard to make him proud. Of me. Or my mother. Or himself.

I told the Oracle all this and how I, always the passive rebel, was raised in an angry world bound by unrelenting rules and judgments, constraints, and violence. I didn't have to tell her the obvious: that I learned very early the danger of believing straight men offering to help me out. Every time a straight man offered to help me out—and they always use exactly those words—it's out of my clothes, my job, or my money. No wonder a lesbian would conjure the faggot as animus. Even in dreams, we seek safety. And what are we all but outcasts reaching to each other across fissures as deep and deadly as those behind my grandfather's barn? Unlike straight men, whose survival and comfort depend on the conformity of women, the faggot walks my dreams and my world as the wise outcast, one who already has found new and successful ways of being in a world in which he, even more than we, is branded pariah.

So that might have been the all of it—wispy dream men warning me away from metaphoric doors, and reasons why I conjured them and accept their guidance—except for this: three times the faggot as animus has manifested itself as real. (*Real!*) As the last female descendant of women who kept their magic casually but well, I'm not surprised, nor was the Oracle. Like my mother, she understands how many things magic come in threes.

## One

I have already said 1989 was a bad year for fault lines and for me. But it didn't start out that way. That spring my first book was published, but by summer, I was on a fraying tightrope without a net. That fall the rope would snap, sending me into a free fall that would last more than two years.

I spent that summer with an old friend in his house that overlooks the sea, perching all-but-precariously high atop the San Andreas Fault. I thought the negative ions would calm my frazzled mind, give me time to think; and he was lonely. The man he loved (then and still) was helping mop up a couple of million gallons of crude oil that the *Exxon Valdez* had so ignobly urped into Alaska's pristine waters. (When crude oil hits cold seawater it resembles black mayonnaise, floating and fouling everything in its path.) They were steam-cleaning the rocks, for god's sake. (For *God's* sake.) If the good old skipper of the good old *Valdez* hadn't decided to tie one on, my friend and his partner would have had their one last perfect summer in California before moving back to New Mexico. As it was, Bob got to spent it with good old, crazy me.

Bob Anderson lives in Santa Fe now, among the middle-aged hippies who call themselves New Age while they fight or welcome—depending on who you talk to—old age. The radio stations there play endless streams of tinkling music designed to make you think of endless streams. It is a sparse and peaceful land, without the excess of California. He is happy there. We seldom speak of the summer of '89, and when we must, we smooth it over, as is the way with longtime friends. And we have known each other a long, a very long time. Long enough to know each other's families and first loves and ex-lovers, long enough to overlook the quirks and peeves, long enough to have a history and no secrets. Twenty years keeps you honest, if nothing else. (I have structured my life in such a way that there are very few such people in it. More's the pity, I think, the older I grow.) Now when I think of that summer and that house and Bob, I remember sitting on the back deck, drinking Pepsi and sometimes cheap wine, making bets on when the fog would come in (you can actually watch it roll toward the coastline there). And I remember the woman I loved (then but no more) leaving me. I even remember hearing the tightrope snap. I remember it all, but none of it clearly. Mostly I remember Bob saying: "Whatever you do, don't go back to that." (*You don't want to go through that door.*)

## Two

Michael Denneny is my editor. I met him on what was supposed to be the happiest day of my life. I suppose in some ways it was. More often, though, I think of it as the beginning of the final slide down, which has nothing to do with him and everything to do with me. In those days, I subscribed to the "if-only-then" theory of relativity: if only I had a master's degree, then I wouldn't feel stupid; if only I had a book published, then I wouldn't feel untalented; if only I could find enough if-onlys, then I would be happy. I signed the contract for my first book the morning of the day I received my master's degree. Fate delivered on the if-onlys. And I waited. (Patience was about the only virtue left in my life.) But then nothing happened; I didn't feel smart or talented, or any different at all, really. I was the butt of the ultimate cosmic practical joke. (Sometimes, I swear, I can still hear the fates chuckling over that one.) Ha-ha.

The book would go on to do quite well without me, probably as well as it would have done with me doing all the things writers are supposed to do, now that writing is entertainment. Nineteen eighty-nine slogged past. I couldn't write for the first time in my life, and I have been a writer all my life. There was nothing left to say. I was not so much blocked as gutted. When I finally started to write again, there were no dreams to spin, only tortured characters who hated me. I was no longer the writer creating the work but a piece of work being created by characters from the singed parts of my mind. On the heels of a book about lesbians who triumph over adversity, I had descended into a very personal hell where triumph was never considered, where even survival was in jeopardy. I thought it was a masterpiece. I was wrong.

There are all kinds of stories we writers circulate among ourselves about the greed of editors who push next books out too soon on the heels of a popular book. *The Bar Stories* was and continues to be popular, even now. (At least I'm still getting royalty checks.) And I am grateful for that. I am more grateful, though, that my torturous dark masterpiece, with its beautiful language and horrific visions, wasn't sent into an already tortured and horrific world. Mostly, I am grateful that Michael Denneny had the great good sense to ask: "Are you really sure you want to go ahead with this project?" (*You don't want to go through that door.*)

# Three

Allan Gidley and I have no history at all. He is the kindest, most compassionate man I know. For a long time now, I have straddled two careers: one in journalism and, more recently, in university public relations; the other as a lesbian writer of fiction. The balance is sometimes difficult to maintain.

Making a book is a very costly proposition for a writer. It takes courage and faith and time and love, all exercised in almost Spartan isolation. Nuns could not live more simply or with more devotion to a cause than do writers at work on a book. And we cannot, as much by our natures as by our too-often-anorexic bank accounts, live the great American dream; our task is to dissect it, examine it, make sense of it when we can, occasionally remaking it if we can. We are not supposed to be seduced by Madison Avenue; but we sometimes are. At least I sometimes am. I met Allan Gidley during one of those times.

Some people call him an angel (although he insists he is much too angry and too naughty to be that) because he has spent almost every evening for the past few years as a hospice volunteer for AIDS patients. (By day, he is the director of a university bookstore, one of those quiet, unassuming jobs that will ultimately change the world very little.) I think of him less as an angel than as Hermes, who had much to do with death and messages. And the dying leave such potent messages. Allan knows this probably better than anyone; he's been with more than a hundred people at the time they've died. (How many of us would do that? How many of us would even try?) And he carries their messages back to the rest of us, who are floundering and toying with ideas of what we Americans call success. None of it matters, the dying say, not the cars or the clothes, not even the condominiums or the summer houses. All that matters is being passionate about some one or some thing. That is the single largest regret of the dying: that they spent too little time on what truly matters and so much on what our sickly insatiable society told them was all-important.

"How tragic," he told me that winter, when corporations were trying to seduce me, "to have spent your whole life chasing something only to find out in the end that it never mattered at all." (*You don't want to go through that door.*)

●━●━●

And so, these are the three. Perhaps they are not the animus manifested into flesh; maybe they are just kind men no different than a dozen others I know. But I don't really believe that, any more than I believe that the dream men are nothing more than shadows of the day's events. Perhaps it would have been easier to ignore their warnings and go through those doors. How much easier it would have been to sink back into yet another disastrous relationship, or to bring out a book that would have ultimately caused me so much pain that I would have been left with no choice but to finally chuck it all and sell myself to the highest bidder, the Chevrons and Exxons of this world. How easy to open that door, to slip down those stairs back to my familiar terrain of shit and dungeons and catacombs. How easy never to climb out again. How easy. How easy? You don't want to go through that door.

(*With appreciation to Betty DeShong Meador, Ph.D., the Oracle in this piece.*)

ROBERT F.
REID-PHARR

# Living as
# a Lesbian

In 1985 Barbara Smith came like a fresh wind into Chapel Hill. She brought with her a vision of home unlike anything I had imagined. Home held out promises of redemption and nurturance, acceptance and love. Home was populated with brothers and sisters so unlike my own "natural" family in their politics, their progressiveness, their passion. At home we would re-create ourselves and our world, fashion a new mode of being, map a way for living in which the vision of the black freedom struggle would be realized in the daily interaction of black lesbians and gays. In coming home, I told myself, I would finally be able to articulate that which I had known all along, the centrality of the black woman, the black faggot, the so-called black underclass, and especially the black lesbian to the project of redeeming America. Armed with strong doses of Audre Lorde, Pat Parker, Cheryl Clarke, and Donna Kate Rushin, I felt, for a brief moment in my life, as if I knew in which direction to place my feet, saw clearly the road before us.

> *The most general statement of our politics at the present time would be that we are actively committed to struggling against racial, sexual, heterosexual, and class oppression, and see as our particular task the development of integrated analysis and practice based upon the fact that the major systems of oppression are interlocking.*
>
> Combahee River Collective, "The Combahee River Collective Statement," in
> Home Girls: A Black Feminist Anthology, ed. Barbara Smith
> (New York: Kitchen Table of Women of Color Press, 1983)

My sister had been in early life the quintessential daddy's girl. To him she was his "heart," the proof of his own self-worth, his princess to be protected from boys, men, and the great unfriendly world. It seemed to all of us that only a moment had passed before her long hair, fancy dresses, and sassy little-girl style gave way to cigarettes, a Jheri curl, unquestioned prowess on the basketball court, and then eventually to her first woman lover, Rose. The news of the passionate love affair between seventeen-year-old bulldaggers hit my family like the news of death or war. After months of histrionics and therapy my parents packed first my sister and then me off to live with our aunt in Brooklyn for a boring summer of softball and Coney Island. When we returned our parents announced their divorce, or rather our mother announced that she would be leaving our father.

My sister's lesbianism had by all indications been cured. She started a tempestuous relationship with Darryl, another impressive basketball player and the father of her child. She suffered through years of drug and alcohol abuse and raised her son, in working poverty, always stuck in the shadow of my parents' smugly secure comfortableness and my own unquenchable thirst for success. She pushed forward, however unfruitfully, into the mystique of heterosexual acceptability until unexpectedly Rose, her ex–high school lover, suddenly reappeared, moved in, and began receiving well-chosen gifts from my parents during the holidays.

> Afraid, jealous, or stuck in some foaming
> funk I learned from her in the circumstances
> of her loneliness, I push away from my lover.
> This hotness, this coldness still in her aging she tricks me.
>
> Cheryl Clarke, "No More Encomiums," in Living as a Lesbian
> (Ithaca, NY: Firebrand, 1986)

My students and I have been discussing Audre Lorde's *Zami* in a monstrously large Harlem building with few windows. We keep the door to the classroom open to save ourselves from roasting inside the six-inch-thick cement walls. I present the text to them like a scarce and delicious morsel. They snatch it up, hungrily consuming what they like, leaving the rest to scavengers.

"I'm not a lesbian, still I can relate."

"I'm Caribbean and these Caribbean writers just get under my skin."

"Was she abused as a child?"

"Was she afraid of black people?"

"I didn't read the whole book, but . . . "

Audre Lorde, Audre—poet, mother, sister, lesbian, warrior, cancer survivor—was for them, and for me, just the third assignment on a fourteen-week syllabus, sandwiched between a collection of Lower East Side writers and Alfred Kazin's *Walker in the City.* They liked her, they said. I talked about her being the poet laureate of New York, one of the great prophets of multiculturalism and the concept of overlapping identities. They blinked back at me and argued among themselves about whether lesbians could walk the streets of Harlem holding hands.

> *To whom do I owe the power behind my voice, what strength I have become, yeasting up like sudden blood from under the bruised skin's blister?*
>
> Audre Lorde, Zami: A New Spelling of My Names
> (*Freedom, CA: The Crossing Press, 1982*)

"He looks just like a girl," well-meaning ladies would giggle as they passed by me, sitting on the front steps, my Afro braided down into neat cornrows. Other children would respond cruelly that indeed I was a boy, that it was only my fat body and long hair that so obfuscated my sex. And yet even they could not resist taking me around by the hand on Halloween nights when, dressed in a skirt and stockings, I would present myself as a rather delectable treat on neighbors' doorsteps.

"Stop acting like a sissy," my father would bark at me, his eyes fixated on my limp wrist as I crossed the street from the school bus.

"*Mira loca!*" my Dominican neighbors would yell years later as I issued forth, in full butch-queen regalia, from my newly rented Washington Heights apartment.

I have acquired this ill-fitting masculinity at considerable cost. There were years during my adolescence when men would start to scream at me as I walked out of public restrooms, assuming that I was some crazy or radical woman breaking into their most sacred domain. In graduate school I became the first male teaching assistant for the "Introduction to Women's Studies" lecture. My sections filled up with the few men taking the course. One of them would eventually break down in class as he recounted the details of his having been sexually abused. Another wrote to me privately that I was the only thing standing in the way of his acting on unspecified rape fantasies. I assigned him the grade *check,* as opposed to *check minus* or *check plus,* and told him that his letter was one of the most interesting things he had written.

> *This anger so visceral I could shit it*
> *and still be constipated.*
> *My ass is sore with the politics*
> *of understanding the best given the circumstances.*
> *I could spit this anger*
> *and still choke on the phlegm.*

Clarke, "No More Encomiums"

My lesbianism takes me to dyke parties in Brooklyn, small clubs hidden away among the West Side warehouses, the odd women's gathering, and a wealth of impromptu therapy sessions. I know all the young black female film and video makers: Cheryl, Shari, Dawn, Vejan, Yvonne, and even Michelle, not to mention Jackie W., the children's writer; Pamela, the performance artist; Cathy, the Ivy League professor and AIDS activist; bald Jackie B., the erotic poet; Jewelle, who needs no introduction; and of course Barbara, the mother of us all. I am asked with a regularity that never ceases to surprise me for my sperm and then asked, ever so gingerly, to step quietly aside.

My files are packed with back copies of *Sinister Wisdom, Off Our Backs, On Our Backs,* and *Conditions.* I have recently removed my copy of J. R. Roberts's bibliography, *Black Lesbians,* from my bookcase, afraid that this most precious piece of lesbian ephemera might be damaged on my crowded shelves. I continue to keep my three issues of *Stallion, Male Pictorial,* and *Honcho,* my two issues of *Drummer* and *Mandate,* my four issues of *Advocate Men,* and my single issues of *Inches* and *Torso* in a box under my bed.

> *The book you are holding in your hands is a kind of miracle. The fact that hundreds of black lesbians have found the courage to commit their lives and words to paper is miraculous.*
>
> Barbara Smith, foreword to Black Lesbians, *comp. by J. R. Roberts (Tallahassee, FL: Naiad Press, 1981)*

To become myself I have become a lesbian, or at least that's what I have been told. I have found my way into dozens of women's beds, been thoroughly schooled in the intricacies of women's relationships, learned to sit quietly and listen as the many vulgarities of "The Man" are rehearsed:

> *how like a man*
> *is the ku klux klan*
> *it comes in the night*
> *to wag its ugly shaft*
> *to laugh at the final climax of its rape*
> *as rope chokes out the final cry of "why?"*
> *blood blurring sight of a naked cross.*
>
> Cheryl Clarke, "How Like a Man," *in* Living as a Lesbian *(Ithaca, NY: Firebrand, 1986)*

And yet. And still. Even as I stand before the bathroom mirror, my dick tucked between my legs so that only the bushy triangle of pubic hair is showing, I continue to smell my own heavy man's smell, a scent not very different from the musky sweetness my father left behind in my childhood memories. Of late I have taken to rubbing my face along the cocks and balls and inside the buttocks of my lovers, hoping that in their scent I might find something of my own, or my father's, or his own unknown father's. I lick the sweat off bellies spilling over too-tight jeans, suck gobs of chest hair, and underarm hair, and scrotum hair into my mouth, gorging on the rough texture, begging to be pinned down to the bed, to be penetrated by a vigorous and vibrant masculinity. My lovers whisper, "Whose pussy is this?" as they struggle to slip their cocks into my ass. I haven't the heart to answer simply that it is my own.

In 1985 Barbara Smith came like a fresh wind into Chapel Hill. She brought with her a vision of home unlike anything I had imagined. It would be years before I would look up to find that as I searched for home I continued in my isolation. It was the death of Pat Parker that first alerted me to the fragility of both our dreams and our community. First her then Joe Beam then Donald Woods then David Frechette then Rory Buchanan then James Baldwin and Roy Gonsalves then Audre Lorde herself. In response I wrote:

> *I could have fucked him*
> *Head on rumpled pillow*
> *Ass lifted towards heaven*
> *Like she cat*
> *In season*
> *In heat*
>
> *I might have cut into flesh*
> *Leeched out blood*
> *Bitten into gristle*
> *And Swallowed*
>
> *And yet*
> *And Still*
>
> *I tried saving him long distance*
> *Tied up phone lines preaching brotherhood*
> *Wrote treatises on community*
> *Debated love and metaphysics at the institute*
>
> *Took clever men to bed*

*Shall I scratch his name onto parchment*
*Press it to my lips*
*Arrange it among the relics on my altar?*

*Shall I build a memorial*
*Great Edifice Reaching forth to God*
*Higher than misery?*

I showed this, my only attempt at poetry as an adult, to my boyfriend at the time, who told me that the "she cat" line made him uncomfortable. We broke up. I left for the comfort of my girlfriends. He started dating women. We both resisted the somewhat Afrocentric, Brooklyn-centered black lesbian and gay community, finding that our own deepest desires had turned back in on themselves.

*I'm a queer lesbian.*
*Please don't go down on me yet.*
*I do not prefer cunnilingus.*
*(There's room for me in the movement.)*

*Cheryl Clarke, "Sexual Preference," in* Living as a Lesbian
*(Ithaca, NY: Firebrand, 1986)*

Cheryl phones on an early weekday morning looking for a hundred dollars and advice. I write a check for fifty and remain on the telephone for hours debating the relative merits of worry versus denial. She complains that too many of the wrong kind of women love her. I answer that that's my problem exactly. We laugh, make plans to see each other, and hang up. The two of us maintain a type of charming delicacy with each other. I respect her boyishness as she cherishes my effeminacy. We are a couple, mentioned in one breath as dinner parties are planned, given to public quarrels over the minutiae of everyday life, constantly aware of each other's steps and jealous of the intrusion of outsiders. Our lesbianism runs deep. We are drawn together because of our profound love of women, our unquenchable thirst for companionship, our hot-blooded sexual passion, and our constant struggle to find and create home. She chides me to help her write her story. I respond by looking hard at her small breasts, pulling from her the details of her menstruation, and resisting the urge to cover my penis, floating in the bathwater, as she passes by the tub.

> *Sweet words and warm this time—*
> *not like the last time salty and frigid*
> *over some money I owed her—*
>
> Cheryl Clarke, "No More Encomiums"

Living as a lesbian continues for me to be a process in which I am constantly brought back, in my search for spiritual perfection, for transcendence, to my body, to the luscious beauty of my heavy thighs and hairy chest, my fleshy ass and strong hands. And still I continue to love and desire "her" body, Cheryl's body, Yevette's body, Joanna, Daphne, Pat, Sabhia, and Nicki's bodies, not simply the image or the promise, but the texture of their hair, the color of their skin, the smell of their sweat.

In 1985 Barbara Smith came like a fresh wind into Chapel Hill. She brought with her a vision of home unlike anything I ever had imagined. It was then that I began the process of becoming a lesbian. It is only recently that I began to understand lesbianism as a state of being that few of us ever achieve. To become lesbian one has to first be committed to the process of constantly becoming, of creatively refashioning one's humanity as a matter of course.

## Coda

*By becoming lesbian, I have done nothing more nor less than become myself.*

I had expected to end this piece with these words, forcing all of us, myself included, to reevaluate what it means to be labeled lesbian, gay, straight, bi, transgendered, asexual. And yet this is not enough. For even as I recognize the difficulty of giving definition and meaning to our various identities, I also realize that as I struggle to lay claim to my lesbianism I am always confronted with the reality of my own masculinity, this strange and complex identity that I continue to have difficulty recognizing as privilege.

It was a Friday afternoon in September when I had my first bathhouse experience. I'm not sure what I expected, or wanted. In truth, I was compelled more than anything else by Samuel Delany's description in *The Motion of Light in Water* of his visit to the St. Mark's Baths in the early sixties. I thought that it would be exciting, that perhaps within this outlaws' territory I could throw off the stifling fears and anxieties that shape and constrain our lives, sexual and otherwise. I even felt that, given the name of the enterprise I was about to visit—"baths"—there had to be something intrinsically cleansing and healing about it.

Now I find myself asking if in the bathhouse—the most sacred of male enclaves, where my masculine body and affected macho style increase my worth in the sexual economy—I am still lesbian. Is it lesbianism that spills out of the end of my cock as bald-headed men with grizzled beards and homemade tattoos slap my buttocks and laugh triumphantly? Is it lesbianism that allows me to walk these difficult streets alone, afraid only that I will *not* be seen, accosted, "forced" into sexual adventure?

All my bravado, my will to adventure is caught up, strangely enough, with the great confidence I have gained from "The Lesbian." And yet, this confidence, this awareness of my own body, of my own independence, takes me to places where she dares not go. Perhaps then I am not a lesbian at all, but rather like a drag queen: by day a more or less effeminate, woman-loving gay man, by night a pussy, a buck, the despoiler of young men recently arrived from the provinces and the careful tutelage of their loving mothers. What I know for certain is that this self, this lesbian-identified gay man, is in constant flux. I live like a lesbian, *as* a lesbian, because I know no better way of life. Still, I live beyond her in a province that continues to be reserved exclusively for men, all the while reaping the many fruits of sexual apartheid.

*Me, I want to escape . . . this dirty world, this dirty body. I never wish to make love again with anything more than the body.*

Perhaps in my next life I will be done with these questions of identity altogether, will cherish fully the body that I am given, begin to see it neither as burden or weapon, but only as the vessel of my existence. Perhaps in my next life I will have given up finally this constant struggle to explain who I am not—not woman, not white, not straight, not you—and start to revel in the limitlessness of my boundaries. Perhaps each one of us will recapture that which has been lost, start again to accept and acknowledge the profound ambiguity and uncertainty of this existence. It is then and only then that we will find home.

In 1985 Barbara Smith came like a fresh wind into Chapel Hill.

**JAMES**

**JOHNSTONE**

**&**

**KAREN X.**

**TULCHINSKY**

# Across the Lines

*Dedicated to the memory of our friends Lea Dawson and Shawn Feeney*

## James

I stop writing for a moment to look at Karen as she concentrates on her ten-minute writing exercise.

Her face is intent, her gaze focused on the pen she skips across her pad. This is our weekly ritual: to get together and write, and share what we have written. It's a miracle that we are even writing this piece together, considering all the stuff we went through. It is hard to imagine that only two years ago we didn't even speak to each other. It feels good to be friends again. So much healing has happened since our friend Shawn died. We have come full circle. Because of him, Karen and other lesbians are back in my life again.

## Karen

The first time I met James I was having a fight with a man on the provincial gay and lesbian conference committee. He wanted to have an ecumenical service on the Sunday morning of the conference.

"Uh, what's an ecumenical service?" I asked.

"Oh," he said, waving his hands in the air, "it's a religious service for all faiths."

"All faiths?"

"Yeah, you know, it's for Catholics, Protestants, and Baptists. You know, nondenominational."

My Jewish heart sunk. Where would I start? Here I was, a new kid in Vancouver, a beautiful place geographically speaking, but a cultural wasteland for a nice Jewish girl like me. This was white-bread country. These people never heard of a bagel or matzo balls or pastrami on rye, hold the mayo. They were strictly ham and cheese with lots of butter. How could I begin to explain my life to them? I considered quitting the conference. I didn't because Lea, another woman on the committee, convinced me to be patient, and for reasons I quite couldn't put a finger on at the time, I wanted to connect with gay men.

Before moving to the West Coast, I had worked at a rape-crisis center in Toronto for four years. After listening to dozens of women every day who were in various stages of recovery from being raped, beaten, abused, harassed, and generally kicked around by people of the male species, I was almost ready to buy a machine gun and run rampaging through the streets of Vancouver shooting men at random.

And yet, I knew they couldn't all be bad. It was time to either find at least one gay man I could like or lead a life of lesbian separatism, never again to enjoy political alliances with gay men, fabulous dinners cooked just for me by the fag of my choice, fashion tips, and the exchange of cruising techniques with homosexuals of the male gender. I knew I would get support and encouragement for my attempts at casual dyke dating from gay men in a way I couldn't always count on from other dykes.

## James

I came out late, comparatively. I was twenty-four when I finally risked hellfire and accepted what I have known since seven and had been fighting all along—that I liked men, that I was gay.

The next few years were spent making up for all that lost time. I earned my pink card learning how to cook, cruise, figure out the hanky code, give and deal with attitude, dance in discos, have sex without guilt, and survive eight-day relationships.

I immersed myself in the gay male world. I spent most of my free time in the bars looking for a husband. After six months of hit-and-miss dating, I was swept off my feet and down the aisle by the eleventh man I slept with. I stayed in that relationship for three and a half years.

I made quite a few good friends in that time, all male. Some were old tricks, and others, like Shawn, I met through my lover. I had little exposure to lesbians. I lived in the West End, Vancouver's high-rise gay ghetto, far removed from the cappuccino bars and pool halls of Commercial Drive in the East End, where most lesbians lived. Every now and then I would meet one at a friend's party, but I didn't go out of my way to talk with them. I was so focused on checking out the men. Back then, I never dreamed that lesbians might become significant in my life.

This all changed in 1985. I was at my first mixed gay and lesbian dance with my lover. There were lots of men there, but my eyes were drawn to the women whirling around me. Look at all those earth mothers, I thought. I was fascinated with how these women moved, how they seemed to draw energy right up out of the earth as they swayed and pounded their feet to the music. There was a magic in their dancing that excited me somehow.

That night I had my first glimpse of the goddess. It was my first inkling that lesbians might be different from what I had heard. Before then, all I knew about lesbians I had gleaned from other gay men. Lesbians were so serious. They didn't have a sense of humor. They ate lots of tofu and their potlucks were political. They listened to depressing music, and most of them hated men. The one positive thing I had heard about them was they were experts at long-term monogamous relationships.

The following year I got dumped by my lover. I was in need of a focus, something to keep me busy. I volunteered to help organize the 1987 provincial gay and lesbian conference and got drafted to cochair with a woman named Lea. Lea became my first lesbian friend.

## Karen

I met James the first time I went to a gay and lesbian conference meeting. I noticed right away that we were wearing the same thing. We both had on blue 501 jeans, white T-shirts under navy flannel button-down shirts, black Reeboks, and black leather jackets. We looked like twin brothers. To my mind he dressed just like a butch dyke.

## James

Karen was among the women Lea brought on board. Within a week, two very different gay women walked into my world. My life and the conference were in for some wonderful changes.

What drew me to Lea was her warmth and openness.

She was intelligent, articulate, and prepared to be patient with me. There was something that felt big-sisterish about her. She inspired me to learn as much as I could about being a sensitive and worthy cochair.

Karen, on the other hand, was my first exposure to the fire of radical feminism. She was Jewish, butch as all hell, and preferred the word *dyke* over *lesbian*.

My memory of Karen at her first meeting is her exploding at the ex-chair of the conference in a debate about the traditional conference ecumenical service. I remember how my anxiety rose. I had never seen anyone so publicly real with her emotions before. I was unnerved and fascinated at the same time. I had to get to know her better. My chance came when we formed a subcommittee together to work on community outreach.


## Karen

"Why don't we meet at my place?" James said over the phone. "I'll cook."

"Okay," I said. "I'll pick up a six-pack."

"Uh," he hesitated, "why don't you make that a bottle of red wine? A cabernet sauvignon perhaps. It will go better with the meal."

"Okay."

He cooked me something fabulous. I can't remember what it was. It might have been beef teriyaki with basmati rice and curry vegetables, or maybe it was cashew chicken and pepper linguini followed by mango and kiwi ice cream for dessert. Who remembers now? The point is, the meal was exquisite and I loved every bite, even after I spilled red wine all over my 501s. Ever-so-gallant James dashed to his bedroom and brought out a pair of his jeans for me to wear, while he hung mine over the shower-curtain rod to dry.

"How many of these do you have?" I asked while looking over his shoulder to snoop in his dresser drawers.

"I don't know. Five or six."

"Hmmm," I said, slipping into the jeans and buttoning up the fly.

"What?"

"Well . . ."

"What?"

"You don't know this yet," I said, "but you're going to give me these jeans."

"What?"

"You have to."

"No I don't."

"Yes you do."

He folded his arms across his chest. "Okay. Why should I?"

"Because I have only one pair and you have five or six," I said, keeping a deadpan face, "and I'm just a poor dyke who makes way less money than you do even though I work just as hard. And I'll keep bugging you about this until it drives you so crazy that you'll tell me to just keep the jeans and get off your back. That's why."

"Hmmm." He stood across from me, his arms still folded across his chest, trying to suppress a smile.

"Or . . . ," I grinned, "you could save yourself a lot of pain and anguish and just give them to me right now."

"More wine?" he said, holding out the bottle.


James

Karen was even more engaging than what my first impression had led me to expect. Physically, she was short and compact. But she had this way of drawing herself up to her full height and cocking her head back in such a manner as to create the illusion that she was taller and somehow looking down at me.

Her life was divided into appointment-book time slots, with most nights of the week devoted to various collective meetings and dates with friends. She even had dates with Suzanne, her lover of three years!

We set it up so that we would make dinner for each other every other Friday.

One by one, Karen destroyed my illusions about lesbians. Sure, she was political, and she was serious, but that's where it ended. She laughed a lot, liked getting silly; she didn't wear Birkenstocks or like depressing music. She liked reggae and disco, and she loved to dance. Heck, the one time I tried to serve her tofu, she told me she didn't eat it.

I loved talking with her. We talked about our different backgrounds, gay and lesbian politics, childhood abuse, lesbian mothers, cruising, what happens in bathhouses, how lesbians have sex—everything. But our favorite topic of conversation was relationships.

My new boyfriend, Keith, wanted us to be nonmonogamous. I needed a lot of convincing. Karen and her lover were moving into separate homes and opening up their relationship after three years of monogamy. Listening to her describe how she and Suzanne looked after each other through this period of change made me more positive about my own relationship, gave me the courage to be open and take each day at a time. Finally I had a reference point of sorts, a couple I liked and respected as role models, and some options to explore.

I couldn't have been happier than when my best friend, Shawn, and Suzanne hit it off. Shawn was my running mate and bar buddy. He had been my main support through my breakup. He was politically conservative and closeted at work, but that was nothing that a little lesbian influence couldn't remedy.

## Karen

I met Shawn for the first time at James's thirty-first birthday party in 1986. Shawn was a leprechaun, Irish, born on Saint Patrick's Day, with flaming red hair and slightly pointy ears. He knew that his pot of gold lay just beyond the rainbow. He was HIV-positive when I met him, but asymptomatic. He was living in a high-rise in the West End that was home to so many gay men that it was known throughout the city as Stack-of-Fags. He was boyfriendless and living with a straight woman friend. He became friends with my lover, Suzanne, and he joined our circle of friends.

## James

Finally Shawn had some "real wimmin" in his life. I marveled at the combination. My best bud, up to now an apolitical, sometimes sexist product of middle-class, Irish Catholic, what-would-the-neighbors-think Oakville ways, had taken up with a proud and fiery working-class, Franco-Manitoban feminist femme and lover of perhaps the most politicized, hot-blooded butch dyke I knew. I was curious to see how things would develop—and develop they did.

My friendships with Karen and Lea blossomed and brought more women into my life. I went out to support women's events. There were Take Back the Night rallies, marches for International Lesbian Week and International Women's Day. I got invited to barbecues and birthday and Hanukkah parties, where Keith and I and sometimes Shawn were often the only men there. It made me think of the lone lesbians I had met years ago who braved those near all-men parties I went to.

I loved working with Lea and Karen on the conference committee. There was a synergy in our friendship and politics. Consensus came easy. May rolled around, and the conference was a tremendous success. Our winter and spring of political work segued into a long hot summer of weekends spent in the buff on Vancouver's Wreck Beach.

## Karen

On the west side of Vancouver, south of the University of British Columbia, lies Wreck Beach. It has been an unofficial nude beach for decades. People come from all over the world to lie naked in the sun, play Frisbee in the buff, and splash in the Pacific Ocean with their tits and cocks and cunts to the wind.

There is no need to bring a picnic basket because there are merchants walking up and down the beach who will sell you anything. You can buy beer, sandwiches, soft drinks, sushi, fruit salad, T-shirts, tarot readings, kiwi-mango kebabs, hot dogs, and G-strings on Wreck Beach.

My lover and I used to go sometimes to lie in the sun. No matter how hard we tried to discourage them, inevitably during the day straight men would approach us, try to sit down, talk to us, stare at our naked bodies, or otherwise harass us. In the summer of 1987 whenever we went to the beach we'd meet James, Shawn, and other dykes and fags we knew. We'd all spread our towels together beside a large rainbow flag that James would bring and plant in the sand. Now we were women with men, and no longer "alone." Straight men stopped bothering us.

## James

We named our spot the Pink Triangle and dubbed the gray granite breakwater beside it the Stonewall. It was our summer of love.

*Life couldn't be much better,* I thought as I lay on my back, surrounded by my lover and my best lesbian and gay friends, watching the seagulls dart and glide over the crowded beach. I remember flipping over and talking to Bet, a close friend, about it. I enthused about how well the conference had gone and how our work had laid firm foundations for a new era of closeness between our gay and lesbian communities. Bet was not as optimistic. "Remember," she said, "that in any relationship, there is a honeymoon period. When that ends, the work and the hard stuff really begins."

I was not daunted by her comment. In my mind it was all set. Karen and Keith would cochair the next conference. We would work to expand and diversify the committee. Things could only get better. From my angle, lying on the beach as I was, the dark clouds on the horizon were out of my line of vision.

## Karen

Question: What happens when you bring together two radical lesbian feminists; one angry young Métis dyke; one furious Quebecoise dyke who consented to speak English only because nobody spoke French half decently in Vancouver anyway; one pissed-off former rape-crisis worker recently recovered man-hating Jewish butch dyke; one Irish Hungarian working-class femme punk lesbian; one lesbian comother; two middle-class, white, apolitical gay women; and six or seven white, middle-class, Gentile, disco-loving, politically naive, law-abiding, financially secure, inadvertently sexist, quiche-eating gay men for the purpose of organizing a provincial gay and lesbian conference?

Answer: Long, drawn-out, frustrating, irritating, infuriating, annoying, exasperating, bitter, passionate, offensive, enraging, insulting, aggravating, blood-boiling, tacky, abusive, outrageous, disorganized meetings.

## James

The clouds rolled in and the storm finally hit. Although it hadn't been the plan, I ended up having to cochair the 1988 conference committee with Karen. This time, I was in way over my head. There were a lot of new women on the committee, radical feminists with years of experience working on all-women collectives. Of the men, there were only two with any long-term political experience, and I wasn't one of them.

From early on, a definite split developed in the group. My lover, some of the lesbians, and most of the men were on one side, while Karen and the radical dykes were on the other. Each side had a very different vision of the conference and of how the meetings should be held. We got bogged down with process. It became a real struggle to come to any kind of consensus.

Over the weeks, our meetings grew more tense as dysfunctional backgrounds won out over common sense and earlier good intentions. We constantly pushed each other's buttons as we blundered along through minefield after minefield of unspoken resentments and hidden agendas. I didn't know how to deal with it. I was completely ineffectual as a cochair. My loyalties were split, and I knew my friendship with Karen was on the line.

## Karen

Somewhere in the process I got mad at James and didn't know how to make up with him. If he had been a woman, it would have been different. We would not have been able to avoid each other, this being a small town and there being only one dyke bar for hundreds of miles and at least one border crossing. Eventually—that is to say, in a matter of days—we would have run into each other on the dance floor and we would have had it out. Like it or not, we would have had to kiss and make up and live happily ever after in this small community of ours.

Being that James was a man, however, it was possible to avoid each other for approximately the next two years. Occasionally I'd see him at Gay Pride Day or the AIDS Vigil or some other demo or parade where fags and dykes gather, and we'd ignore each other from across the street or park or auditorium. Secretly I'd feel sad and nostalgic, because when I saw him he'd be wearing the same thing as me and I'd remember the good times.

## James

We pulled off the conference in the end. My speech for the opening ceremony was lame and uninspired, someone else's voice. Karen's speech sounded like a harangue against the men and the middle-class lesbians on the committee. Our conference theme was supposed to be "Building Bridges." More bridges were burned that week than built.

I heard that some people thought the conference was a success. For me, it was a personal disaster. By the time it was all over, the two groups in the committee had written each other off. I never wanted to be involved in community politics again.

What's worse, the bad blood in the committee spilled over into my private life. It was bad enough that my friendship with Karen was on the rocks, but my friendship with Shawn suffered as well.

He had strong connections with some of the women on the "other side," and he felt caught in the middle. Shawn wouldn't talk about the conference or any of the people involved. That left us with little to share with one another. We continued to spend time together, but there was always an underlay of unease in our relationship. We began to drift apart.

The next two years were the worst I can remember in my life. Karen had cut me off completely, and there didn't seem to be any way to pick up the pieces. Shawn was diagnosed with full-blown AIDS. And just when I thought that things couldn't get worse, Lea took her life. She had always seemed so strong, resilient—a survivor, not a victim. Lea had been a friend, mentor, and role model. Where was hope if a person like Lea chose suicide?

Loss upon loss was leaving me numb inside. My new world, which had expanded and been so enriched through knowing Lea in the first place, shattered and collapsed in on me. Constantly bumping into Karen didn't make things any easier. She lived and shopped nearby. We attended a lot of the same events. Seeing her was a constant reminder of a sore that wouldn't heal.

I remember attending a demonstration against proposed provincial quarantine legislation that we felt would be used against people with AIDS. Karen made an articulate and impassioned speech at the rally. It was one of the proudest moments of my life, watching and listening to her, with her head cocked back, stretching her five-foot-two frame so that she towered above the crowd. When it ended, I wanted to run over and congratulate her. But I couldn't. Our wall of silence still stood between us.

## Karen

Late in 1990, we knew that Shawn was dying. He was completely blind now from CMV retinitis and had been in and out of the hospital many times with bouts of PCP. He was losing weight, and now he had a tumor in his brain. It was in the hospital corridors that I started seeing James again. There it was impossible to ignore each other.

## James

Shawn didn't make it to Christmas. He died in a bubble bed on the seventh floor of the new wing of Saint Paul's Hospital. Don, his lover, and a few of his friends were there when Shawn rattled out his last breath. I arrived five minutes after. I walked into a room of tear-flushed faces. He was gone. I hadn't had a chance to say good-bye.

I went over and touched Shawn's face. His eyes were still open. Someone came in and unplugged his bed. Ten minutes later they wheeled his body out of the room and I plodded home. It's funny: I expected to feel something, but I didn't. I couldn't. My mind was a fog, my whole body numb. I knew I didn't want to be alone. I needed someone to talk to. I wanted to be around Shawn's friends. There was only one thing to do.

## Karen

On a Friday afternoon I was coming home from work when I found James standing in front of my building with a wine bottle under his arm. I knew at once why he was there. It could only be one thing.

"Shawn's dead," I said to him, and it was more of a statement than a question. He nodded.

## James

Karen reached up and touched my shoulder, the first time we had touched since the conference.

"I didn't know if you or Suzanne had heard yet so I thought I would come over," I mumbled.

She led me into the apartment. Suzanne and her friend Mickey were sitting quietly at the kitchen table. Don had phoned earlier. They already knew.

## Karen

The four of us sat around my dining-room table drinking the wine James brought, crying, toasting Shawn, breathing collective sighs of relief that our friend was out of his misery, wondering what we would do without him, remembering the good times, feeling sad, and getting just a little drunk.

## James

I remember the warmth of Suzanne's body and the softness of her long hair as we hugged. I stared over her shoulder at a picture taken at one of Shawn's last birthdays. Shawn, Suzanne, and Mickey were clinking very large martini glasses. It felt so right to be there, with Shawn smiling down at us, toasting our reunion. Suzanne and I did most of the talking. Karen sat beside her lover in silence, her hand resting gently on her shoulder. Every so often she would look at me and I could see the concern in her eyes, not just for Suzanne, but for me as well. Something had changed. Her wall was crumbling.

## Karen

Every so often I would sneak a peek at James, sitting there at my table for the first time since I disowned him, and I was struck all at once with a revelation.

People can die. It was that simple. You might be expecting it or you might not. They can die just like that and you might never have the chance to see them again, or tell them something important, or fight with them, or steal their jeans, or eat their food, or go to the hospital with them the next time another friend is sick. You don't always have all the time in the world.

It was one of the most important moments in my life. It was the moment I grew up and knew what I wanted to be.

I wanted to be a mensch, a decent person, someone who is big enough to forgive the mistakes of others, like my uncle Sam, who survived Hitler's concentration camps and still does not hate all Germans.

"There were good Germans and there were bad Germans," he said to me often enough that I remember. "Most of them were very bad, they'd spit on a Jew who lay dying in the streets. But it was a good German who helped me escape. Therefore, how can I hate them all?" he'd say as he shrugged his shoulders.

I wanted to be someone who sticks by my friends through the good and the bad, someone who is brave enough to be honest, to be real, to fight and struggle through the hard times, to be there whether they're waiting on me hand and foot or pissing me off or thrilling me or boring me. And though I wouldn't be inviting Ronald Reagan or Arnold Schwarzenegger over for tea, my man-hating days were over.

I drank some more wine and half smiled at James. I knew I wouldn't say anything about my revelation just then, even though I was bursting with it. It would have to wait.

"To Shawn," Suzanne was saying, and we all held our glasses high and drank to our recently fallen friend.

## James

Later, Karen saw me off at the door. We hugged and said good-bye. Shawn's long struggle was over, and our two years' silence was finally broken.

A few weeks after the funeral, I went down to the seawall for a walk. I stared out at the freighters anchored in the still gray waters of English Bay. I thought about Shawn and all the unfinished business we had left hanging, like a shroud of Vancouver rain clouds, over our five-year friendship. It was too late to do anything about that now. I still wished that somehow I could tell him that I loved him, and let him know how much his friendship had meant to me.

I picked up a shiny black rock and skipped it across the water. I turned around and recognized a familiar form, jumping from log to log along the beach, as she made her way toward me. It was Karen, of course.

## Karen

James and I smiled at each other and then sat down on a log facing the ocean.

I pulled a hash joint out of my pocket.

"Smoke?" I asked.

"Sure."

I lit the joint and we smoked in silence for a few minutes.

"Isn't that my shirt?" James asked me finally. I was wearing a royal blue sweatshirt with a hood.

"No. It was Shawn's. Don was cleaning out his closet and gave me some clothes. See?" I pointed to the jeans I was wearing that were cuffed up at the ankles. "These were his jeans, too."

"No," James reached for my shirt cuff to feel the material. "This was mine. I lent it to Shawn."

"Oh," I said. "So? Do you want it back or something?"

"No. You keep it. It looks good on you."

"I miss you," I said, and I realized I was crying. He looked over to me, and I saw he was crying too.

"I've missed our friendship, too, Karen."

"I don't even remember why I was mad at you." I went on. "It doesn't seem important anymore, whatever it was."

"Yeah."

We sat there for a while, watching the waves come in, thinking about life and death and AIDS and friends and lovers. People walked by, seagulls squawked at each other above our heads. The sun was going down and the tide coming in. We both knew that something important had happened, and it was bigger than just the two of us. On the gay and lesbian conference committee we all forgot who the real enemy was and acted out our rage against an unjust world on each other. It was a downward spiral that, once we got on, we couldn't get off of until we hit bottom. It took Shawn's death for us to see how fragile our lives were, how precious friends could be, and how little time there really was for any of us. It was his last gift to us, and we felt humbled by its enormity. If there was life after death, we hoped that Shawn was watching; then he'd know that we'd never forget him or the lesson we had learned. The ocean before us reflected our mood, which was quiet and pensive. We felt sorry for our mistakes and a bit ridiculous, but most of all, we felt hopeful. We didn't know what would happen next, but we knew we were at a starting place, and our optimism for the future returned. In the sky, big thick rain clouds were clearing up, just as the sun was setting. We were sure it was a sign that we were on the right track and sure that, even if it was just a coincidence, the moment held meaning for us and always would.

GERRY

GOMEZ

PEARLBERG

&

STEPHEN

WILDER

# The Cultural Exchange

## Introduction

We met and became close friends in high school, lived together for two years after college, and continue to play important roles in one another's lives to this day. What follows are our two perspectives on a seventeen-year friendship between a lesbian and a gay man who have influenced, guided, and cared deeply for each other for more than half of their lives.

## Stephen: Coming Out

My coming out was a murky process. I have early memories of being strongly physically attracted to other boys as well as feeling some attraction to and a great deal of affection for some girls. Somehow I didn't let my more powerful attraction to boys interfere with the assumption that I would one day get married and have children. I dated women in high school and became physically involved with several women during my first two years of college. Meanwhile, my attraction to men was growing stronger: no longer just the objects of heart-rending crushes, these men became the focus of increasingly vivid sexual fantasies. Somehow I managed to live with this stressful conflict for years, until at the end of my sophomore year of college, provoked by a passing comment, I was forced, or allowed myself, to realize that I might in fact be gay.

I had a very difficult summer following this realization. With the support of my family, the few friends I confided in, and a therapist my parents found for me, I managed to get through it. By the end of the summer I had determined that life was worth living even if I did turn out to be gay, and that I didn't have to make a permanent decision at that time. I returned to school for my junior year ready, willing, and eager to have sex with men. By the time I graduated it was clear to me that my homosexuality was too powerful a force to be suppressed or subverted and that this was, in fact, okay.

Interestingly, Gerry's perception of my coming-out process is slightly different from my own. She remembers an incident during our senior year of high school when, at her apartment, late at night, I tearfully told her that I was gay. I vaguely remember that night. I think she asked me if I was "interested" in any of the women in our class. I remember starting to shake, clutching my knees to my chest, chokingly telling her that I was more attracted to some of the men in our class, and breaking down in racking sobs. While I managed to totally block that night from my memory for years because I couldn't handle what deep down I already knew, Gerry came away from that evening with the understanding that I had come out to her. The differences in our interpretations of that event were to have interesting repercussions a couple of years later when Gerry came out to me as a lesbian.

## Gerry: Coming Out

As far as I was concerned, Stephen came out to me in high school, at my house, after who knows how many rum and cokes. I don't remember exactly what he said, only that he was very distraught, literally shaking and crying. I remember being not in the least surprised, feeling very tender toward him, and thinking, *My favorite person in the world is gay and therefore this is a desirable thing to be.* I was sleeping with my boyfriend at the time, although in some very abstract way I thought of myself as bisexual because the crowd I was hanging out with perceived bisexuality as a higher form of life. During this same period I vividly recall hearing—and feeling deeply validated by—a radio program on which Janis Ian, David Bowie, Joan Baez, and several others came out as bisexual. This was around 1978.

Although Stephen had relationships with women for a few years following his drunken declaration in my room, I continued to see him as gay. I sent him a coming-out letter the summer after our first year of college in which I wrote: "Sit down for this one. I wanted to talk about this when I saw you but the words just didn't form themselves. Stephen, I'm gay. . . . I wanted you to know because you're one of the people I love and trust most in the world." Even if he didn't think of himself as gay at that point, he was, in my own mind, my gay peer. I remember being surprised and a little hurt by what I considered to be his luke-warm response to my letter. In rereading Stephen's letter recently, I real-ize that it was actually a perfectly appropriate reply. But at the time, I was disappointed that he didn't seem as thrilled about my lesbianism as I'd expected him to be.

In any case, unbeknownst to Stephen, he was a role model for me, living proof that being gay didn't make one a "bad" or unappealing per-son. The fact of his homosexuality helped allay my youthful fears about what it meant to be gay, even if at the time he was seeing women. On a deeper level, I saw Stephen, in some essential and unalterable way, as a gay comrade. So when he came out to me again during college, I re-member being baffled and thinking, *I already know this. He already told me. Why is he telling me again?*

## Stephen: Living Together

Gerry and I kept in touch throughout college, writing letters during the school year and hanging out together during the summers. After grad-uation we took a two-bedroom apartment in Park Slope, Brooklyn, where we lived for two and a half years.

This was one of the most glorious periods in my life, and I know Gerry shares some of my nostalgia for that time: we were young and free and got along fabulously. I think some of my sense of freedom re-lated to a new perspective on my sexuality. Out of college, away from a predominantly straight and claustrophobically small environment, no longer financially dependent on my parents, and living with my best friend who happened to be a supportive, nonjudgmental lesbian, I fi-nally felt free to pursue a totally liberated sex life.

Unfortunately, this is just when the AIDS crisis entered the pub-lic's awareness and mine. At that time, we were told that AIDS was af-fecting "promiscuous" gay men and that it could be avoided by limiting the number of one's sex partners. I did what many other gay men did in response: scrambled to get into a relationship with one sexual partner. Unfortunately, the chances of maintaining a relationship with a partner snatched in haste to avoid disease or celibacy were slim, so these monogamous pairings changed fairly often.

During this time Gerry was pursuing her own romances, serious and otherwise. Sometimes she was "attached" and I was single, sometimes the reverse—but in any case we always seemed to have time for each other, providing twenty-four-hour counseling, living vicariously through each others' sexual adventures, and bolstering each other creatively.

We also learned from each other. Gerry was involved in a reproductive-rights organization and a women's literary magazine, while I was barhopping and contemplating art school. Gerry persuaded me to sign up with her to attend a class on gay American history, and we both got involved with a short-lived organization planning an international march for lesbian and gay rights—things I probably would not have gotten involved with on my own. In the meantime, I dragged her to East Village clubs and taught her the fine art of cruising—on subways, in the streets, in coffee shops, wherever. Gerry exposed me to books on gay history and politics. I exposed her to some of the more "frivolous" aspects of gay male culture: music, clothes, drag queens. Because we were so close, so trusting, so receptive to each other, our differences did not alienate us, but enhanced us both.

Gerry and I became, in some ways, like a couple. People referred to us as a unit. We hosted a seemingly endless series of now notorious parties that began as a way of luring our friends out to Brooklyn. The parties were held about once every six weeks, with increasingly elaborate invitations passed out to virtual strangers, resulting in bizarre, fascinating, and sometimes disturbing combinations of partygoers in our home.

After we had lived together for a couple of years, we both began to feel isolated in Brooklyn, and looked—without success—for an affordable Manhattan apartment to share. When Gerry told me that she had been offered a good deal on a studio apartment sublet in the East Village and would be moving out on her own, I was saddened, but I understood. After trying to find a new roommate I realized that I couldn't share that apartment with anyone else and ultimately let it go.

Prior to moving out, Gerry had started what was to be a serious long-term relationship, while I was just ending a less serious one. Because of Gerry's commitment to her developing relationship, we had already begun to drift apart, spending less time together, growing more emotionally independent from one another. Gerry's moving out was hard on me, but at the time I felt that this change would be good for me because being so close to her had prevented me from getting really close to another man in a romantic relationship. Gerry had been my primary relationship, and my sexual relationships were secondary. I think one reason for this was that I was still in the process of coming out, and a commitment to a homosexual relationship was a commitment to homosexuality that I probably wasn't yet able to make.

## Gerry: Living Together

Stephen's influence on me during the years we lived together after college was vast. For one thing, he modeled an unashamed "I'm into sex with men" attitude. In the lesbian feminist culture I came out into, it wasn't acceptable to say, "I'm a dyke because I love having sex with women." Stephen's comfort with a *sexualized* homosexuality was a big thing for me. I remember the way he'd talk about how cute some guy was, how much fun we'd have on the subway ogling some attractive androgynous person and arguing about whether we were looking at an adolescent boy or a dyke. I learned from him a whole new—and very enjoyable—way of gazing, of looking. Cruising was a totally foreign element that I admired and emulated; it offered me a means to express myself as a sexual person without apologizing for or rationalizing it. Stephen demonstrated lustfulness combined with affection for and appreciation of the men he was attracted to—a balance I found extremely appealing.

Another wonderful thing about those days was how immersed we were in developing our own little culture: every inch of our walls, not to mention the floors, was covered with stuff we collected from the streets, cut out from magazines, painted or drew or wrote or built. The little boy I used to baby-sit for once came to our house and said, "Gerry's house is like a museum." And it *was* like a very personal, very idiosyncratic museum, a lesbian/gay, Stephen/Gerry aesthetic amalgam. Stephen was in art school doing totally exciting work, and I was writing a lot. We'd have wild parties every six weeks where everyone would come and stand around staring at the walls. We were incredibly productive, and I think we inspired that in one another. People I don't know still come up to me and say, "Are you the one who used to have those parties with your roommate in that incredible apartment in Brooklyn?" There seems to be a whole subculture of people who went to our parties—people I don't even know, people *Stephen* doesn't even know. We created something that had a life of its own, even if it was very temporal. That's the beauty of it in my mind: we were completely unselfconscious about what we were doing, but we did it with a vengeance.

In retrospect, I think I felt myself to be—and was—in a primary relationship with Stephen during the years we lived together. He was in committed relationships with men, while I was having a series of affairs, but no matter what, I would come home pretty much every night, and pretty much every night he'd be there making us dinner—pork chops and rice, chicken and rice—which was delightful. My sense of that time is totally centered on that unkempt railroad apartment, more of a home than any I've ever had since. Because ours wasn't a sexual relationship, with all the conflict and staidness that can accompany that, there was a wonderful combination of intimacy, stability, and unpredictability. We enjoyed an endless series of escapades—mouse-catching episodes, the details of each other's sexual adventures, late-night high jinks in the East Village, artistic collaborations. An especially fond memory is one of dragging the TV set onto the roof and watching it up there with Stephen one hot summer night. We matched each other's need for pleasure, adventure, and strangeness. It was very romantic in many ways—a classic romantic friendship.

## Stephen: The Impact of HIV/AIDS

In the time after Gerry and I lived together I had two fairly disastrous relationships; one good one, which ended for various reasons; and a brief affair with a married man who ended up returning to his wife and children. The breakup of that last affair two years ago brought on a bit of an identity crisis for me. It left me questioning my commitment to my sexual preference and desperately longing for children of my own. I began considering the possibility of fathering or adopting a child. I realized that if I was going to have a biological child I would need to first find out my HIV status; even were I to adopt, I felt that I should first find out my long-term health prospects.

I didn't think, after so many healthy years of practicing safer sex, that I would test positive. Still, it was a possibility, and that possibility brought fear. I was, however, serious about having a child and for that reason felt ready to face AIDS anxiety, my old fearsome enemy.

But first I had to consult Gerry. Aside from being my most sage and valued adviser on any subject, she was also the best expert I knew on HIV/AIDS, a field she had been working in as a writer and educator for several years. Up until that time HIV was a subject we did not discuss because, like an ostrich who sticks his head in the sand, I felt that by not acknowledging AIDS, it did not exist. In earlier years, Gerry had opposed testing because of the lack of effective treatments and discrimination considerations. But when we discussed it this time, she felt that important advances had been made in the medical and antidiscrimination arenas and offered me any support necessary throughout the testing process and whatever the results might be. I took advantage of her offer by asking her to be with when I got the results back.

After an excruciating two weeks of waiting, my results were ready and I left to meet Gerry at my doctor's office. I arrived early. Gerry wasn't there yet, so I waited outside—much to the concern of the receptionist—rather than wait inside without her, such was my need for her presence at that time. When Gerry arrived I went in to see the doctor and found out much to my surprise that I had tested positive. I have to say that this was one of the worst moments of my life. My doctor was as reassuring as possible, and eventually I felt ready to go back out into the waiting room. After a surreal exchange with the receptionist, I stumbled outside into the rain with Gerry, lit a cigarette, and told her what she'd already gathered. We took a cab to my place and talked for a while. She waited in the living room while I made some calls; then we talked some more. Finally, when I was all talked out and simply numb, she kissed me, hugged me, and left.

I'll never forget that night. As opposed to the other traumatic events in my life, this was one during which I had total unconditional love and support. As I remember that night I am overwhelmed with love and gratitude to Gerry. I know I will never be able to sufficiently thank her or repay her for what she gave me that night by being there in a way that only she could be.

Aside from an inevitably rocky month or two, I feel I've handled the news of my HIV status very well. I believe that the support I received on the night I found out my test results was crucial in setting the tone for the time that followed. I am grateful for the support of my family, my friends, and my lover, Brian, whom I adore. For the first time I feel totally loved by and loving toward a man, enjoying a relationship in which we accept each other for who we are and respect our differences.

I cherish the important parts of my life, and Gerry is certainly one of them. We've had wonderful times at the requisite parties we have thrown, although separately, at the last twelve consecutive Lesbian and Gay Pride marches, and in collaborating on this project. Gerry is a friend for life. What we have learned from each other and what she means to me can never be captured in words.

## Gerry: The Impact of HIV/AIDS

I have a vivid memory from the time when Stephen and I lived together: *he's looking intensely into the bathroom mirror, neck craned, checking for swollen glands.* That image encapsulates my first awareness of the depth of Stephen's AIDS-related terror and its mirror image, my own fears about his health. I would later realize that in many ways my AIDS work, which began around 1985 and continues today, was a kind of semiconscious bargain with the universe to keep Stephen safe, a kind of magical thinking that by committing "good acts" in response to the epidemic I could somehow keep it from touching him.

I remember being baffled during those years by the fact that Stephen never seemed to want to discuss my work in ACT UP and AIDS education, which had become central to both my professional and personal lives. At times I resented this; I wanted him to recognize the work I was doing, to know I was doing it partly for him, to approve of what I was doing. His silence about it was frustrating, and it became increasingly alienating as my life became more and more about AIDS, as my losses and fears accumulated. At the same time, I clearly understood that the whole subject was just too scary for him to approach. Whereas I dove into AIDS work to manage my intense feelings about what was happening around me, Stephen managed his anxiety by keeping AIDS at arm's length—both of us postmodern queers engaged in our own acts of superstition, getting by as best we could under extremely trying circumstances.

I was both honored and terrified when Stephen asked me to accompany him to receive his HIV test results last year. At some point during my wait in the doctor's office, it hit me that he'd been in with the doctor too long for the test results to have been anything but positive. That moment and the hours following it are still emblazoned in minute detail in my mind's eye. It was unquestionably the most emotionally challenging moment of my life, a kind of crisis of faith in which my private bargain with the universe was brutally betrayed. It was also the moment in which my love for Stephen was distilled into an element of extraordinary clarity and power.

In the time since, I've seen Stephen face his diagnosis with action, optimism, and humor in such a distinctly Stephen way that it makes me smile with admiration to think of it. This frightening experience has made it possible for me to more fully recognize who Stephen is and has brought about a deepening of my feelings for him. It is wonderful, too, that even in these distressing times, we continue to find ways to care for each other, to teach each other strengths we did not know we had, and to still be silly together in all the unique expressions of frivolity we've so diligently devised over these seventeen years of friendship. There is much to be grateful for.

# Contributors to
## Sister & Brother

ALAN BELL was born in Sacramento, California, in 1956. He is a graduate of UCLA, where he edited the gay and lesbian student newspaper, *Ten Percent*. He is currently working on a collection of short stories and a novel. He lives in Los Angeles.

LUCY JANE BLEDSOE is the editor of *Goddesses We Ain't*, a collection of writing from women in San Francisco's Tenderloin district. Her work has been published in anthologies including *Women on Women 2, Tickled Pink, SportsDykes,* and *Afterglow,* and in *New York Newsday, Northwest Literary Forum, Evergreen Chronicles, Girljock,* and *Conditions.* She has been awarded an NEH Youth grant, a PEN Syndicated Fiction Award, and a Barbara Deming Memorial Money for Women grant.

CLIFFORD CHASE has written a book about his brother, who died of AIDS in 1989, *The Hurry-Up Song.* His work has appeared in the *Yale Review, Threepenny Review,* and *Boulevard,* and in anthologies including *A Member of the Family: Gay Men Write About Their Families.* A former resident of the MacDowell Colony and Yaddo, he studied creative writing at the City College of New York. He grew up in California and currently lives in Brooklyn, where he is working on a novel.

BERNARD COOPER's first book, *Maps to Anywhere,* received the 1991 PEN/USA Ernest Hemingway Award. He is the author of the novel *A Year of Rhymes.* His work has appeared in such periodicals as the *Paris Review, Harper's,* and the *Yale Review,* as well as in several anthologies including *The Penguin Anthology of Gay Literature, Flash Fiction,* and *A Member of the Family: Gay Men Write About Their Families.* "Truth Serum" is from a forthcoming collection of memoirs.

LISA DAVIS lived the first twenty-three years of her life in Georgia. She then made her way to Greenwich Village via Long Island. She is at present finishing the second draft of a novel about gay life in the Village in the roaring forties.

NISA·DONNELLY is best known as the author of *The Bar Stories: A Novel After All,* which won the Lambda Award for Lesbian Fiction, and *The Loves Songs of Phoenix Bay.* Her short fiction has appeared in *Women on Women 2* and *Erotic Interludes* and in various magazines.

KATHERINE V. FORREST is the author of seven novels, which include the Lambda Award–winning Kate Delafield mystery series, a collection of short stories, and articles and book reviews that have appeared in a number of publications. She is supervising fiction editor at Naiad Press. Born in Canada, she has been a full-time writer and editor since 1979.

PHILIP GAMBONE is the author of a collection of short stories, *The Language We Use Up Here.* He has been a fellow at the MacDowell Colony. His essays and reviews have appeared in *Bay Windows, Lambda Book Report, Frontiers,* and the *New York Times Book Review.* He has also contributed to *Hometowns: Gay Men Write About Where They Belong* and *A Member of the Family: Gay Men Write About Their Families.* He teaches at the Park School, in Brookline, Massachusetts, and in the writing program at Harvard University. He makes his home in Boston and Provincetown.

GABRIELLE GLANCY's work has appeared in such publications as the *American Poetry Review,* the *Paris Review, New American Writing, Agni,* the *Kenyon Review,* and *Ploughshares.* She is the recipient of a New York Foundation for the Arts Fellowship and a Writers at Work prize. In addition to writing poetry and fiction, she is translating a book by Marguerite Dumas (much of which has appeared in *Fiction*) and one by Jean Genet. She is currently at work on a novel. Born and raised in New York City, she now lives in San Francisco.

JEWELLE GOMEZ is the author of a novel, *The Gilda Stories*, and a collection of essays, *Forty-three Septembers*. Formerly the director of the Literature Program of the New York State Council on the Arts, she is currently living and teaching in San Francisco.

JAMES JOHNSTONE was educated in Canada and Japan. A translator and interpreter, he bailed out of the corporate nine-to-five to concentrate on metaphysical studies, writing, reading, and friends. He lives in Vancouver's West End, where his community work includes organizing and emceeing the Vancouver AIDS Candlelight Memorial. A poet since high school, he now writes short stories and is working on his first novel.

ARNIE KANTROWITZ is associate professor of English at the College of Staten Island. He is a former vice president of Gay Activists Alliance, New York, and a founding member of the Gay and Lesbian Alliance Against Defamation. He is the author of *Under the Rainbow: Growing Up Gay*. His writing has appeared in the *Village Voice*, the *New York Times*, the *Advocate*, *OutWeek*, *QW*, the *New York Native*, and *Christopher Street*. His poetry has appeared in numerous magazines and in the volume *Poets for Life*; his essays have appeared in *Hometowns*, *Leatherfolk*, and *A Member of the Family*. He lives in New York City with his lover, Larry Mass.

STEVEN F. KRUGER teaches medieval studies and gay/lesbian studies at Queens College and the Graduate Center of the City University of New York. He is author of *Dreaming in the Middle Ages*, has recently published an article called "Claiming the Pardoner: Toward a Gay Reading of Chaucer's *Pardoner's Tale*" in *Exemplaria*, and is currently completing a book tentatively titled *Gender and Sexuality in the Literature of AIDS*.

BIA LOWE has lived in Los Angeles since she attended Cal Arts in 1970. Her publishing credits include articles in *Harper's* and the *Kenyon Review*. Her work has been anthologized in *Turning Toward Home: Reflections on the Family from "Harper's" Magazine*, *Indivisible: New Short Fiction by West Coast Gay and Lesbian Writers*, and *Helter Skelter: L.A. Art in the 1990s*. She has compiled a volume of her essays, *Wild Ride*.

MICHAEL LOWENTHAL graduated in 1990 as the first openly gay valedictorian from Dartmouth College, where he received awards for his fiction and poetry. His writing has appeared in *Flesh and the Word 2*, the *James White Review, Lambda Book Report, Gay Community News, OutWeek*, and other publications. He is a freelance writer and editor in New Hampshire, where he lives with his lover, Koko.

WILLIAM J. MANN has gone from having no lesbian friends in his life to living in Lesbianville, U.S.A.—Northampton, Massachusetts. Life there is good, with his lover, Tim, two cats, friendly neighbors, lots of dykes, and a budding gay male population. He's the copublisher of *Metroline*, the queer news and features magazines for Connecticut and western Massachusetts, and his stories and articles have appeared in the *Advocate, Gay Community News*, the *Washington Blade, Guys*, and the anthology *Shadows of Love*. He's currently working on a novel.

JAMES MERRETT is a contributing writer at the *Advocate* and *Frontiers*. He has also published articles in the *Village Voice*, the *New York Times*, the *Charlotte News and Observer*, the *Guide, Windy City Times, Seattle Gay News, Au Courant*, and others. He was a contributor to *Flesh and the Word 2*. He has published poetry in the *James White Review, Bay Windows, First Hand* and *Ellipsis . . .*, and a short story in *RFD*. He would like to thank his partner of seven years for pushing him to work harder than he'd like to.

PAUL MONETTE is the author of sixteen books—poems, novels, and memoirs. He is especially well known for a series of books about the AIDS calamity, including *Borrowed Time*. His memoir *Becoming a Man* was the winner of the 1992 National Book Award for Nonfiction.

CHERRÍE MORAGA is a poet, playwright, and essayist. She is the co-editor of *This Bridge Called My Back: Writings by Radical Women of Color*, which won the Before Columbus American Book Award in 1986. She is the author of numerous plays, including *Shadow of a Man*, winner of the 1990 Fund for New American Plays Award, and *Heroes and Saints*, winner of the Will Glickman Prize and the Pen West Award in 1992. Her most recent book is a collection of poems and essays entitled *The Last Generation*. Ms. Moraga is also a recipient of the National Endowment for the Arts' Theatre Playwright's Fellowship.

MERRIL MUSHROOM is an old-timey dyke and a prolific writer of lesbian stories.

JOAN NESTLE is cofounder of the Lesbian Herstory Archives, author of *A Restricted Country,* editor of *The Persistent Desire: A Femme-Butch Reader,* and coeditor of *Women on Women 1* and *Women on Women 2.* For the past twenty-eight years she has been a teacher of writing in the SEEK Program at Queens College, City University of New York. She has just begun teaching courses in gay and lesbian literature, and for this she thanks the younger generation of gay men and lesbians who are demanding that respect be given to their culture.

ELISABETH NONAS is the author of three novels, *For Keeps, A Room Full of Women,* and *Staying Home.* She has written articles for the *Advocate* as well as the screenplay adaptation of Paul Monette's *Afterlife.* She teaches fiction writing at the Institute of Gay and Lesbian Education in West Hollywood and at UCLA Extension, where she developed and taught the first lesbian and gay fiction-writing classes offered there. Elisabeth is coauthoring, with Simon LeVay, a book on lesbian and gay life. She lives in Los Angeles.

MARTIN PALMER lives in Anchorage, Alaska, where he practices medicine and teaches at the University of Alaska. His work has appeared in *Men on Men 3, Hometowns: Gay Men Write About Where They Belong, A Member of the Family: Gay Men Write About Their Families,* and *Flesh and the Word 3.* He is working on a volume of poetry.

GERRY GOMEZ PEARLBERG is a poet who lives in Brooklyn with her dog, Otto. She supports herself as a freelance writer specializing in HIV/AIDS prevention and health.

JOHN PRESTON wrote and edited over forty books. He was editor of the *Advocate* and contributed to a wide range of periodicals including *Harper's, Interview,* and *Lambda Book Report.*

ROBERT F. REID-PHARR is a cultural critic who teaches in the Department of English at the City College of New York. His work has appeared in *Callaloo,* the *African American Review, Fuse, Outlook, Radical America,* and the collection *Black Masculinity.* He is currently completing a manuscript on the effects of gender and sexuality in the development of African American national literature.

SUSAN FOX ROGERS is the editor of *SportsDykes* and *Cutting Loose: New Outdoor Writing by Women.* She is a writer whose work rarely strays from the subject of rock climbing, which she has been doing for the past eighteen years. Her work has appeared in *Leading Out: Women Climbers Reaching for the Top* and various magazines, including *Girljock* and *Climbing.* She lives in the mid–Hudson Valley of New York, on the west side of the Schawangunk Ridge.

MICHAEL ROWE was born in Ottawa, Ontario, and raised in Beirut, Havana, and Geneva. He attended the University of Toronto and studied creative writing at Harvard University. He is a journalist and essayist and the author of a volume of poetry, *When the Town Sleeps.* He lives in Milton, Ontario.

WICKIE STAMPS is a writer who has contributed to numerous gay and lesbian publications, including the *Advocate, Gay Community News, On Our Backs, OutWeek,* and *Bad Attitude.* Other published works appear in *Dykescapes: Short Fiction by Lesbians, Leatherfolk,* and *For Shelter and Beyond.* More recent work is scheduled for publication in *Daddy Is a Girl,* edited by Pat Califia.

JUDITH P. STELBOUM is associate professor at the College of Staten Island, City University of New York, where she teaches literature and women's studies. She is the founder and director of the Chinese American Educational Exchange. Her nonfiction has appeared in *Sinister Wisdom,* her fiction and poetry in *Common Lives/Lesbian Lives.* She is currently working on a novel.

KAREN X. TULCHINSKY is a Jewish lesbian political activist writer who lives in Vancouver, Canada, with her lover, Suzanne. Her work has appeared in *Getting Wet, Lovers, Sister/Stranger, Afterglow, Love's Shadow & Breaking Up Is Hard to Do,* and *OutRage.*

CANDACE LEE VAN AUKEN has long been active in the Boston lesbian and gay community. Positions she has held include cochair of WORDS/NWU, the lesbigay caucus of the National Writers Union,

Boston Local; chair of the Greater Boston Lesbian and Gay Political Alliance; and host of the cable TV show *Gay Boston*. She has edited several community publications, including *Bay Windows,* the *Center Times,* and most recently, the *WORDS/NWU Newsletter.* By day she is director of information systems for a management consulting firm. Her first novel, *Kite Maker,* was published in 1991.

STEPHEN WILDER lives with his lover, Brian, in the East Village. He works at a women's magazine and sees his friend Gerry as often as possible.

"CHRIS WYLER" is a pseudonym for a well-known gay writer who lives happily in Houston.

JOYCE ZONANA teaches Victorian literature and women's studies at the University of New Orleans. She is the author of *The Underground Gourmet Cookbook;* she has reviewed books, film, and theater for *Philadelphia Gay News.* She has published numerous scholarly essays, including an article on feminist orientalism in *Signs* that won the 1992 Florence Howe Award. She is currently working on a book of personal essays exploring gender, ethnicity, and sexuality. She lives with her two cats in a little house on the bayou.